THE LITTLE FLOWERS OF ST. FRANCIS OF ASSISI

Translated by
W. HEYWOOD

FV ÉDITIONS

CONTENTS

Introduction	1
Translator's Note	17
THE LITTLE FLOWERS OF ST. FRANCIS	19
OF THE MOST HOLY STIGMATA OF ST. FRANCIS	189
THE LIFE OF FRIAR JUNIPER	249
THE LIFE OF FRIAR GILES, THE COMPANION OF ST. FRANCIS	283
TEACHINGS AND SAYINGS OF FRIAR GILES	307
ADDENDA TAKEN FROM THE MANUSCRIPTS	359

INTRODUCTION

I. ST. FRANCIS OF ASSISI

FRANCIS, son of Peter Bernardone, a wealthy cloth merchant, was born at Assisi in or about the year 1182 during the absence of his father on business in France. From his mother he had received the name of John, but his father on his return changed it to Francis (*Francesco*, *i.e.*, Frenchman), by which name he was ever afterwards called. Of his mother, whose name was Pica, scarcely anything is known. It is probable that she was of higher social standing than her husband, and certain that Francis was much more in sympathy with her than with his harsh, close-fisted father. Francis was taught some Latin, and also acquired a knowledge of French; and the *Chansons de Geste* fired his mind with a love of chivalrous adventure. He also learnt to write; but was not at any time a ready penman, and generally resorted to dictation. When he grew up he was put to his father's trade. Of a singularly genial, open-handed disposition, he was "given to sports and singing, going about Assisi by day and night with young fellows like himself". Indeed his extravagance, both in personal indulgence and in giving to the needy, made him conspicuous in the town and neighbourhood. In 1202, Perugia having declared war against its smaller neighbour Assisi, a battle was fought in which Francis was taken prisoner, and he remained in captivity for about a year. Not long after his return he had a serious illness, by which he was first led to turn his thoughts to a change of life. The process of his conversion was slow, and it was a good two years before his path was made plain before him. This period was marked by several well-known incidents. Still thirsting for worldly renown, Francis had made costly preparations for joining a military expedition to Apulia, but had not proceeded farther than to Spoleto when he was turned back by a vision. Again, one night after a banquet, as he and his comrades were going through the town singing, he suddenly fell into an ecstasy and stayed behind, and in answer to the mocking inquiry "What he was thinking of?" and "Whether he was thinking of taking a wife?" he made the significant reply: "You have said the truth, for I have thought to take a bride nobler, richer and fairer than you ever saw." The incident of his changing clothes with a beggar and asking alms in French on the steps of St. Peter's at Rome also belongs to this period. His mental state at this time is thus described: "It repented him that he had so grievously sinned, nor could he take pleasure either in the past or in the present: for he had not yet received assurance that he would refrain from sin in the future" (*Legenda Trium Sociorum*, 12). The following passage tells us in his own words how he was put on the right track: "It was thus that the Lord granted to me Brother Francis to begin repentance: for while I was in sin it seemed to me exceeding bitter to look upon lepers; but the Lord brought me among them and I showed them kindness. And as I withdrew from them, that which had seemed to me bitter was turned to sweetness of soul and body. And not long after I came out from the world" (*Opuscula S. Francisci*, p. 77, ed. Quaracchi). About this time, while he was praying in the little ruinous church of St. Damian, by Assisi, before a painted figure of the Crucified, he heard these words: "Francis, seest thou not that My house is being destroyed? Go, therefore, and repair it for Me." And he, trembling and astonished, said: "Gladly will I do it, O Lord". "From that hour his heart was bruised and melted within him, and ever after he bore the wounds of the Lord Jesus in his heart, as clearly appeared afterwards by the wondrous renewing of them in his body" (*Legenda Trium Sociorum*, 14). The close of the period of his conversion is marked by the memorable scene before the Bishop of Assisi's palace, when Francis renounced his father and all his possessions, stripped himself naked, and was covered by the Bishop's mantle while Peter Bernardone walked off with his son's clothes.

Taking in a literal sense the command to "repair God's house," Francis went to live with the priest of St. Damian, and began to beg in the city for stones (which he carried on his shoulders) for the reparation of the church; withal "praising God and uttering simple words in fervour of spirit," so that some mocked at him for a madman, and others were moved to tears of compassion. Now, too, he began the wooing of Lady Poverty, and set himself to live on the scraps of food which he could beg from door to door. At first he looked with loathing at the food he gathered in this way; but he conquered himself and at last preferred such fare to any dainties. By the year 1208 the repair of St. Damian was finished, and Francis set about repairing the little church of S. Maria de Portiuncula (or degli Angeli) below Assisi, which work was completed by the early part of 1209. In this church (probably on 24th February, 5209), hearing in the Gospel for the day the passage *Matt.* x. 9, 10 ("Provide neither gold nor silver," etc.), Francis committed it to memory and resolved to fulfil it to the letter. He had been wearing a hermit's dress with a leathern girdle, and shoes, and a staff in his hand. These he discarded, and made himself a single tunic of coarsest stuff, substituting a cord for the girdle, and going barefoot. Forthwith he began to preach repentance, always beginning his address with the greeting "The Lord give you peace"; and soon his first few disciples joined him, giving up all their worldly possessions to the poor, and dwelling in hovels round the church of Portiuncula and at Rivo Torto (also in the neighbourhood of Assisi).

Before long, when his disciples numbered eleven, Francis determined to obtain the Pope's sanction for his work. He and his little band of laymen, devoted though they were to the Church, had no locus standi as preachers, and were liable to be confounded with the many sectaries, also professing evangelic poverty, by whom Christendom was infested at this time (see Sabatier, *Vie de S. François*, c. 3): without the support of the Church's authority his efforts must be sorely hampered. This is his own account of his action: "After that the Lord gave me brethren no one showed me what I ought to do; but the Most High revealed to me that I should live according to the pattern of the Holy Gospel. And I got this written down simply and in few words; and the Lord Pope confirmed it to me" (*Opusc.*, p. 79). This was in 1210; the "Lord Pope" was that Innocent III. before whom the Kings of England and Aragon had grovelled in the dust; his "confirmation" of the rule was verbal only, and in some sort provisional; he authorised Francis and his disciples to preach repentance; blessed them, and caused them all to receive the tonsure, which conferred on them the status of clerks. Francis, it may be mentioned, never proceeded to priest's orders. On their way back to Umbria Francis and his brethren tarried for a while at a solitary place near Orte. Speaking of their brief sojourn here, Thomas of Celano says (i., 35): "Great was their exaltation at neither having, nor seeing, anything which might give them carnal delight. Here they began to have intercourse with holy Poverty, and being exceedingly comforted in the want of all things that are of the world, they determined to cleave to her everywhere and always." Indeed, they even discussed the question whether they should not altogether forsake the society of men, and dwell in solitude. "But holy Francis . . . chose not to live for himself alone, but for Him who died for all, knowing that he had been sent to win souls for God".[1] And so, fixing their abode in a deserted lepers' hospital at Rivo Torto, they went forth to preach "repentance for the remission of sins". Fortified by the Pope's commission they preached with confidence and vast numbers were converted. In 1211 the church of S. Maria de Portiuncula (or degli Angeli) was given them by the Benedictines, and this tiny chapel (now engulfed in the Palladian church of S. Maria degli Angeli) with a few poor huts round it became the headquarters of the new Order. In 1212 the Benedictines also gave them the little church of St. Damian, which soon afterwards became the abode of St. Clara, who had forsaken the world at the preaching of Francis, and the Poor Ladies her companions. The incident related below of the gift of the mountain of La Verna (otherwise La Vernia or Alvernia) to Francis belongs to the year 1213, and not, as there stated, to 1224. The numbers of the Brethren rapidly increased, and the Order began to assume a settled organisation. Twice a year, at Whitsuntide and Michaelmas, the Brethren met in Chapter General; and at the Whitsuntide Chapter of 1217 Brethren were first sent out to foreign countries. The success of the Order began to arouse ill-will, especially on the part of the prelates and the secular clergy. In 1217 Cardinal Ugolino, Bishop of Ostia (afterwards Pope Gregory IX.), who was warmly attached to Francis and the Brethren, sent for Francis, bidding him come to Rome and plead his own cause before Pope Honorius III., who had succeeded Pope Innocent III. the year before. Thomas of Celano (i., 73) has left us a graphic description of Francis' audience of the Pope and Cardinals, of the simple earnestness of his address, and of the agonised suspense of his patron Cardinal Ugolino, who feared that the holy man's simplicity might only arouse contempt. In 1218 was held the Chapter General described below. In the following year Francis, who had twice before essayed to go and preach the faith of Christ to the unbelievers, first in Syria and afterwards in Morocco, accomplished his purpose and preached before the Soldan in Egypt. He remained abroad for more than a year, returning to Italy in the summer of 1220. During his absence there had been serious trouble in the Order, and the two Brethren whom he had left in charge had begun "to mitigate the vow of poverty and to multiply observances " (Sabatier, *Vie de S. François*, 268). On 22nd September the Pope issued a Bull imposing a year's novitiate on all who would enter the Order. This Bull marks the close of the first phase of the Franciscan movement. The old happy days at Orte and Rivo Torto, where Francis and his companions did indeed form a family, were gone for ever. The Order was now spreading its branches over all the world; and the time was come when a closer organisation and a more direct connection with the Holy See were become inevitable. Francis himself felt that he could no longer control the situation, and at the Michaelmas Chapter of 1220 resigned his office of Minister-General to Peter dei Cattani, flinging himself at his successor's feet with touching humility and promising him obedience. Peter died a few months later, and was succeeded by Brother Elias. On 29th November, 1223, the Rule of the Order, which had undergone various modifications since its verbal approbation by Innocent

III., was confirmed by a Bull of Honorius III. After the Whitsuntide Chapter of 1224 Francis withdrew to the mountain of La Verna for that fast of forty days during which those transcendent experiences were vouchsafed to him which are described at length below. From this time St. Francis' health began rapidly to fail, though he was still able to go about preaching. The incident related below (Chapter XIX.) belongs to the following year, 1225, when Francis, much against his will, had been induced by Brother Elias to go to Rieti (where the Papal court then was) for the cure of his eyes. Subsequently he went to Siena to consult a physician there; but his condition became so alarming that he was brought back to Assisi. At first he lodged at the Bishop's palace, where he was nursed by his loved companions—Leo, Angelo, Rufino and Masseo. For several months he lingered in great suffering; at last, as his end was approaching, they took him to Portiuncula, where, on 3rd October, 1226, he died.[2] Very shortly before his death he had caused himself to be placed on the bare ground; then he stripped off his poor garments, and received them back as a loan from one of the Brethren, who said to him: "That thou mayest know that thou hast no property in these garments, I deprive thee of the power of giving them away to any one." Whereat the holy man rejoiced, for he had kept faith with his Lady Poverty even till the end (2 *Cel.*, 215). On 26th July, 1228, he was canonised by Pope Gregory IX.

II. THE INFLUENCE OF ST. FRANCIS

The influence of St. Francis has been very grew. and far-reaching, but its manifestations have not always been such as he expected, and have often been such as he would have sternly condemned. The dominant note in his character after his conversion was absolute devotion to the person of his Lord and Master; and his espousal of Poverty signified the getting free from all worldly preoccupations so that nothing might stand between him and the literal fulfilment of the commands and counsels of the Gospel. On those who perceived what he was really aiming at the fascination of his character wrought with extraordinary power. Many instances of this occur in the *Little Flowers*, but special reference may be made to the humiliation of Friar Masseo (below, Chapters XI., XII.), and to the strange scenes of Friar Bernard, a man of mature age and high standing in the world, sitting in the piazza of Bologna to be mocked at as a madman by the rabble of the place, and of Friar Rufino, compelled to preach naked in a church at Assisi. But the true significance of Francis' life and example was apprehended by few. The ideal of a life of voluntary poverty was no new invention of St. Francis: it was generally diffused at that period; and was carried into practice by the Cathari and other heretics whose influence threatened irreparable damage to the Church (see Sabatier, *Vie de S. François*, 45, 51). Hence it may be surmised that many of Francis' contemporaries deemed that destitution in itself constituted "a title clear to mansions in the skies" and joined the Order, though "their hearts were not right with God". The realisation of Francis' intentions was in fact to a great extent frustrated by the very success of the movement. He did not intend that all the world should take upon themselves the vows of Religion. If, instead of assuming the habit of the Order, the more part of those who crowded into it had been content to live the Gospel life in the world as "brethren of penitence" (sec Sabatier, *op. cit.*, 307), the lamentable events which followed on Francis' death would have been averted. The personal fascination of the founder swept into the Order many who were not prepared to act up to the stringency of his Rule. Hence a relaxation of it was inevitable, and the only cause for wonder is the rapidity with which the Order was transformed. As to the permanent results of the preaching of St. Francis it is impossible to speak with certainty. Very many no doubt were turned to God; but the age was one of crass superstition, and what appealed to the people were too often the accidents rather than the substance of Francis' life. His ecstatic visions, his personal austerities, the miracles which he wrought in his life and those which he was expected to work after his death —these were the things which caused him to be canonised by the popular voice even in his lifetime. When he was brought back to Assisi to die "the city held high festival on the arrival of the blessed father . . . and the tongues of all the people praised God for it: for all the multitude foresaw that the saint of God would shortly die; and this was the subject of such great rejoicing" (1 *Cel.*, 105). All they cared for was to secure possession of his corpse. The transient character of St. Francis' spiritual influence is only too apparent from the most cursory survey of Italian history. Had his gospel of love really taken root among the people there would have been an end to the civil strife and bloodshed which had so long prevailed in every part of the country; but even in Assisi itself after his death "the story of the city becomes, as it had never been before, a list of murders, of struggles to the death for individual power, and of wars which made the fair Umbrian country a desolate and cruel waste for months and even years" (*The Story of Assisi*, by L. Duff Gordon, p. 59). Still, though the visible result of Francis' life fell so far short of his aim, something was achieved. The heretical sects were combated with their own weapons and lost much of their influence; the secular clergy were forced by the example of Francis and his friars to preach, a duty they had long neglected; and in Southern Umbria, the Abruzzi and the March of Ancona (see below, Chapter XLII.) his simple teaching was kept alive by a race of Brethren whom he would have owned as his "Knights of the Round Table who lurk in deserts and remote places that they may the more diligently attend to prayer and meditation, living a simple life, men of humble conversation" (*Spec. Perf.*, 72). The mission of St. Francis was in large measure a failure; but if Italy was no better disposed to receive the spiritual liberty he preached than it was a hundred years later to acknowledge the righteous government of the Emperor Henry VII. (see Dante, *Par.*, xxx., 137, 138), the charm of St. Francis' character, the devotion of his life, seized at once on the hearts of the Italian people who to this day have never forgotten him and never ceased to love him; and the spread of this affection to other nations also is witnessed by the extraordinary multiplication of Franciscan literature of late years in England and elsewhere.

One aspect of St. Francis' influence cannot be entirely passed over, and that is, its effect on Italian art. This is surely the result of his life which would have amazed and displeased him more than any other. In violation of his expressed wishes, Brother Elias immediately after his death set himself to rear that splendid basilica at Assisi, which is one of the most notable examples of mediæval architecture in Italy. Here, some seventy years later, Giotto executed his famous frescoes illustrating St. Francis' life and miracles, and from thenceforth the "little poor man" becomes one of the most familiar figures in Italian painting. "To the painters the life of St. Francis came as a new inspiration, full of dramatic possibilities, and offering an entirely new field for original and imaginative treatment" (*Franciscan Legends in Italian Art*, by E. G. Salter, p. 2).

III. EARLY WRITINGS ABOUT ST. FRANCIS

Of the earlier writings about St. Francis the most important are the *Speculum Perfectionis* (Mirror of Perfection), first published as a separate work by M. Paul Sabatier in 1898; the *Legenda Trium Sociorum* (Legend of the Three Companions); the two *Lives of St. Francis* by Brother Thomas of Celano; and the *Life* by St. Bonaventura. Of these five works the first two are unofficial; they are written without any pretension to literary elegance and with absolute simplicity, and bring us into direct personal contact with St. Francis. The two *Lives* by Celano are official works, the first having been composed by order of Pope Gregory IX. in 1228, and the second (first part) at the instance of the Chapter General held at Genoa in 1244. In 1247 the author was invited by John of Parma (who had just been appointed Minister-General) to continue his work, and the second part of the second *Life* was accordingly added. These *Lives* show greater literary skill than the *Speculum Perfectionis* and the *Legenda Trium Sociorum*, but are less spontaneous, and the author makes considerable use of the material of other informants.[3] They occupy, in fact, a position intermediate between the *Speculum Perfectionis* and the *Legenda Trium Sociorum*, on the one hand, and the *Life* by St. Bonaventura on the other. This last was written by order of the Chapter General at Narbonne in 1260; and six years later the Chapter at Paris ordered the suppression of all former "Legends". St. Bonaventura's Life thenceforth remained the official record of St. Francis. The "Seraphic Doctor's" ornate and rather luscious style is strangely out of keeping with the story of the "little poor man of Assisi"; and though the book is not to be neglected, it is of far less value in helping us to picture St. Francis as he was than the works previously referred to.

One other work must be mentioned, the *Sacrum Commercium B. Francisci cum domina Paupertate*, in which the espousals of Francis and Poverty are narrated in allegorical form. This little book, one of the gems of mediæval literature, is believed to have been written in July, 1227, by John Parenti, who had just been elected Minister-General of the Order in the room of Brother Elias; and consequently to be the earliest work about St. Francis.

IV. THE FIORETTI, OR LITTLE FLOWERS OF ST. FRANCIS[4]

The *Little Flowers* have more of the character of legend (in the modern sense of the word) than the writings already mentioned; but though facts are here embellished with fabulous additions, the narratives are to a great extent based on authentic tradition, written and oral. Account must, however, be taken of the strong antipathy displayed towards Brother Elias. Thus the story of the "blessing of the firstborn" in Chapter VI. is in flat contradiction with 1 *Celano*, 108 (written before the apostasy of Elias, where St. Francis lays his *right* hand on Elias' head. Chapter IV. also, in which we read how Brother Elias slammed the door in the face of an angel, is manifestly fabulous (see also Chapters XXXI. and XXXVIII.). Still, in spite of inaccuracies and of the prominence given to miraculous occurrences, the *Fioretti*, as Sabatier remarks, do set forth with a vivid colouring not to be found elsewhere the atmosphere and surroundings amid which St. Francis and his companions lived.

The Italian text, of which a translation is given in the present volume, is itself a translation of more ancient records. The translator is not known, but there is some ground for thinking that he was Friar John of S. Lorenzo, a Florentine of the Marignoli family, who was Bishop of Bisignano, in Calabria, from 1354 to 1357. As regards the original material, the fifty-three chapters to which the title Fioretti strictly belongs are selected from a Latin compilation, the *Actus B. Francisci et sociorum ejus*. This compilation dates from the first half of the fourteenth century, and was probably the work of Ugolino, of the noble family of Brunforte, a Franciscan friar, generally described as Ugolino of Monte Giorgio, after the name of the convent (near Fermo, in the March of Ancona) wherein he spent part of his life. He was appointed Bishop of Teramo, in the Abruzzi, by the hermit-Pope Celestine V., but this appointment was annulled by Celestine's successor, Boniface VIII., in 1295. The fifty-three chapters of the *Fioretti* divide themselves into two parts, the first comprising Chapters I.-XL., which are concerned with St. Francis and his first companions; the second comprising Chapters XLI.-LIII., which are concerned with the brethren of the March of Ancona. In the first part Ugolino founds himself on oral and written tradition, and especially on information given to Brother James of Massa by Brother Leo, St. Francis' beloved companion. In the second part the author relates what he saw, or rather what he admired, among the brethren dwelling in the convents in the neighbourhood of Monte Giorgio.

Two passages in which the sources of the book are referred to may here be noticed. In Chapter XLV, after telling how Friar John of Penna prevented a novice from leaving the Order, the author states that "Friar John himself told all this to me Ugolino".[5] Again, in Chapter LII, reference is made to the experience of "that friar who first wrote of these things". The *Considerations on the Stigmata*, the *Lives* of Friars Juniper and Giles, and the *Sayings* of the latter form a sort of appendices to the *Fioretti*. Their compiler is unknown. "In the first, the compiler has divided into five chapters all the information he could collect touching the Stigmata. . . . The second, entitled the Life of Friar Juniper, is but very indirectly related to St. Francis; it deserves, however, to be studied, for it presents the same kind of interest as the principal collection, than which it is doubtless but a little later. . . . The third, the Life of Friar Giles, appears to be the most ancient document we possess on the life of the famous ecstatic. . . . The first seven chapters form a complete whole; the last three are doubtless a first attempt to complete them. The fourth appendix comprises the favourite Sayings of Friar Giles; they are only important as showing the tendencies of primitive Franciscan teaching" (Sabatier, *Vie de S. François d'Assise*, pp. cxi.-cxiii.).

The most ancient extant MS. of the *Fioretti* in Italian is believed to be that in the National Library at Florence which was written by Amaretto Manelli in 1396. It contains the *Considerations on the Stigmata*, but not the Lives of Juniper and Giles nor the Sayings of the latter. It is described, together with forty-three other MSS., by Luigi Manzoni in his *Studi*. The popularity of the *Little Flowers* began even from the first: the book was printed at a very early date, and the subsequent editions have been extremely numerous. The earliest dated edition was printed at Vicenza in 1476; other editions, undated, appeared at about the same time, and no less than sixteen were published before 1500. None of these contain the *Lives* of Juniper and Giles or the *Sayings* of the latter. At least thirteen editions appeared in the sixteenth century. Of the later editions reference may be made to that edited by the Senator Filippo Buonarroti (Florence, 1718), to the highly esteemed edition of Antonio Cesari (Verona, 1822), and to the recent illustrated editions of Passerini (Florence, 1903) and of Luigi Manzoni (second edition, Rome, 1902). Passerini follows the text of a fifteenth century MS. in the Riccardi Library at Florence, and includes certain "examples and miracles" of St. Francis contained in that MS. and not before printed. Manzoni prints the text of the MS. of Amaretto Manelli (above mentioned). Owing to the lamented death of Signor Manzoni, only the first volume of his edition, containing the *Fioretti* proper and the *Considerations on the Stigmata*, has appeared.

A. G. FERRERS HOWELL

---

1. The incidents there related are referred by Sabatier to the year 1215.
2. 4th October, according to the style of Assisi.
3. The authorship, date and subject-matter of the *Speculum Perfectionis* and the *Legenda Trium Sociorum*, and the relation of these works to one another and to Celano's*Lives*, furnish problems of extreme intricacy, of which the solutions have not yet been attained. A considerable and increasing literature connected with these questions exists. Reference may be made to a useful article by Mr. A. G. Little on the "Sources of the History of St. Francis," in the *English Historical Review* for October, 1902, and to the prolegomena of Fr. E. d'Alençon's edition of Celano's *Lives* (Rome, 1906).
4. The information given in this section is founded on Luigi Manzoni's *Studi sui Fioretti*, published in vols. 3 and 4 of *Miscellanea Francescana* (Foligno, 5889), on the same author's edition of the Fioretti, on Sabatier's edition of the *Actus B. Francisci* (Paris, 1902), and on Sabatier's *Vie de S. François d'Assise* (31st ed., Paris, 5904). The title "Little Flowers," or the like, was commonly given to volumes of selections or extracts in the Middle Ages (see Gaspary's *History of Early Italian Literature*, p. 183, Œlsner's translation; Manzoni, Studi, p. 551).
5. I quote from the *Actus* (p. 200), the Italian text of the *Fioretti* being ambiguous.

TRANSLATOR'S NOTE

WHERE not otherwise indicated, the following translation has been made from the text of the *Fioretti di San Francesco con Prefazione* di PAOLO SABATIER, Assisi, Tip Metastasio, 1901. I have, however, consulted various other versions, among which the following are the more important:—

I Fioretti di S. Francesco, Testo di Lingua secondo la lezione adottata dal P. ANTONIO CESARI, Milano, Casa editrice Guigoni, 1893.

Floretum S. Francisci Assisiensis. Liber aureus qui italice dicitur I Fioretti di San Francesco, Edidit PAUL SABATIER, Paris, Librairie Fischbacher, 1902.

I Fioretti del Glorioso Messere Santo Francesco e de' suoi Frati, a cura di G. L. PASSERINI, Firenze, G. C. Sansoni, 1903.

THE LITTLE FLOWERS OF ST. FRANCIS

1
―――――――

In the name of our Lord Jesus Christ the Crucified, and of His Mother the Virgin Mary. In this book are contained certain Little Flowers, Miracles and devout ensamples of the glorious mendicant of Christ, Messer St. Francis, and of certain of his Holy Companions, to the praise of Jesus Christ. Amen

FIRST, it is to be considered that the glorious Messer St. Francis in all the acts of his life was conformed to Christ the blessed: in that as Christ, at the beginning of His preaching, chose Twelve Apostles to despise every earthly thing and to follow Him in poverty and in the other virtues; so did St. Francis, at the beginning, choose for the foundation of his Order twelve companions, possessors of most high Poverty. And as one of the Twelve Apostles of Christ, being rejected of God, finally hanged himself by the neck; so likewise one of the twelve companions of St. Francis, whose name was Friar Giovanni della Cappella, apostatised and finally hanged himself by the neck. And unto the elect this is a great ensample and cause of humility and of fear; considering that no man can be certain that he will persevere unto the end in the grace of God.

And as those Holy Apostles were of marvellous sanctity and humility before all the world and full of the Holy Ghost, so these most holy companions of St. Francis were men of so much sanctity, that, from the time of the Apostles until now, the world had never such marvellous and holy men; for one of them was caught up into the third heaven, like St. Paul, and this was Friar Giles; one of them, to wit Friar Filippo Lungo, was touched upon the lips by an angel with a live coal, as was Esaias the prophet; one of them, and he was Friar Sylvester, spake with God, as one friend speaketh with another, after the manner that Moses did; one, by reason of the subtlety of his intellect, soared even unto the light of the Divine wisdom, as did the eagle, to wit John the Evangelist; the which was the most lowly Friar Bernard, who with very great understanding expounded the Holy Scriptures; one of them was sanctified of God and canonised in heaven, while yet he lived in the world; this was Friar Ruffino, a gentleman of Assisi; and in like manner every each of them was granted a singular seal of sanctity, as is hereinafter set forth.

2

Of Friar Bernard Of Quintavalle, First Companion Of St. Francis

THE first companion of St. Francis was Friar Bernard of Assisi, who was converted after this manner. St. Francis, being still clothed with lay garments, albeit he had already renounced the world, lived utterly scorned and mortified for penance, on such wise that by many he was deemed mad and was scoffed at as a madman and driven away with stones and mud by kinsfolk and by strangers. Nevertheless, he ever bore himself patiently, as one who is deaf and dumb, under every insult and derision. Wherefore it came to pass that Messer Bernard of Assisi, who was among the most noble and rich and wise of that city, began to consider attentively St. Francis' very great patience of injuries under such extreme contempt of the world; and beholding how, after having been thus abhorred and despised by every one for two years, he ever appeared more constant, he began to think and to say within himself: "Of a truth it is impossible that this Francis hath not great grace from God".

And so he invited him to supper in the evening and to lodge in his house; and St. Francis accepted and supped with him and lodged. Then Messer Bernard was minded to contemplate his sanctity; and thereunto he caused a bed to be prepared in his own chamber, in the which, at night, a lamp was always kept burning. And St. Francis, to conceal his sanctity, having entered into the chamber, forthwith cast himself upon the bed and feigned to sleep; and in like manner, Messer Bernard, after a little while, laid himself down and began to snore loudly as if he were fast asleep. Whereupon, believing that in very truth Messer Bernard slept, St. Francis presently rose from his bed and betook himself to prayer, lifting up his eyes and hands to heaven, and saying, with great devotion and fervour: "My God, my God". And so saying and weeping continually, he abode even until morning, always repeating: "My God, my God," and nothing else. And this St. Francis said, contemplating and marvelling at the excellence of the Divine Majesty which vouchsafed to give grace to the perishing world, and, through His mendicant Francis, to provide a remedy of salvation for his soul and for the souls of others. Wherefore, illuminated by the Holy Ghost or else by the spirit of prophecy, and foreseeing the great things that God would do through him and through his Order, and mindful of his own insufficiency and little worth, he called unto God and prayed Him that of His pity and omnipotence, without which human weakness can do nothing, He would supply, aid and complete that which, of himself, he (St. Francis) could not do. Now, when Messer Bernard had seen by the light of the lamp the very devout actions of St. Francis, and had reverently considered the words which he spake, he was touched and inspired by the Holy Ghost to change his life. Wherefore, when day was come, he called St. Francis and said unto him: "Friar Francis, I am altogether disposed in my heart to renounce the world and to follow thee in that which thou shalt command me". Hearing this St. Francis rejoiced in spirit and said: "Messer Bernard, this which you speak of is so great and difficult a work, that we ought to seek the counsel of our Lord Jesus Christ touching the same, and to pray Him to vouchsafe to show us His will therein and teach us how we may bring the same to good effect. Wherefore let us go together to the house of the bishop, where there is a good priest, and him will we cause to say Mass, and afterward we will continue in prayer until terce, beseeching God that, in three openings of the missal, He may show us the way which it is His will that we should choose." Thereto Messer Bernard made answer that he was well content. Wherefore they presently departed and gat them to the bishop's house; and after they had heard Mass and had continued in prayer until terce, the priest, at the request of St. Francis, took the missal, and having made the sign of the most holy cross, opened it three times in the name of our Lord Jesus Christ. At the first opening, they found that saying which Christ spake in the Gospel to the young man which inquired the way of perfection: *If thou wilt be perfect, go and sell that thou hast, and give the to poor and follow Me*. At the second opening, they found that saying which Christ spake to the Apostles, when He sent them forth to preach: *Take nothing for your journey, neither staff, nor scrip, nor shoes, nor money;* intending thereby to teach them that they ought to set all their hope of living upon God, and to turn all their thoughts to preaching the Holy Gospel. At the third opening of the missal they found that saying which Christ spake: *If any man will come after Me, let him deny himself and take up his cross and follow Me*. Then said St. Francis to Messer Bernard: "Behold the counsel which Christ gives us. Go then, and do thoroughly that which thou hast heard, and blessed be our Lord Jesus Christ who hath vouchsafed to show us His evangelic way". When he had heard this,

Messer Bernard departed and sold all that he had; and he was very rich. And with great rejoicing he gave everything to widows, to orphans, to prisoners, to monasteries, to hospitals and to pilgrims; and in everything St. Francis faithfully and providently aided him. Now a certain man whose name was Messer Sylvester, when he saw that St. Francis gave and caused to be given so much money to the poor, was moved by avarice and said:

"Thou didst not pay me in full for those stones which thou boughtest of me to repair the church; wherefore, now that thou hast money, pay me".

Then St. Francis, marvelling at his avarice and not wishing to contend with him, as a true follower of the Holy Gospel, put his hands into the bosom of Messer Bernard and, having filled them with money, put them into the bosom of Messer Sylvester, saying that if he wanted more he would give him more.

Messer Sylvester, being content with that which he had received, departed and went to his house; and in the evening bethinking him of that which he had done during the day, and considering the zeal of Messer Bernard and the sanctity of St. Francis, he repented him of his avarice; and on the night thereafter and on the two following nights, he had a vision from God, wherein he beheld how from the mouth of St. Francis issued a cross of gold, the top whereof reached to heaven, and the arms whereof extended from the East even unto the West.

By reason of this vision he gave away all that he had for love of God and became a minor friar; and he was of such holiness and grace in the Order, that he spake with God even as one friend speaketh with another, according as St. Francis many times approved, and as shall be hereinafter set forth. In like manner Messer Bernard had so much grace from God that he was ofttimes carried away in contemplation to God; and of him St. Francis said that he was worthy of all reverence, and that he had founded this Order, because he was the first who had left the world, keeping back nothing for himself, but giving everything to Christ's poor; and, when he began evangelic poverty, offering himself naked in the arms of the Crucified; the which be blessed by us for ever and ever. Amen.

3
———

How For An Evil Thought Which St. Francis Had Against Friar Bernard, He Commanded The Said Friar Bernard To Tread With His Feet Three Times Upon His Throat And Upon His Mouth

THE most devout servant of the Crucified, Messer St. Francis, by the severity of his penance and by his continual weeping, had become almost blind and saw but little. Upon one occasion among others, he left the Place where he was and went to the Place where Friar Bernard was, to speak with him of Divine things; and on reaching the Place, he found that he was in the wood in prayer, all uplifted and joined with God. Then St. Francis went into the wood and called him. "Come," said he, "and talk to this blind man;" and Friar Bernard answered him never a word; because, being a man of great contemplation, his mind was transported and raised to God; and because he had singular grace in speaking of God, as St. Francis had ofttimes proved, he therefore desired to speak with him. After waiting a little, he called him a second and a third time, in the same manner, and never a time did Friar Bernard hear him, and therefore he answered him not neither went unto him, so that St. Francis departed thence, somewhat cast down and marvelling and lamenting within himself that Friar Bernard, albeit he had been called three times, had not come unto him. Departing with this thought, St. Francis, after he had gone a little way, said unto his companion: "Await me here"; and he betook himself to a solitary place hard by, and casting himself upon his knees, besought God that He would reveal to him the reason why Friar Bernard had not answered him; and, while he yet prayed, there came to him a voice from God which spake thus: "O poor manikin, why art thou disquieted? Should a man leave God for a creature? Friar Bernard, when thou calledst him, was joined unto Me; and therefore he could not come to thee nor answer thee; marvel not then if he could not answer thee; because he was beside himself, and heard nothing of thy words." St. Francis, having received this answer from God, immediately and with great haste returned toward Friar Bernard, to accuse himself humbly of the thought which he had had concerning him. And when Friar Bernard saw him coming towards him, he went to meet him and cast himself down at his feet; then did St. Francis lift him up, and with great humility he told him of the thought and tribulation which he had had concerning him, and of the answer which God had given him touching the same; and he made an end of speaking after this manner: "I command thee in the name of holy obedience to do that which I bid thee." Now Friar Bernard, fearing lest St. Francis should command something excessive, as he was wont to do, sought a way to escape from that obedience honestly; wherefore he made answer on this wise: "I am ready to do your obedience, if you promise me to do that which I shall command you". And when St. Francis had promised him, Friar Bernard said: "Now, father, tell me that which you wish me to do". Then said St. Francis: "I command thee in the name of holy obedience that, to punish my presumption and the arrogance of my heart, when now I shall cast myself down upon my back upon the earth, thou shalt set one foot on my throat and the other on my mouth and so pass over me three times, from one side to the other, crying shame and infamy upon me, and especially say thou unto me: 'Lie there, thou churl, son of Pietro Bernardoni, whence hast thou so much pride, thou that art a very abject creature?'" Hearing this, Friar Bernard, albeit it was exceeding hard for him to do so, for the sake of holy obedience, fulfilled that which St. Francis had commanded him, as courteously as he was able; and when he had so done, St. Francis said: "Now do thou command me that which thou wouldest that I should do unto thee; for I have promised thee obedience". Said Friar Bernard: "I command thee in the name of holy obedience that every time that we are together thou shalt rebuke me and correct me harshly for my faults".

Thereat St. Francis marvelled much because Friar Bernard was of so great sanctity that he held him in exceeding reverence and deemed him not blameworthy in anything. Wherefore, from thenceforward, St. Francis was careful to avoid being much with him by reason of the said obedience, to the end that he might speak no word of correction to one whom he knew to be of so great sanctity; but when he desired to see him or to hear him speak of God, he left him as quickly as possible and gat him thence. And it was a passing edifying thing to see with what love and reverence and humility, St. Francis, the father, conversed and spake with Friar Bernard, his first-born son. To the praise and glory of Jesus Christ and of the mendicant Francis. Amen.

4

How the Angel of God proposed a question to Friar Elias, guardian of a Place of Val di Spoleto, and because Friar Elias answered him proudly, departed and went on his way to St. James, where he found Friar Bernard and told him this story

AT the beginning and commencement of the Order, when there were few friars and the Places were not yet taken, St. Francis, for his devotion, went to St. James of Galicia, and took with him certain friars, among whom one was Friar Bernard; and, as they thus journeyed together, he found in a town a sick mendicant, upon whom he had compassion, and he said unto Friar Bernard: "Son, I desire that thou abide here to tend this sick man"; and Friar Bernard, humbly kneeling and bowing his head, received the obedience of the holy father, and remained in that place. And St. Francis with his other companions went to St. James. Now, when they had arrived there, while they passed the night in prayer in the Church of St. James, it was revealed by God to St. Francis that he would take many Places throughout the world, inasmuch as his Order would increase and grow into a great multitude of friars; and, by reason of this revelation, St. Francis began to take Places in those regions. Thereafter, returning by the way whereby he had come, St. Francis found Friar Bernard and the sick man, with whom he had left him, perfectly healed. Wherefore St. Francis gave leave to Friar Bernard to go to St. James in the following year; and so St. Francis returned to the Val di Spoleto, and abode in a desert place, he and Friar Masseo and Friar Elias and others, all of whom were exceeding careful not to annoy or interrupt St. Francis when he was at prayer; and this they did for the great reverence which they bore him, and because they knew that God revealed great things to him in his prayers. Now it befel upon a day that, while St. Francis was at prayer in a wood, a goodly youth, clad as for a journey, came to the door of the Place and knocked thereon so impatiently and loudly, and for so long a time, that the friars marvelled greatly at such unwonted knocking. Friar Masseo went and opened the door and said to that youth: "Whence comest thou, my son, for it seemeth that thou hast never been here before, in so unwonted a manner hast thou knocked?" The youth replied: "And how ought one to knock?" Friar Masseo said: "Knock three times with an interval between each knock, and then wait long enough for the friar to say the Paternoster and to come unto thee, and, if in this space he cometh not, knock again". The youth replied: "I am in great haste and therefore do I knock so loudly, because I have a long journey to make, and hither am I come to talk with Friar Francis; but he is now in the wood in contemplation, and therefore I would not disturb him; but go and send me Friar Elias whom I wish to ask a question, because I hear that he is very learned". Thereupon, Friar Masseo went and told Friar Elias to go and speak to that youth, and thereat was he wrath and would not go. Wherefore Friar Masseo knew not what to do, nor what answer to carry back, in that, if he said: Friar Elias cannot come, he lied; and if he said that he was angered and would not come, he feared to set a bad example. And because Friar Masseo delayed to return the youth knocked again as at the first, and after a while Friar Masseo returned to the door and said unto him: "Thou hast not observed my teaching with regard to knocking". The youth replied: "Friar Elias is not willing to come to me. Go therefore and tell Friar Francis that I have come to speak with him; but, because I would not hinder him from prayer, bid him send Friar Elias to me." Then Friar Masseo went to St. Francis, who was praying in the wood with his face upraised to heaven, and told him of the message of the youth and the reply of Friar Elias; and that youth was the angel of God in human form. Then, St. Francis, neither moving from his place nor lowering his face, said: "Go and tell Friar Elias, for obedience sake, to go at once to that youth". Now when Friar Elias had heard the commandment of St. Francis, he went to the door in great wrath and opened it with much fury and noise, and said to the youth: "What dost thou want?" The youth made answer: "Look to it, friar, that thou art not wrath, as thou seemest to be, because anger clouds the mind and prevents the discernment of the truth". Said Friar Elias: "Tell me what thou wantest with me". The youth replied: "I ask thee whether it be lawful for those who observe the Holy Gospel to eat that which is set before them even as Christ said to His disciples; and I ask thee further whether it be lawful for any man to prefer anything contrary to the liberty of the Gospel". Friar Elias answered haughtily: "This I know well, but I will not answer thee. Go about thy business". Said the youth: "I could answer this question better than thou". Then was Friar Elias wrath and he slammed the door and departed. Thereafter he began to think over the said question and to doubt thereof within himself; and he knew not how to answer it, because he was vicar of the Order and had commanded and made an ordinance beyond the Gospel and beyond the Rule of St. Francis, that no friar of the Order should eat meat; so that the said question was expressly intended for him. Wherefore, not knowing how to decide the matter himself, and considering the modesty of the youth and that he had said that he knew how to answer that question better than he, he returned to the door and opened it to inquire of the youth touching the aforesaid question; but he was already gone, because the pride of Friar Elias was not worthy to speak with an angel. This done, St. Francis, to whom everything had been revealed by God, returned from out the wood and sternly and with a loud voice rebuked Friar Elias, saying: "Ill do you, proud Friar Elias, that you drive away from us the holy angels who come to teach us. I tell thee that I fear much lest thy pride should make thee end thy days outside this Order". And so it befel thereafter, even as St. Francis had said unto him, in that he died outside the Order. On that same day, and in that hour wherein the angel departed, he appeared in that same form to Friar Bernard who was returning from St. James; and he had reached the bank of a great river; and he saluted him in his own tongue, saying: "God give thee peace, O good friar"; and the good Friar Bernard, marvelling greatly at the beauty of the youth and at hearing the speech of his native country, with salutation of peace and with joyful countenance, asked of him: "Whence comest thou, good youth?" The angel made answer: "I come from the Place where St. Francis dwells; and I went thither to have speech with him and was not able to do so, because he was in the wood, wrapped in contemplation of Divine things, and I desired not to disturb him. And, in that Place dwell Friar Masseo and Friar Giles and Friar Elias: and Friar Masseo hath taught me how to knock at the door after the manner of a friar;

but Friar Elias, because he would not answer the question which I asked him, afterward repented, and wished to hear me and to see me, and could not." After these words, the angel said to Friar Bernard: "Wherefore dost thou not pass over to the other side?" Friar Bernard answered: "Because I am fearful of danger by reason of the depth of the waters which I see". Said the angel: "Pass we over together; doubt thou not"; and he took him by the hand and in the twinkling of an eye he set him on the other side of the river. Then Friar Bernard knew that it was the angel of God, and, with great reverence and joy, he cried in a loud voice: "O blessed angel of God, tell me thy name". The angel made answer: "Why askest thou my name, which is Wonderful?" And when the angel had thus said he vanished away and let Friar Bernard greatly comforted, insomuch that he made all that journey with rejoicing, and he gave thought to the day and the hour when the angel appeared unto him. And, when he arrived at the Place where was St. Francis with the aforesaid companions, he told them everything in order, and they knew certainly that that same angel in the day and hour in which he had appeared unto them appeared also unto him.

5

How the Holy Friar Bernard of Assisi was sent by St. Francis to Bologna, and there founded a monastery

BECAUSE St. Francis and his companions were called by God and chosen to bear in their hearts and in their works, and to preach with their tongues the Cross of Christ, they seemed and were men crucified, touching their habit and their austere life and their deeds and works; and because they desired rather to bear shames and insults for the love of Christ than the honours of the world and the respect and praise of men; yea, being reviled they rejoiced, and at honours they were afflicted; and so they went through the world as pilgrims and strangers, bearing nothing with them save Christ Crucified. And because they were true branches of the true vine, that is Christ, they brought forth great and good fruit of souls which they had won for God. It came to pass at the beginning of the Religion that St. Francis sent Friar Bernard to Bologna to the end that there, according to the grace, which God had given him, he might bring forth fruit to God; and Friar Bernard signing himself with the sign of the most holy cross, for holy obedience, departed and came to Bologna. And the children, seeing him clad in mean and unwonted garments, made a great scoff of him and despitefully used him, even as though he were a madman; and Friar Bernard patiently and gladly bore everything for the love of Christ; yea, to the end that he might be mocked the better, he steadfastly abode in the public square of the city, whereby there gathered about him as he sat there many children and men; and one pulled at his cowl from behind and another in front, one cast dust at him and another stones, one pushed him this way and another that; and ever unmoved and patient, with joyful countenance, Friar Bernard complained not nor disquieted himself, and for many days returned to the same place to endure like things. And because patience is a work of perfection and a proof of virtue, a learned doctor of law, seeing and considering the very great constancy and virtue of Friar Bernard, which, in so many days, neither insult nor injury could disturb, said within himself: "It is impossible that this is not a holy man"; and drawing nigh unto him he asked him: "Who art thou, and wherefore art thou come hither?" For answer, Friar Bernard put his hand into his bosom and drew forth the Rule of St. Francis and gave it to him that he might read it; and when he had read it, considering its most excellent state of perfection, he turned to his companions with very great amazement and wonder, and said: "Truly, this is the most excellent state of perfection whereof I have ever heard, and because this man and his companions are the most holy men in this world, whoso doth him wrong committeth a very grievous sin. Rather should we honour him above measure, as a true friend of God". And he said to Friar Bernard: "If you wish to take a Place in which you may seemly serve God, I for my soul's health would gladly give it to you." Friar Bernard answered: "Sir, I believe that our Lord Jesus Christ hath inspired you hereunto; and therefore do I accept your offer willingly to the honour of Christ". Then the said judge, with great joy and charity, led Friar Bernard to his house, and thereafter he gave him the Place which he had promised, and made it ready and finished it at his own expense; and from thenceforward he became the father and special defender of Friar Bernard and his companions. And Friar Bernard, by reason of his holy conversation, began to be held in high honour by the people, insomuch that he who was able to touch or see him held himself blessed; but he, as a true disciple of Christ and of the holy Francis, fearing lest the honours of the world should hinder the peace and salvation of his soul, departed one day and returned to St. Francis and said unto him: "Father, the Place is taken in the city of Bologna; send thither friars who may maintain it and may dwell therein; because, as for me, I no longer profited aught there, in that by reason of the too great honour that was done me, I fear that I have lost more than I have gained". Then St. Francis, when he had heard everything in order, how God had wrought by Friar Bernard, gave thanks to God who had thus begun to enlarge the mendicant disciples of the Cross; and thereafter he sent certain of his companions to Bologna and into Lombardy, the which took many Places in divers parts.

6

How St. Francis blessed the holy Friar Bernard, and left him as his vicar, when he came to pass from this life

FRIAR BERNARD was of such great sanctity that St. Francis held him in great reverence, and ofttimes praised him. On a day St. Francis, being and continuing devoutly in prayer, it was revealed unto him of God that Friar Bernard, by the Divine permission, must bear many and bitter assaults of the fiends; wherefore St. Francis, having great compassion for the said Friar Bernard, whom he loved as his own son, prayed many days with tears, beseeching God for him, and committing him to Jesus Christ that He might give him victory over the demon. And while St. Francis was thus devoutly praying, on a day God answered him: "Francis, fear not; because all the temptations wherewith Friar Bernard must be assailed are permitted him by God for proof of virtue and for a crown of reward; and finally he shall have the victory over all his enemies, because he is one of the Commissaries of the Kingdom of Heaven". Of this answer St. Francis had very great joy and gave thanks to

God, and from that hour he bore him ever increasing love and reverence. And well was the same made manifest, not only in his life but also in his death. For when St Francis came to his death, after the manner of the holy patriarch Jacob, his loving sons standing about him, grieved and tearful for the departure of so sweet a father, he asked: "Where is my firstborn? Come unto me my son that my soul may bless thee before I die." Then Friar Bernard said to Friar Elias in secret, the which was vicar of the Order: "Father, go thou to the right hand of the saint that he may bless thee". And when Friar Elias had set himself upon his right hand, St. Francis, who had lost his sight by reason of excessive weeping, laid his hand upon the head of Friar Elias and said: "This is not the head of my firstborn son Bernard". Then Friar Bernard went unto him upon his left hand, and St. Francis thereupon set his arms in the form of a cross and so laid his right hand on the head of Friar Bernard and his left on the head of Friar Elias, and said unto Friar Bernard: "God the Father of our Lord Jesus Christ bless thee with every spiritual and heavenly blessing in Christ; in that thou art the firstborn, chosen in this holy Order to give an evangelical example and to follow Christ in evangelic poverty; because not only didst thou give thy possessions to be distributed wholly and freely among the poor for the love of Christ; but also thou didst offer thyself unto God in this Order for a sacrifice of a sweet savour. Be thou therefore blessed by our Lord Jesus Christ and by me his mendicant servant with eternal benedictions; going, abiding, waking, sleeping, living and dying. May he who shall bless thee be fulfilled with benedictions; may he who shall curse thee not remain unpunished. Be thou the chief among thy brethren, and let all the friars be obedient unto thy commandment. Have thou licence to receive into this Order whomsoever thou wilt, and let no friar have dominion over thee; and be it lawful unto thee to go and to abide wheresoever thou shalt please." And after the death of St. Francis the friars loved and reverenced Friar Bernard as a venerable father; and when he drew nigh unto death, many friars came unto him from divers parts of the world, among whom came that hierarchical divine Friar Giles, the which beholding Friar Bernard, with great joy, said: "*Sursum corda*, Friar Bernard, *sursum corda*". And Friar Bernard secretly bade a friar prepare for Friar Giles a place fit for contemplation; and so was it done. And Friar Bernard, being at the last hour of death, caused himself to be lifted up, and spake unto the friars that were before him saying: "Most dear brethren, I desire not to speak many words unto you; but ye ought to consider that the state of Religion which I have had ye have, and this which I now have ye too shall have, and I find this in my soul that for a thousand worlds equal to this, I would not have served any other Lord than our Lord Jesus Christ; and of every wrong that I have committed I accuse myself and confess myself guilty to Jesus my Saviour and to you. I beseech you, my dearest brethren, that ye love one another." And after these words, and other admonitions, he laid him down again upon his bed, and his face became splendid and beyond measure glad, so that all the friars marvelled greatly, and in that gladness his most saintly soul, crowned with glory, passed from this present life to the blessed life of the angels.

7
———

How St. Francis passed a Lent in an island of the lake of Perugia, where he fasted forty days and forty nights, and ate no more than one half loaf

INASMUCH as the faithful servant of Christ, St. Francis, was in certain things well-nigh another Christ, given to the world for the salvation of mankind, God the Father willed to make him in many actions conformed and like unto His Son Jesus Christ; as is made manifest in the venerable College of the Twelve Companions, and in the admirable mystery of the sacred stigmata, and in the unbroken fast of the holy Lent which he made on this wise. On a time, St Francis being, on the day of Carnival, hard by the lake of Perugia, in the house of one of his disciples, with whom he had lodged during the night, he was inspired by God to go and keep that Lent in an island of the lake; wherefore St. Francis besought this disciple of his that, for the love of Christ, he would carry him in his skiff to an island of the lake, whereon no man dwelt, and that he, would do this on the night of Ash Wednesday to the end that none might know thereof; and he, for the love of the great devotion which he bare St. Francis, diligently fulfilled his request and carried him to the said island; and St. Francis took with him nothing save two small loaves. And, when he had landed upon the island, and his friend was about to depart and to return to his house, St. Francis besought him lovingly that he would not reveal to any man that he was there, and that he would not come for him until Holy Thursday; and so he departed. And St. Francis remained alone, and, in that there was no dwelling there, wherein he might find shelter, he entered into a very dense thicket, which many brambles and bushes had made like unto a cave or little hut; and in this place he set himself in prayer to contemplate celestial things. And there he abode all Lent without eating and without drinking anything save only half of one of those little loaves, according to that which his disciples found on Holy Thursday when he returned to him; for he found of the two little loaves one whole and half of the other. It is believed that St. Francis ate for reverence of the fast of Christ the blessed, who fasted forty days and forty nights without taking any earthly food; and on this wise, with that half loaf, he cast forth from himself the poison of vainglory, and after the ensample of Christ fasted forty days and forty nights. Thereafter, in that place where St. Francis had shown such marvellous abstinence, God did many miracles through his merits; for which cause men began to build houses there and to dwell there; and, in a little while, a walled village, fair and great, was made there, and withal the Place of the friars, which is called the Place of the Island, and the men and women of that village still have kept great reverence and devotion for that place where St. Francis kept the said Lent.

8

How while St. Francis and Friar Leo were on a journey, he expounded unto him those things which are perfect joy

ONCE when St. Francis was coming from Perugia to Santa Maria degli Angeli with Friar Leo in the winter, and the very great cold vexed him sore, he called Friar Leo, who was going before, and spake after this manner: "Friar Leo, albeit the minor friars in every land set a great example of holiness and of good edification, nevertheless, write and note diligently that therein is not perfect joy". And when St. Francis had gone farther, he called unto him the second time: "O Friar Leo, although the minor friar should give sight to the blind, make straight the crooked, cast out devils, make the deaf to hear, the lame to walk, and the dumb to speak, and, what is a greater thing, should raise those who have been dead four days; write that therein is not perfect joy". Going a little farther, he shouted loudly: "O Friar Leo, if the minor friar knew all tongues, and all sciences, and all the Scriptures, so that he was able to prophesy and to reveal not only things to come but also the secrets of consciences and souls; write that therein is not perfect joy". Going a little farther, St. Francis yet again shouted loudly: "O Friar Leo, little sheep of God, albeit the minor friar should speak with the tongue of angels, and knew the courses of the stars and the virtues of herbs, and albeit all the treasures of the earth were revealed to him and he knew the virtues of birds and of fishes and of all animals and of men, of trees, of stones and of roots and of waters; write that therein is not perfect joy". And going yet farther a certain space, St. Francis shouted loudly: "O Friar Leo, although the minor friar should know to preach so well that he should convert all the infidels to the faith of Christ; write that therein is not perfect joy". And this manner of speech continuing for full two miles, Friar Leo, with great wonder, asked and said: Father, I pray thee in the name of God to tell me wherein is perfect joy". And St. Francis answered him: "When we shall be at Santa Maria degli Angeli, thus soaked by the rain, and frozen by the cold, and befouled with mud, and afflicted with hunger, and shall knock at the door of the Place, and the doorkeeper shall come in anger and shall say: 'Who are ye?' and we shall say: 'We are two of your friars,' and he shall say: 'Ye speak not truth; rather are ye two lewd fellows who go about deceiving the world and robbing the alms of the poor: get you hence'; and shall not open unto us, but shall make us stay outside in the snow and rain, cold and hungry, even until night; then, if we shall bear such great wrong and such cruelty and such rebuffs patiently, without disquieting ourselves and without murmuring against him; and shall think humbly and charitably that that door-keeper really believes us to be that which he has called us, and that God makes him speak against us; O Friar Leo, write that here is perfect joy. And if we persevere in knocking, and he shall come forth enraged and shall drive us away with insults and with buffetings, as importunate rascals, saying, 'Get you hence, vilest of petty thieves, go to the hospice. Here ye shall neither eat nor lodge.' If we shall bear this patiently and with joy and love; O Friar Leo write that herein is perfect joy. And if, constrained by hunger and by cold and by the night, we shall continue to knock and shall call and beseech for the love of God, with great weeping, that he open unto us and let us in, and he, greatly offended thereat, shall say: 'These be importunate rascals; I will pay them well as they deserve,' and shall come forth with a knotty club and take us by the cowl, and shall throw us on the ground and roll us in the snow and shall cudgel us pitilessly with that club; if we shall bear all these things patiently and with cheerfulness, thinking on the sufferings of Christ the blessed, the which we ought to bear patiently for His love; O Friar Leo, write that here and in this is perfect joy; and therefore hear the conclusion, Friar Leo; above all the graces and gifts of the Holy Spirit, which Christ grants to His friends, is that of self-conquest and of willingly bearing sufferings, injuries and reproaches and discomforts for the love of Christ; because in all the other gifts of God we cannot glory, inasmuch as they are not ours, but of God; whence the Apostle saith: *What hast thou that thou didst not receive from God! and if thou didst receive it from Him, wherefore dost thou glory therein as if thou hadst it of thyself!* But in the cross of tribulation and of affliction we may glory, because this is our own; and therefore the Apostle saith: *I would not glory save in the Cross of our Lord Jesus Christ.*

9

How St. Francis taught Friar Leo to make answer; and how he was never able to speak save the contrary to that which St. Francis desired

ON a time in the beginning of the Order, St. Francis being with Friar Leo in a Place where they had not books for the saying of the divine office, when the hour of matins came, St. Francis said to Friar Leo: "Most dear companion, we have no breviary wherewith we can say matins; but to the end that we may spend the time to the praise of God, I will speak and thou shalt answer as I will teach thee: and look to it that thou changest not the words otherwise than I shall teach thee. I will say thus: 'O Friar Francis, thou hast done so many evils and so many sins in the world that thou art worthy of hell'; and thou shalt make answer: 'It is a true thing that thou meritest the lowest hell'." And Friar Leo with dove-like simplicity replied: "Willingly, father. Begin in the name of God." Then St. Francis began to say: "O Friar Francis, thou hast done so many evils and so many sins in the world, that thou art worthy of hell". And Friar Leo answered:

"God shall do through thee so much good that by reason thereof thou shalt go to paradise". Said St. Francis: "Say not so, Friar Leo, but when I shall say, 'Friar Francis, thou hast done so many wicked things against God, that thou art worthy to be accursed from God,' answer thou thus: 'Verily thou art worthy to be set among the accursed'". And Friar Leo answered: "Willingly father". Then St. Francis, with many tears and sighs and beatings of the breast, said with a loud voice: "O my Lord of heaven and earth, I have committed so many wickednesses and so many sins against Thee that I am altogether worthy to be accursed from Thee"; and Friar Leo answered: "O Friar Francis, God will make thee such an one that among the blessed thou shalt be singularly blessed". And St. Francis, marvelling that Friar Leo answered contrary to that which he had bidden him, rebuked him saying: "Wherefore dost thou not answer as I teach thee! I command thee by holy obedience to answer as I shall teach thee. I will speak thus: 'O Friar Francis, miserable sinner, thinkest thou that God will have mercy upon thee, seeing that thou hast committed so many sins against the Father of mercy and God of every consolation that thou art not worthy to find mercy?' And thou, Friar Leo, little sheep, shalt answer: 'On no wise art thou worthy to find mercy'." But afterward when St. Francis said: "O Friar Francis, miserable sinner," etc., Friar Leo answered: "God the Father, whose mercy is infinitely greater than thy sin, will show thee great mercy, and thereabove will add unto thee much grace". At this reply, St. Francis, sweetly angered and patiently disquieted, said to Friar Leo: "And wherefore hast thou had the presumption to do against obedience, and already so many times hast replied contrary to that which I have commanded thee?" Friar Leo answered very humbly and reverently: "God knoweth, my father, that every time I have resolved in my heart to answer as thou hast bidden me; but God maketh me to speak as it pleaseth Him, and not according to that which pleaseth me". Thereat St. Francis marvelled and said to Friar Leo: "I beseech thee very lovingly that this time thou answer me as I have told thee". Friar Leo answered: "Speak in the name of God, because of a surety this time I will answer as thou wouldst have me". And St. Francis weeping said: "O Friar Francis, miserable sinner, thinkest thou that God will have mercy upon thee?" Friar Leo answered: "Yea, and not only so, but great grace shalt thou receive from God, and He shall exalt thee and glorify thee for ever, because *whosoever humbleth himself shall be exalted*, and I cannot speak otherwise in that God speaketh through my mouth". And on this wise, in that humble strife, with many tears and much spiritual consolation, they watched even until day.

10

How Friar Masseo, as if in raillery, said to St. Francis that all the world followed after him; and he replied that that was to the confusion of the world and grace of God

ONCE while St. Francis dwelt in the Place of Porziuncula with Friar Masseo of Marignano, a man of great sanctity, discretion and grace in speaking of God; wherefore St. Francis loved him much; it came to pass that, one day, when St. Francis was returning from the wood and from prayer, and was already come to the place of egress from the wood, the said Friar Masseo desired to prove how great was his humility and drew nigh unto him and, as if in raillery, said: "Why after thee? why after thee? why after thee?" St. Francis answered: "What is this that thou wouldst say?" Said Friar Masseo: "I say, why doth all the world follow after thee, and why doth every man seem to desire to see thee and to hear thee and to obey thee? Thou art not a man beautiful of body, thou art not greatly learned, thou art not noble: wherefore then should all the world follow after thee?" Hearing this St. Francis rejoiced greatly in spirit, and raising his face to heaven, stood for a long time with his mind uplifted in God, and thereafter, returning to himself, kneeled down and gave praise and thanks to God, and then with great fervour of spirit turned to Friar Masseo and said: "Wouldst know why after me? wouldst know why after me? why all the world follows after me? This have I from those eyes of the most high God, which in every place behold the good and the wicked: because those most holy eyes have not seen among sinners any more vile, or more insufficient, or a greater sinner than I am; and since to do that marvellous work which He meaneth to do, He hath not found a viler creature upon earth; therefore hath He chosen me to confound the nobility and the pride and the strength and the beauty and wisdom of the world, to the end that it may know that every virtue and every good thing is of Him and not of the creature, and that no one may be able to glory in His sight; but whosoever shall glory, let him glory in the Lord, to whom is all honour and glory for ever." Then Friar Masseo, at so lowly an answer, spoken with so much fervour, was afraid and knew of a surety that St. Francis was stablished in humility.

11
___

How St. Francis made Friar Masseo turn round and round many times, and thereafter gat him to Siena

ONE day, while St. Francis journeyed with Friar Masseo, the said Friar Masseo went a little before: and arriving at a certain place where three roads met which led to Florence, to Siena and to Arezzo, Friar Masseo said: "Father, by which way must we go?" St. Francis made answer: "By that which God shall will". Said Friar Masseo: "And how shall we be able to know the will of God?" St. Francis answered: "By the sign which I shall show thee. Wherefore I command thee by the duty of holy obedience, that in this place where three roads meet, on the spot where now thy feet are set, thou turn round and round, as children do, and stop not from turning thyself unless I bid thee do so." Then Friar Masseo began to turn himself round, and so much did he turn that, by reason of the dizziness of the head which is wont to be generated by such turning, he fell divers times to the ground: but, in that St. Francis did not bid him stop; he, desiring to obey faithfully, gat him up again (and resumed the said turning). At the last, while he was turning round manfully, St. Francis said: "Stand still, and move not"; and he stood; and St. Francis asked him: "Toward which part is thy face set?" Friar Masseo answered: "Toward Siena". St. Francis said: "That is the way whereby God wills that we go". Now, as they went by that way, Friar Masseo marvelled that St. Francis had made him do even as children do, before the worldly folk who were passing by: nevertheless, for reverence' sake, he ventured not to say anything to the holy father. As they drew nigh unto Siena, the people of the city heard of the coming of the saint, and went forth to meet him; and for devotion they bare him and his companion even unto the bishop's house, so that they touched no ground with their feet. In that hour certain men of Siena fought together and already two of them were slain; but when St. Francis arrived there, he preached to them so devoutly and holily that he brought them all to peace and to great unity and concord. For the which thing the Bishop of Siena, hearing of that holy work which St. Francis had done, invited him to his house and lodged him with great honour that day and also the night. And, on the morning of the following day, St. Francis, who, with true humility, in all his actions sought only God's glory, rose up early with his companion and gat him thence without the knowledge of the bishop. For which cause the said Friar Masseo went by the way murmuring within himself, and saying: "What is it that this good man hath done? He made me turn round like a child, and to the bishop who hath shown him so much honour he hath spoken never a word nor thanked him;" and it seemed to Friar Masseo that therein St. Francis had borne himself indiscreetly. But afterward, returning to his right mind by Divine inspiration, and reproaching himself in his heart, he said: "Friar Masseo, too proud art thou who judgest Divine works, and thou art worthy of hell for thy indiscreet pride; for yesterday Friar Francis wrought such holy deeds that if an angel of God had done them they could not have been more marvellous; wherefore, if he should bid thee throw stones, thou oughtest so to do and to obey him; and that which he did upon the way proceeded from Divine inspiration as is shown by the good result which followed thereupon; in that if he had not made peace between them who fought together, not only would the sword have devoured the bodies of many, even as it had already begun to do, but also the devil would have carried away many souls to hell; and therefore art thou very foolish and proud who murmurest against that which manifestly proceedeth from the will of God". And all these things which Friar Masseo said in his heart, as he went before, were revealed of God to St. Francis. Wherefore St. Francis drew nigh unto him and spake thus: "Hold fast to those things which now thou thinkest, in that they arc good and useful and inspired of God; but the first murmuring which thou madest was blind and vain and proud, and was put in thy mind by the demon". Then Friar Masseo perceived clearly that St. Francis knew the secrets of his heart, and he understood certainly that the spirit of Divine wisdom guided the holy father in all his actions.

12

How St. Francis laid upon Friar Masseo the service of the gate, of alms-giving and of the kitchen; and thereafter, at the prayer of the other friars, relieved him of them

ST. FRANCIS, desiring to humble Friar Masseo, to the end that he might not become puffed up by reason of the many gifts and graces which God was giving him, but by virtue of humility might increase thereby from virtue to virtue; once when he was dwelling in a solitary place with those true saints, his first companions, among whom was the said Friar Masseo, he spake on a day to Friar Masseo before all his companions, saying: "O Friar Masseo, all these thy companions have the grace of contemplation and of prayer; but thou hast the grace of preaching the Word of God to the satisfying of the people; and therefore, to the end that these thy companions may be able to give themselves to contemplation, I will that thou perform the office of the gate and of alms-giving and of the kitchen; and when the other friars shall eat thou shalt cat without the gate of the Place, so that thou mayest satisfy those who come to the

Place with some good works of God or ever they have knocked; thus it will not be necessary for any other to go forth save thee alone; and this do thou for the merit of holy obedience". Thereupon, Friar Masseo drew back his cowl and bowed his head and humbly received this obedience and persevered therein for many days, performing the office of the gate, of almsgiving and of the kitchen. Wherefore his companions, as men illuminated of God, began to feel great remorse in their hearts, considering that Friar Masseo was a man of great perfection even as they or more so, and upon him was laid all the burthen of the Place and not on them. For which cause they were all moved with one desire and went to beseech the holy father that he would be pleased to distribute among them those offices; inasmuch as their consciences might in no wise bear that Friar Masseo should endure so great labour. Hearing this St. Francis inclined his ear unto their counsels and consented unto their wish. Calling Friar Masseo he spake to him after this manner: "Friar Masseo, thy companions desire to share the offices which I have given thee; and therefore I will that they be divided among them." Said Friar Masseo, with great humility and patience: "Father, that which thou layest upon me, whether in whole or in part, I esteem it altogether done of God". Then St. Francis, beholding the charity of those others and the humility of Friar Masseo, preached unto them a marvellous sermon touching most holy humility; teaching them that the greater the gifts and graces which God bestows upon us, the greater should our humility be; because without humility no virtue is acceptable to God. And whey: he had finished preaching, he distributed the offices with very great love.

13

How St. Francis and Friar Masseo placed the bread which they had begged upon a stone hard by a fountain, and St. Francis praised Poverty much. Thereafter, he prayed God and St. Peter and St. Paul, that He would cause him to be enamoured of holy Poverty; and how St. Peter and St. Paul appeared to him

THE marvellous servant and follower of Christ, Messer St. Francis, to the end that in everything he might conform himself to Christ, who, according to the Gospel, sent His disciples by two and two to all those cities and places whither He Himself was about to go; inasmuch as after the example of Christ he had gathered together twelve companions, sent them through the world to preach by two and two. And to set them an ensample of true obedience, he himself was the first to go, after the ensample of Christ, who began to do before He began to teach. Wherefore, having assigned to his companions the other regions of the world, he, taking Friar Masseo as his companion, journeyed toward the province of France. And coming one day to a village and being very hungry, they went, according to the Rule, begging bread for the love of God; and St. Francis went through one street and Friar Masseo through another. But because St. Francis was a man too despicable and small of body, and was esteemed a vile mendicant therefor by those who knew him not, he gat only some mouthfuls and fragments of dry bread; whereas to Friar Masseo, because he was tall and beautiful of body, were given good pieces and large and in plenty and fresh cut from the loaf. And so when they had finished begging they met together to eat outside the village in a place where there was a beautiful fountain with a fair large stone beside it, whereupon each of them laid all the bread which he had begged; and when St. Francis saw that the Friar Masseo's pieces of bread were more plentiful and better and larger than his, he showed very great joy thereat, and spake after this manner: "O Friar Masseo, we are not worthy of so great treasure"; and when he had repeated these words many times, Friar Masseo replied: "Father, how is it possible to speak of treasure where there is such great poverty and lack of all things needful? Here is neither tablecloth, nor knife, nor trencher, nor porringer, nor house, nor table, nor man-servant, nor maidservant." Said St. Francis: "And this is that which I esteem great treasure, where there is nothing prepared by human industry; but that which there is, is prepared by the Divine Providence, as may be manifestly seen in the bread which we have begged, in this beautiful table of rock and in this clear spring. Wherefore I will that we pray God that He make us to love with our whole heart the so noble treasure of holy Poverty, which hath God to servitor." And when he had said these words and had prayed and partaken for bodily sustenance of these fragments of bread and of that water, they rose up to journey into France; and coming to a church, St. Francis gat him behind the altar and betook himself to prayer: and in that prayer he received by Divine visitation such exceeding fervour, the which kindled his soul so mightily to love of holy Poverty, that by the heat of his face and by the unwonted gaping of his mouth it seemed that he breathed forth flames of love. And coming thus enkindled to his companion, he spake to him on this wise: "Ah! Ah! Ah! Friar Masseo, give me thyself"; and so spake he three times; and the third time St. Francis raised Friar Masseo into the air with his breath, and cast him before him a great spear's length. Thereat was Friar Masseo filled with very great wonder; and thereafter, he related to his companions that when St. Francis thus lifted him up and cast him from him with his breath he experienced such great sweetness of spirit and consolation of the Holy Ghost, that never in his life had he felt the like. And when this was done, St. Francis said: "Companion mine, let us go to St. Peter and St. Paul and pray them that they will teach us and aid us to possess the immeasurable treasure of most holy Poverty; for she is a treasure so surpassing and so Divine that we are not worthy to possess it in our most vile vessels; for this is that celestial virtue whereby all earthly things and transitory are trodden under foot and every barrier is removed which might hinder the soul from freely uniting itself to the eternal God. This is that virtue which enableth the soul, while yet on earth, to hold converse in heaven with the angels; this is she, who bare Christ company upon the cross, with Christ was buried, with Christ was raised again, and with Christ ascended into heaven; who even in this life grants to the souls which are enamoured of her nimbleness to fly to heaven; seeing that it is she who guards the weapons of true humility and charity. Therefore, I pray we the most holy Apostles of Christ, who were perfect lovers of this evangelic pearl, that they may beg this grace for us from our Lord Jesus Christ that, of His most Holy pity, He may grant us to be worthy to be true lovers, observers and humble disciples of most precious, most beloved and evangelic Poverty." And thus discoursing, they came to Rome and entered into the Church of St. Peter; and St. Francis betook himself to prayer in one corner of the church and lf Masseo in another; and they abode long time in prayer with great devotion and many tears, until, at the last, the most holy Apostles Peter and Paul appeared to St. Francis in great splendour, and said: "Because thou askest and desirest to observe that which Christ and His Apostles observed, the Lord Jesus Christ sends us to thee to make known unto thee that thy prayer is heard, and that the treasure of most holy Poverty is granted unto thee of God in fullest perfection, to thee and to thy followers. And further we tell thee in His name that whosoever, after thy example, shall perfectly follow this desire, he is assured of the beatitude of life eternal; and thou and all thy followers shall be blessed of God." And when they had thus spoken, they vanished away, leaving St. Francis full of consolation. Thereafter, he rose up from prayer and returned to his companion and asked him if God had revealed aught unto him; and he answered "No". Then St. Francis told him how the holy Apostles had appeared to him and what they had revealed unto him. Wherefore each of them was fulfilled with joy; and they determined to return to the Val di Spoleto and to leave their journeying into France.

14

How while St. Francis and his friars spake of God, He appeared in the midst of them

IN the beginning of the Religion, what time St. Francis and his companions were gathered together to speak of Christ, he, in fervour of spirit, commanded one of them that, in the name of God, he should open his mouth and speak of God that which the Holy Ghost inspired him. Now, while the friar was fulfilling that commandment and was discoursing marvellously of God, St. Francis imposed silence upon him and bade another friar speak in like manner. He yielding obedience and discoursing subtly of God, St. Francis, in like manner, imposed silence upon him, and commanded a third to speak of God, who, in his turn, began to speak so profoundly of the secret things of God that, of a verity, St. Francis knew that he, like the other two, spake through inspiration of the Holy Ghost; and this also was shown by example and by a clear sign; in that, while they were thus speaking, Christ the blessed appeared in the midst of them in the likeness and form of a youth, exceeding beautiful, and blessing them, fulfilled them all with so much grace and sweetness, that they were all rapt away out of themselves and lay like dead men, wholly insensible to the things of this world. And thereafter, when they had come to themselves, St. Francis said unto them: "My dearest brethren, let us thank God, who hath willed to reveal the treasures of Divine wisdom through the mouths of the simple; for it is God who openeth the mouth of the dumb and maketh the tongues of the simple to talk very wisely".

15

How St. Clare ate with St. Francis and with the friars, his companions, in Santa Maria degli Angeli

ST. FRANCIS, when he abode at Assisi, ofttimes visited St. Clare and gave her holy admonishments; and she having very great longings to eat once with him, and thereto beseeching him many times, he was never willing to give her this consolation; wherefore his companions perceiving the desire of St. Clare, said to St. Francis: "Father, to us it seems that this severity is not in accordance with Divine charity, in that thou hearkenest not to Sister Clare, a virgin so holy and so beloved of God, in so small a matter as is this of eating with thee; and the more so considering that she through thy preaching abandoned the riches and pomps of the world; and, of surety, if she asked of thee a greater boon than this is, thou oughtest to grant it to thy spiritual offspring". Then St. Francis made answer: "Doth it seem to you that I ought to grant her prayer?" The companions replied: "Yea, father; it is a fitting thing that thou grant her this grace and consolation". Then St. Francis said:

"Since it seemeth so to you, it seemeth so also to me. But to the end that she may have the greater consolation, I desire that this meal be eaten in St. Mary of the Angels, because she hath been long shut up in St. Damian, and thus will she have joy in beholding the Place of St. Mary, where a she was shorn and made the bride of Jesus Christ; and there will we eat together in the name of God." Accordingly, the day thereunto appointed being come, St. Clare went forth from the convent with one companion, and, accompanied by the companions of St. Francis, came to St. Mary of the Angels, and after she had devoutly saluted the Virgin Mary before her altar, where she had been shorn and veiled, they took her to see the Place until the dinner hour was come. And, in the meantime, St. Francis caused the table to be set upon the bare ground, as he was wont to do. And when the dinner hour was come, St. Francis and St. Clare sat down together, and one of the companions of St. Francis with the companion of St. Clare; and thereafter all the other companions sate them humbly down at the table. And, at the first dish, St. Francis began to speak of God so sweetly, so highly and so marvellously, that abundance of Divine grace descended upon them and they were all rapt in God. And while they were thus rapt, with eyes and hands raised to heaven, the men of Assisi and of Bettona, and they of the district round about, saw that St. Mary of the Angels, and all the Place, and the wood which was then hard by the Place, were burning fiercely; and it seemed to them that there was a great fire which encompassed the church and the monastery and the wood together; for the which cause the men of Assisi ran down thither with great haste to quench the fire, believing that verily everything was burning. But when they reached the Place they saw that there was no fire at all, and they went in and found St. Francis and St. Clare and all their company rapt in God through contemplation, and sitting about that lowly board. Whereby they understood of a surety that that had been Divine fire and not material, the which God had made to appear miraculously to show forth and signify the fire of Divine love wherewith were enkindled the souls of those holy friars and holy nuns; wherefore they departed thence with great consolation of heart and holy edification. Then, after a long while St. Francis and St. Clare, together with the others, returned to themselves and being greatly comforted with spiritual food they gave but little thought to bodily food; and so, that blessed meal being ended, St. Clare, well accompanied, returned to St. Damian; whereof, when they beheld her, the nuns had great joy, in that they feared lest St. Francis should have sent her to rule some other convent, even as he had aforetime sent Sister Agnes, her holy sister, to be abbess of Montecelli in Florence; and St. Francis had once said to St. Clare: "Hold thyself in readiness, that, if need be, I may send thee to some other Place"; whereto she as a daughter of holy obedience had made answer: "Father, I am ready to go whithersoever you shall send me"; and therefore the nuns rejoiced greatly when they received her back again; and from thenceforward St. Clare abode in much consolation.

16

How St. Francis received the counsel of St. Clare, and of the holy Friar Sylvester, that he ought by preaching to convert much folk; and how he founded the Third Order and preached to the birds and made the swallows keep silence

SHORTLY after his conversion, the humble servant of Christ, St. Francis, having already gathered many companions and received them into the Order, stood in great anxiety and in great doubt as to that which he ought to do; whether to devote himself wholly to prayer or sometimes also to preaching; and touching that matter he desired greatly to know the will of God; and because the holy humility which was in him suffered him not to trust to himself nor to his own prayers, he bethought him to inquire of the Divine will through the prayers of others; wherefore he called Friar Masseo and said: "Go thou to Sister Clare and tell her in my name that, together with certain of the most spiritual of her companions, she should devoutly pray God that He may vouchsafe to show me whether it be better that I give myself to preaching or to prayer alone. And thereafter go to Friar

Sylvester and tell him to do the like." Now, in the world, this had been that Messer Sylvester who had seen a cross of gold proceeding out of the mouth of St. Francis, the which was high even unto heaven and wide even unto the ends of the earth; and this Friar Sylvester was of so great devotion and of so great sanctity that by prayer he prevailed with God and all that he asked was granted him, and ofttimes he talked with God; and therefore St. Francis had great devotion toward him. Friar Masseo departed and, according to the bidding of St. Francis, did his embassage first to St. Clare and thereafter to Friar Sylvester; who, as soon as he had received it, forthwith gat himself to prayer, and while he was yet praying he obtained the Divine answer, and turned him to Friar Masseo and said: "Thus doth God bid thee say to Friar Francis; that God hath not called him to this estate for himself alone, but that he may have much fruit of souls, and that many through him may be saved". And when he had heard this, Friar Masseo returned to St. Clare, to know what answer she had received from God; and she replied that she and the other companions had had the self same answer from God which Friar Sylvester had had. Therewith Friar Masseo returned to St. Francis; and St. Francis welcomed him with very great charity, washing his feet and setting food before him. And when he had eaten, St. Francis called Masseo into the wood; and there he kneeled down before him, and drew back his cowl, and making a cross of his arms, asked him: "What doth my Lord Jesus Christ bid me do?" Friar Masseo made answer: "To Friar Sylvester as to Sister Clare and to her companion, Christ hath made answer and revealed that His will is that thou go through the world to preach, because He hath not chosen thee for thyself alone but also for the salvation of others".

Then St. Francis, when he had had this answer and knew thereby the will of Jesus Christ, rose up with exceeding great fervour and said: "Let us go in the name of God"; and he took as his companions Friar Masseo and Friar Agnolo, holy men. And going with impetuosity of spirit, taking thought neither of way nor path, they came to a walled place which is called Savurniano; and St. Francis began to preach; but first he bade the swallows which were twittering to keep silence until such time as he should finish preaching; and the swallows obeyed him; and there he preached with so great fervour that for devotion all the men and women of that town were minded to follow him and to abandon the town; but St. Francis suffered them not, saying: "Be not over hasty to depart; and I will ordain that which it behoves you to do for the salvation of your souls"; and then he bethought him to institute the Third Order for the universal salvation of all men: and so, leaving them greatly comforted and with minds turned to repentance, he gat him thence and came betwixt Cannaio and Bevagno. And passing on, full of fervour, he lifted up his eyes and saw certain trees hard by the road, whereupon was an almost infinite number of birds; whereat St. Francis marvelled, and said to his companions: "Ye shall await me here on the road, and I will go and preach to the birds my sisters"; and he went into the field and began to preach to the birds which were upon the ground; and anon those which were in the trees came to him, and all of them stood still together until St. Francis finished preaching; and even then they departed not until he gave them his blessing; and according to that which Friar Masseo afterward related to Friar James of Massa, when St. Francis went about among them touching them with his mantle, none of them moved therefor. Now the preaching of St. Francis was on this wise: "My sisters the birds, much are ye beholden unto God your creator, and alway and in every place ought ye to praise Him, because He hath given you liberty to fly wheresoever ye will, and hath clothed you on with twofold and threefold raiment. Moreover, He preserved your seed in the ark of Noah that your race might not be destroyed. Again, ye are beholden unto Him for the element of the air which He hath appointed for you; furthermore, ye sow not neither do ye reap; yet God feedeth you and giveth you rivers and fountains wherefrom to drink; He giveth you mountains and valleys for your refuge, and high trees wherein to build your nests; and, in that ye know not how to sew nor spin, God clotheth you and your little ones; wherefore doth your Creator love you seeing that He giveth you so many benefits.

Guard yourselves, therefore, my sisters the birds, from the sin of ingratitude and be ye ever mindful to give praise to God." And, as St. Francis spake these words unto them, all those birds began to open their beaks, and to stretch out their necks, and to open their wings, and reverently to bow their heads even unto the ground, and to show by their motions and by their songs that the holy father gave them very great delight: and St. Francis rejoiced with them and was glad and marvelled much at so great a multitude of birds, and at the most beautiful diversity of them, and at their attention and fearlessness; for which cause he devoutly praised the Creator in them.

Finally, when he had made an end of preaching, St. Francis made over them the sign of the Cross and gave them leave to depart; whereupon all those birds rose into the air with wondrous songs; and thereafter, according to the form of the Cross which St. Francis had made over them, they divided themselves into four bands; and one band flew towards the East, and one towards the West, and one towards the South and the fourth towards the North, and each company went singing marvellous songs; signifying thereby that, even as St. Francis, the Standard-bearer of the Cross, had preached to them, and made over them the sign of the Cross, according whereunto they separated themselves toward the four quarters of the world, so the preaching of the Cross of Christ, renewed by St. Francis, was about to be carried through all the world by him and by his friars; the which friars, like unto the birds, possess nothing of their own in this world but commit their lives wholly to the providence of God.

17

How a boy friar, while St. Francis was praying by night, saw Christ and the Virgin Mary and very many other saints hold converse with him

WHILE St. Francis yet lived, a boy very pure and innocent was received into the Order; and he abode in a little Place, wherein the friars, of necessity, slept on rugs. Once St. Francis came to the said Place, and, in the evening, when compline had been said, betook himself to sleep to the end that he might be able to rise up at night and pray, while the other friars slept, as he was wont to do. Now the said boy settled it in his heart to observe carefully the ways of St. Francis, if so be he might know his sanctity and especially that which he did at night when he rose up. Wherefore, that sleep might not betray him that boy laid himself down to sleep close to St. Francis and tied his cord to the cord of St. Francis that he might perceive when he rose up. And of this St. Francis felt nothing. But during the night, in the first watch while all the other friars slept, he rose up and found his cord thus tied, and he loosed it gently that the boy might not perceive it, and so St. Francis gat him alone to the wood which was hard by the Place, and entered into a little cell which was there and betook himself to prayer; and, after a certain time, the boy awoke and finding the cord untied and St. Francis gone away, he rose up and went to seek him; and finding the gate which led into the wood open, he bethought him that St. Francis might have gone thither, and he entered into the wood. And coming nigh unto the place where St. Francis was praying, he began to hear a sound as of many folk talking, and drawing nearer to see and to understand that which he heard, he beheld a wonderful light which encompassed St. Francis round about, and in the midst thereof he saw Christ and the Virgin Mary and St. John the Baptist and the Evangelist and a very great multitude of angels who spake with St. Francis. When he saw and heard this, the boy fell to the ground in a swoon. Thereafter, the mystery of that holy vision being ended, St. Francis, as he returned to the Place, stumbled upon the said boy, lying as if dead; and for compassion he lifted him up and carried him in his arms, even as the good shepherd carrieth his lambs. And then, learning from him how he had beheld the said vision, he commanded him to tell no man as long as he lived. Afterward the boy, increasing in great grace with God and in devotion to St. Francis, became a worthy man in the Order; and after the death of St. Francis he revealed the said vision to the friars.

18

Of the marvellous chapter which St. Francis held at Santa Maria degli Angeli, where there were more than five thousand friars

ONCE the faithful servant of Christ, Francis, held a general chapter at Santa Maria degli Angeli, to which chapter were gathered more than five thousand friars; and thither came St. Dominic, head and founder of the Order of Preaching Friars, the which at that time was journeying from Burgundy to Rome. And hearing of the congregation of the chapter which St. Francis was holding in the plain of Santa Maria degli Angeli, he betook himself thither to see the same, with seven friars of his Order. There was then at the said chapter a cardinal who was greatly devoted to St. Francis who had prophesied to him that he would be Pope, and so thereafter it befel; the which cardinal had come specially from Perugia, where was the court, to Assisi; every day he came to see St. Francis and his friars, and sometimes he sang mass and sometimes he preached to the friars in chapter; and the said cardinal took very great delight and was filled with devotion when he came to visit that holy college. And seeing the friars seated round about Santa Maria, company by company, here forty, there a hundred and there eighty together, all employed in speaking of God, in prayers, in tears and in exercises of charity, behaving themselves with so great silence and with such sobriety that no clamour was heard there, nor any disturbance, he marvelled to behold so great discipline in so vast a multitude, and, with tears and great devotion, said: "Verily this is the camp of tie army of the knights of God". In all that great multitude no one was heard to tell stories or to jest; but, wherever a company of friars was gathered together, they either prayed, or said the office, or bewailed their own sins or those of their benefactors, or reasoned of the salvation of souls. In that encampment were booths made of withes and of rushes, separate for each company, according to the diverse provinces of the friars: and therefore that chapter was called the Chapter of the Withes or of the Rushes. Their beds were the bare ground and some had a little straw; their bolsters were of stone or wood. For which cause whoever heard or saw them had so great devotion toward them, and such was the fame of their sanctity that, from the court of the Pope, which was then in Perugia, and from other places in the Val di Spoleto, there came many counts, barons, knights and other gentlemen, and many common folk, and cardinals, and bishops and abbots, with many other clerks, to see that so holy and great and humble congregation of so many holy men, the like whereof the world had never; and chiefly they came to see the head and most holy father of that holy folk, who had robbed the world of so fair a prey, and gathered so goodly and devout a flock to follow in the footsteps of the true Shepherd Jesus Christ. All this general chapter, then, being gathered together, the holy father of all and minister-general St. Francis, in fervour of spirit, expounded the word of God and preached unto them in a loud voice that which the Holy Spirit made him say; and he set forth the argument of his sermon in these words: "My sons, great things have we promised unto God; but greater are the promises of God to us-ward, if we observe those promises which we have made unto Him; and we await with confidence those things which are promised unto us. Short is the pleasure of the world; the pain which follows it is eternal; small is the pain of this life, but the glory of the other life is infinite." And most devoutly preaching upon these words, he comforted and urged the friars to obedience and reverence of Holy Mother Church, and to fraternal love, and to pray God for all men, to have patience in the adversities of the world and temperance in its prosperities, and Ito hold fast purity and angelic chastity, and to be at peace and concord with God, and with men, and with their own consciences, and to love and observe most holy Poverty. And touching the same he said: "I command you for the merit of holy obedience, all of you, who are here met together, that not one of you take any thought or care of anything to eat or to drink, or of things necessary for the body, but give yourselves wholly to prayer and to praising God; and all the care of your bodies leave ye to Him, for of you He hath peculiar care".

And all of them received this commandment with joyful hearts and happy faces: and when St. Francis had finished his sermon, they all with one accord betook themselves to prayer. Wherefore, St. Dominic, who was present while all these things were done, marvelled greatly at the commandment of St. Francis, and deemed him indiscreet, being unable to think how so great a multitude could be provided for, without taking any thought of the things necessary for the body. But the Chief Shepherd, Christ the Blessed, willing to show that He careth for His sheep and hath singular love for His poor, presently inspired the inhabitants of Perugia, of Spoleto, of

Foligno, of Spello and of Assisi, and of the other places round about, to bring food and drink to that holy congregation. And lo! immediately, from the aforesaid towns came men with pack animals, horses and carts laden with bread and wine and beans and cheese and other good things to eat, according to that which was necessary for the poor of Christ.

Besides this, they brought tablecloths, pitchers, bowls, glasses and other vessels which were needful for so great a multitude; and blessed was he esteemed who could bring the most, or who could serve most diligently; so that even knights, barons, and other gentlemen, who came to see, waited upon them at table with great humility and devotion. For the which cause, St. Dominic, beholding these things and knowing of a surety that Divine Providence showed forth itself therein, humbly acknowledged that he had wrongly judged St. Francis to have given an indiscreet commandment, and going before him, he kneeled down and humbly confessed his fault, and said: "Verily God hath special care of these holy mendicants, and I knew it not; and from henceforward I promise to observe the holy gospel poverty; and in the name of God do I curse all the friars of my Order, who in the said Order shall presume to have private property". Thus was St. Dominic greatly edified by the faith of the most holy Francis, and by the obedience and poverty of so great and ordered an assembly, and by the Divine Providence and by the great abundance of every good thing. In that sanie chapter, St. Francis was told that many friars wore a mail-shirt next the skin and iron rings whereby many fell sick and died and many were hindered from prayer. Wherefore St. Francis, as a most discreet father, commanded in the name of holy obedience that whosoever had either mail-shirt or iron ring should take it off and place it before him, and they did so; and there were counted more than five hundred iron shirts, and many more rings, both for the arms and for the belly; so that they made a great heap; and St. Francis caused them to be left there. Thereafter, the chapter being ended, St. Francis, exhorting them all to well doing, and teaching them how they ought to keep themselves unspotted from this evil world, sent them back to their provinces, with God's blessing and with his, full of consolation and of spiritual joy.

19

How from the vineyard of the priest of Rieti, in whose house St. Francis prayed, the grapes were taken away and gathered by the much folk which came unto him, and how thereafter that priest miraculously made more wine than ever before, even as St. Francis had promised him. And how God revealed to St. Francis that he would have paradise for his portion

UPON a time, St. Francis being grievously diseased in his eyes, Messer Ugolino, Cardinal Protector of the Order, for the great love which he had toward him, wrote to him that he should go to hint at Rieti, where were very excellent physicians for the eyes. Then St. Francis, having received the letter of the Cardinal, betook himself first to St. Damian, where was St. Clare, the most devoted bride of Christ, to give her some consolation; and afterward to go to the Cardinal. Now, the night after St. Francis came thither, his eyes became so much worse, that he saw no light at all. Wherefore, in that he could not depart, St. Clare made for him a little cell of reeds, wherein he might the better rest himself. But St. Francis, through the pain of his infirmity and by reason of the multitude of mice, which caused him very great annoyance, was not able on anywise to find rest, either by day or by night. And enduring for much time that pain and tribulation, he began to think and to know that that was a scourge from God for his sins: and he began to thank God with all his heart and with his mouth, and thereafter he cried with a loud voice and said: "My Lord, I am worthy of this and of much worse. My Lord Jesus Christ, the Good Shepherd, who showest forth Thy mercy to us sinners through divers pains and bodily afflictions, grant grace and virtue to me, Thy little sheep, that by no infirmity or anguish or pain I may depart from Thee." And, while he was thus praying, there came unto him a voice from heaven, saying: "Francis, answer Me: if all the earth were gold, and all the seas and fountains and rivers were balm, and all the mountains and hills and rocks were precious stones; and thou shouldst find another treasure more excellent than these things are, even as gold is more excellent than earth, and balm than water, and precious stones than mountains and rocks, and if instead of this infirmity that most excellent treasure were given unto thee, wouldst thou not be well content therewith and full of mirth?" St. Francis answered: "Lord, I am not worthy of so precious a treasure". And the voice of God said unto him: "Rejoice, Francis, because that is the treasure of life eternal which I keep for thee, and from this very hour I invest thee therewith, and this infirmity and affliction is the earnest of that blessed treasure". Then St. Francis, full of very great joy at so glorious a promise, called his companion and said: "Let us go to the Cardinal". And having first consoled St. Clare with holy words, and having humbly taken leave of her, he set out towards Rieti, and when he drew nigh thereto, so great a multitude of people came forth to meet him that he did not wish to enter the city, but betook himself to a church which was distant from the city peradventure two miles. The citizens, knowing that he was in the said church, thronged it round about to look upon him, on such wise that the vineyard of the church was laid waste and all the grapes thereof were carried away; whereat the priest was sore grieved in his heart, and repented him that he had received St. Francis into his church. The thought of the priest being revealed of God to St. Francis, he sent to call him and said unto him: "Most dear father, how many measures of wine doth this vineyard yield thee a year, when it yieldeth its best?" He made answer: "Twelve measures". St. Francis said: "I pray thee, father, bear patiently my sojourning here for certain days, because I find here much repose; and do thou permit every man to take the grapes of this thy vineyard, for the love of God and of me a mendicant; and I promise thee in the name of my Lord Jesus Christ that it shall yield thee this year twenty measures". And this St. Francis did in return for his sojourn there, by reason of the great salvation of souls which was manifestly being wrought among the folk which came thither, of whom many departed drunk with Divine love, and abandoned the world. The priest, trusting to the promise of St. Francis, abandoned his vineyard freely to those who came to him. When, behold a marvel! Albeit the vineyard was wholly wasted and despoiled so that scarcely were there left therein any bunches of grapes; yet when the time of the vintage was come, the priest gathered those few bunches and put them in the winepress and trode upon them; and, according to the promise of St. Francis, drew therefrom twenty measures of excellent wine. By which miracle it was made manifest that, as, by the merits of St. Francis, the vineyard despoiled of grapes abounded in wine, so likewise the Christian people, barren of virtue through their sins, through the merits and doctrine of St. Francis, abounded in the good fruits of repentance.

20

Of a very beautiful vision which was seen by a young friar, who held the cowl in so great abomination that he was minded to put off the habit and to leave the Order

A YOUNG man very noble and dainty entered the Order of St. Francis: the which, after certain days, by the instigation of the demon, began to hold the habit that he wore in such abomination, that it seemed to him that he wore a most base sack; he had a horror of the sleeves, he abominated the cowl, and the length and roughness of the habit appeared to him an intolerable burden. And his disgust for the Religion ever increasing, he finally resolved to abandon the habit and return to the world. Now he had already accustomed himself, according to that which his master had taught him, whenever he passed before the altar of the convent, wherein was kept the Body of Christ, to kneel with great reverence and to draw back his cowl and with his arms crossed upon his breast to bow himself down. It befel that, on the night on which he was about to depart and leave the Order, it was necessary for him to pass before the altar of the convent, and, according to his custom, he kneeled him down and did reverence. And, anon, he was rapt in spirit and a marvellous vision was showed him by God; for he saw before him an almost infinite number of saints, after the fashion of a procession, two and two, clad in very beautiful and precious vestments of silken stuffs; and their faces and hands shone like the sun, and they moved to the sound of angelic songs and music; among which saints were two more nobly clad and adorned than all the rest; and they were encompassed round about by so bright a light that whosoever looked on them was filled with very great amaze; and, almost at the end of the procession, he saw one adorned with so great glory that he seemed a new-made knight, more honoured than his peers. Beholding the aforesaid vision, this young man marvelled thereat and knew not what that procession might mean, and he dared not ask but stood dazed with keen delight. Nevertheless, when all the procession had passed by, he took courage and ran after the last of them and with great dread enquired of them, saying: "O most dear ones, I beseech you that it may please you to tell me, who are these so marvellous folk which go in this procession so majestical". They made answer: "Know, son, that we be all minor friars, who now are coming from paradise". Whereupon he asked: "Who are those two who are more resplendent than the rest?" They answered: "These be St. Francis and St. Anthony; and he who goeth last, whom thou seest so highly honoured, is a holy friar who is newly dead, whom; because he fought valiantly against temptations and persevered even unto the end, we are leading in triumph to the glory of paradise; and these beautiful silken vestments which we wear, are given us of God in exchange for the rough habits which we wore patiently in the Religion; and the glorious resplendence which thou seest in us, is given us of God for the humility and patience, and for the holy poverty and obedience and chastity which we observed even unto the end. Wherefore, son, deem it not a hard thing to wear the sackcloth of the Religion which bringeth so great a reward; because if, with the sackcloth of St. Francis, for the love of Christ, thou shalt despise the world and mortify the flesh, and shalt fight valiantly against the demon, thou, together with us, shalt have like vestments, brightness and glory." And when these words had been spoken, the young man came to himself, and, comforted by the vision, drove away from him every temptation and confessed his fault before the guardian and the friars; from thenceforward he desired the roughness of penance and of raiment, and ended his life in the Order in great sanctity.

21

Of the most holy miracle which St. Francis wrought when he converted the very fierce wolf of Agobio

DURING the time that St. Francis dwelt in the city of Agobio, there appeared in the territory of Agobio a very great wolf, terrible and fierce, the which not only devoured animals but also men and women, so that all the citizens stood in great fear, because ofttimes he came nigh unto the city; and all men went armed when they went forth from the city, as if they were going to battle; and therewithal they were not able to defend themselves from him, when haply any man encountered him alone; and for dread of this wolf things came to such a pass that no one dared to leave the city. Wherefore, St. Francis, having compassion on the men of the city, was minded to go forth to meet this wolf, albeit the citizens altogether counselled him not to do so; and, making the sign of the cross, he went forth from the city with his companions, putting all his trust in God. And because the others feared to go farther, St. Francis alone took the road toward the place where the wolf was. And lo! while many citizens who had come out to behold this miracle were looking on, the said wolf made at St. Francis with open mouth. Whereupon St. Francis advanced towards him, and making over him the sign of the most holy Cross, called him unto him and spake to him after this manner: "Come hither, friar wolf. I command thee in Christ's name that thou do no harm to me nor to any other." O marvellous thing! Scarcely had St. Francis made the sign of the cross than the terrible wolf instantly closed his mouth and stayed his running; and, in obedience to that command, came, gentle as a lamb, and laid himself down at the feet of St. Francis. Then St. Francis spake unto him thus: "Friar wolf, thou dost much damage in these parts, and thou hast committed great crimes, destroying and slaying the creatures of God without His licence: and not only hast thou slain and devoured beasts, but thou hast also had the hardihood to slay men, made in the image of God; for the which cause thou dost merit the gallows as a thief and most iniquitous murderer; and all men cry out against thee and complain, and all this city is thine enemy. But I desire, friar wolf, to make peace between thee and them; to the end that thou mayest no more offend them and that they may forgive thee all thy past offences and neither men nor dogs may pursue thee any more." At these words, the wolf, by movements of his body and tail and eyes, and by bowing his head, showed that he accepted that which St. Francis said and was minded to observe the same. Thereupon St. Francis spake unto him again saying: "Friar wolf, inasmuch as it seemeth good unto thee to make and keep this peace, I promise thee that, so long as thou shalt live, I will cause thy food to be given thee continually by the men of this city, so that thou shalt no more suffer hunger; for I know full well that whatever of evil thou hast done thou hast done it through hunger. But seeing that I beg for thee this grace, I desire, friar wolf, that thou shouldst promise me that never from henceforward wilt thou injure any human being or any animal. Dost thou promise me this?" And the wolf, by bowing his head, gave evident token that he promised it. And St. Francis said: "Friar wolf, I desire that thou swear me fealty touching this promise, to the end that I may trust thee utterly". Then St. Francis held forth his hand to receive his fealty, and the wolf lifted up his right fore-foot and put it with friendly confidence in the hand of St. Francis, giving thereby such token of fealty as he was able. Thereupon St. Francis said: "Friar wolf, I command thee in the name of Jesus Christ to come now with me, nothing doubting, and let us go and stablish this peace in the name of God". And the wolf went with him obediently, like a gentle lamb; wherefore the citizens beholding the same marvelled greatly. And anon, the fame thereof was noised abroad through all the city, and all the people, men and women, great and small, young and old, thronged to the piazza to see the wolf with St. Francis. And when all the folk were gathered together, St. Francis rose up to preach unto them, saying, among other things, how, by reason of sin, God permits such pestilences; and far more perilous is the fire of hell, the which must for ever torment the damned, than is the fury of a wolf which can only kill the body; how much then are the jaws of hell to be feared when the jaws of a little beast can hold so great a multitude in fear! "Turn ye then, most dear ones, turn ye to God, and do befitting penance for your sins, and God will save you from the wolf in this present world and from the fire of hell in that which is to come". And when he had done preaching, St. Francis said: "Hear ye, my brethren. Friar wolf, who is here before you, hath promised and sworn fealty to me, that he will make peace with you and never more offend you in anything; do ye now promise him to give him every day that whereof he hath need; and I become surety unto you for him that he will faithfully observe this covenant of peace." Then all the people with one voice promised to provide him food continually, and St. Francis spake unto the wolf before them all, saying: "And thou, friar wolf, dost thou promise to observe the covenant of peace which thou hast made with this folk, that thou wilt offend neither men nor beast nor any creature?" And the wolf kneeled him down and bowed his head, and, with gentle movements of his body and tail and ears, showed as far as he was able his determination to keep that covenant wholly. Said St. Francis: "Friar wolf, as thou didst me fealty touching this promise, without the gate, so now I desire that thou do me fealty, before all the people, touching thy promise, and that thou wilt not deceive me concerning my promise and surety which I have given for thee". Then the wolf, lifting up his right foot, put it in the hand of St. Francis. By which act, and by the other acts aforesaid, all the people were fulfilled with so great joy and wonder, alike for devotion toward the saint, and for the strangeness of the miracle, and for the peace with the wolf, that they all began to shout to heaven, praising and blessing God who had sent them St. Francis, who, by his merits, had freed them from the jaws of the cruel beast. And thereafter, the said wolf lived two years in Agobio, and entered familiarly into the houses, going from door to door, neither doing injury to any one nor receiving any; and he was courteously nourished by the people; and, as he thus went through the town and through the houses, never did any dog bark after him. Finally, after two years, friar wolf died of old age; whereat the citizens lamented much, because as long as they saw him going so gently through their city, they recalled the better the virtue and sanctity of St. Francis.

22

How St. Francis tamed the wild turtle-doves

ONE day, a youth had taken many turtle-doves, and as he was carrying them to sell them, St. Francis, who ever had singular compassion for gentle creatures, chanced to meet him, and looking upon those turtle-doves with compassionate eye, said to the youth: "Good youth, I pray thee give them to me, that birds so gentle, which in the Scriptures are likened unto chaste and humble and faithful souls, come not into the hands of cruel men who would slay them". Whereupon, inspired of God, he forthwith gave them all to St. Francis; and he receiving them in his bosom, began to speak to them sweetly: "O my sisters, simple, innocent, chaste turtle-doves, why do you let yourselves be taken? Now I desire to save you from death and to make nests for you, so that ye may bring forth fruit and multiply, according to the commandments of our Creator." And St. Francis went and made nests for them all, and they resorted thereunto, and began to lay eggs and to hatch forth their young, in the presence of the friars; and so tame were they and so familiar with St. Francis and with the other friars that they might have been domestic fowls which had always been fed by them; and never did they depart until St. Francis with his blessing gave them leave to do so. And to the young man, which had given them unto him, St. Francis said: "Son, thou wilt yet be a friar in this Order, and thou wilt serve Jesus Christ with all thy heart"; and so it came to pass, for the said youth became a friar and lived in the Order in great sanctity.

23

How St. Francis set free the friar who was in sin with the demon

ONCE when St. Francis was praying in the Place of Porziuncula, he saw by Divine revelation, the whole Place encompassed about and besieged by the demons after the fashion of a great army; but none of them could enter into the Place, inasmuch as these friars were of so great sanctity that the demons found none into whom they might enter. But while they thus persisted, it fell upon a day that one of those friars was offended with another, and thought within his heart how he could accuse him and avenge himself on him; for the which cause, while yet he cherished this evil thought, the devil, the door being opened, entered into the Place and set himself upon the neck of that friar. Thereupon the compassionate and careful shepherd, who ever watched over his flock seeing that the wolf had entered in to devour his little sheep, immediately caused that friar to be called to him, and bade him forthwith reveal the poison of hatred conceived against his neighbour, through the which he had come into the hands of the enemy. Wherefore, he, full of fear at seeing himself thus discovered by the holy father, disclosed all the venom and rancour of his heart, and confessed his fault and humbly besought penance and mercy; and when he had so done, and was absolved of his sin, and had received penance, anon, in the presence of St. Francis, the demon departed; and the friar, thus delivered from the hands of the cruel beast, through the loving-kindness of the good shepherd, gave thanks to God, and returning, corrected and admonished, to the flock of the holy shepherd, lived afterward in great sanctity.

24

How St. Francis converted the Soldan of Babylon to the faith

ST. FRANCIS, urged thereto by zeal for the faith of Christ, and by the desire of martyrdom, went once across the seas with his twelve most holy companions, to betake himself straight to the Soldan of Babylon; and being come unto a country of the Saracens, where the passes were guarded by certain cruel men to the end that no Christian who went thereby might be able to escape death; they, as it pleased God, were not slain, but taken, beaten and bound, and so led into the presence of the Soldan. And being in his presence, St. Francis, taught by the Holy Ghost, preached so divinely of the faith of Christ, that for that faith he even wished to enter into the fire. Wherefore the Soldan began to have very great devotion toward him, alike for the constancy of his faith and for the contempt of the world which he saw in him (inasmuch as he would receive no gift from him, albeit he was exceeding poor), and also for the zeal of martyrdom which he saw in him. From thenceforward the Soldan heard him gladly and prayed him that he would often return to him; granting, to him and to his companions, leave to preach wheresoever they pleased; and he gave them a token to the end that they might not be offended by any man. [Having this leave then, St. Francis sent his chosen companions, two by two, into divers regions of the Saracens to preach the faith of Christ. And he, with one of them, chose a street and, arriving thereat, entered into an inn to rest himself. And there he found a woman, most beautiful of body but foul of soul, the which accursed one tempted him to sin. And St. Francis said: "I accept, let us to bed," and she led him into a chamber. Then St. Francis said: "Come with me"; and he conducted her to a very great fire which was burning in that chamber; and in fervour of spirit he stripped himself naked and cast himself down beside that fire, on the hot hearthstone; and he invited her to go and undress herself and to lie with him in that downy and beautiful bed. And, when St. Francis had thus lain there for a long time, with cheerful face and without being burned or singed at all, that woman, terrified at so great a miracle and pricked in the heart, not only repented her of her sin and evil intent, but also turned perfectly to the faith of Christ, and became of so great sanctity that, through her, many souls were saved in those lands.] At last St. Francis, seeing that he could have no more fruit in those parts, prepared, by Divine revelation, to return with all his companions to the land of the faithful; and, having gathered them all together, he returned to the Soldan and took leave of him. Then the Soldan said unto him: "Friar Francis, I would willingly be converted to the faith of Christ, but I fear to be so now, because, if these heard thereof, they would slay both thee and me, with all thy companions: and seeing that thou canst yet do much good and that I have certain matters of great moment to conclude, I would not now bring about thy death and mine; but do thou teach me how I may save myself; I am ready to do that which thou mayest lay upon me". Then St. Francis said: "Sir, I now go from thee; but after I shall be come into my own country and, through the grace of God, shall have ascended into heaven, after my death, according as it shall please God, I will send thee two of my friars from whom thou mayest receive the holy baptism of Christ, and thou shalt be saved, as my Lord Jesus Christ hath revealed unto me. And do thou, in the meantime, free thyself from every hindrance, to the end that, when the grace of God shall come unto thee, it may find thee prepared to faith and to devotion." And this he promised to do, and so did he. Now when this was done, St. Francis returned with that venerable college of his holy companions; and after certain years, St. Francis by bodily death rendered his soul to God. And the Soldan, falling sick, awaited the fulfilment of the promise of St. Francis, and set guards at certain passes and ordered that, if two friars should appear in the habit of St. Francis, they should immediately be brought to him.

At that time St. Francis appeared to two friars, and commanded them to go without delay to the Soldan to provide for his salvation, according as he had promised him; the which friars set out immediately, and crossing the sea, were led before the Soldan by the aforesaid guard; and when the Soldan saw them, he was exceeding glad and said: "Now know I of a truth that God hath sent me His servants for my salvation, according to the promise which St Francis made me by Divine revelation." And, when he had been instructed in the faith of Christ and baptised by the said friars, thus born again in Christ, he died of that sickness and his soul was saved through the merits and prayers of St. Francis.

25

How St. Francis miraculously healed one who was a leper both in soul and body; and that which the soul said unto him as it went into heaven

THE true disciple of Christ, Messer St. Francis, while he lived in this miserable life, sought with all his strength to follow Christ, the perfect Master; whence it ofttimes befel, through Divine operation, that, in the selfsame hour that he healed men's bodies, their souls were healed by God, even as we read of Christ. And, inasmuch as he not only himself willingly served lepers, but, furthermore, had commanded that the friars of his Order, wheresoever they went or sojourned throughout the world, should serve lepers for the love of Christ, who for our sake willed to be accounted leprous; it came to pass upon a time, that, in a certain Place, near to that wherein St. Francis then dwelt, the friars served the lepers and the sick in a hospital; wherein was a leper so impatient and so intolerable and so forward, that every one believed most certainly that he was possessed of the devil, and so in truth he was; for not only did he revile and shamefully belabour whomsoever served him, but (what is far worse) he blasphemously railed upon Christ the blessed and His most holy Mother the Virgin Mary, so that on nowise could any one be found who was able or willing to serve him. And albeit the friars strove to endure patiently the insults and injuries to themselves, that they might increase the merit of patience; nevertheless, because their consciences were unable to bear those which were uttered against Christ and His Mother, they resolved to abandon the said leper altogether; but they were unwilling to do so until they had duly given notice to St. Francis, who was then dwelling in a Place near at hand. And when they had told him thereof, St. Francis betook himself to this perverse leper, and coming unto him saluted him, saying: "God give thee peace, my dearest brother". The leper made answer: "What peace can I have from God, who hath taken from me peace and every good thing, and hath made me all rotten and stinking?" And St. Francis said: "Son, have patience; for the infirmities of our bodies are given us of God, in this world, for the salvation of our souls, because they are of great merit when they are borne with patience". The sick man answered: "And how can I bear patiently the continual pain which torments me day and night? And not only am I afflicted by my sickness, but yet worse by the friars whom thou gayest me that they might serve me, for they do not serve me as they ought." Then St. Francis, knowing by revelation that this leper was possessed by an evil spirit, departed and betook himself to prayer and devoutly besought God for him. And when he had done praying he returned and spake thus: "Son, I would serve thee myself, since thou art not satisfied with the others". "I am content," said the sick man, "but what canst thou do for me more than the others?" Said St. Francis: "That which thou desirest I will do". Said the leper: "I desire that thou wash me all over because I stink so greatly that

I cannot endure my own self". Then St. Francis forthwith caused water to be heated with many sweet-smelling herbs; thereafter he undressed him and began to wash him with his own hands, while another friar poured on the water; and by Divine miracle, where St. Francis touched him with his holy hands, the leprosy departed and the flesh remained perfectly sound. And even as the flesh began to heal, so the soul began to heal also; wherefore the leper, seeing that he was beginning to be made whole, began to feel great remorse and repentance for his sins, and to weep very bitterly; so that, while the body was cleansed outwardly of the leprosy by washing of water, so the soul was cleansed inwardly of sin by amendment and by tears. And when he was completely cured, both in body and in soul, he humbly confessed his fault and said, weeping aloud: "Woe is me, for I am worthy of hell for the injuries and revilings which I have done and spoken against the friars, and for my impatience against God and the blasphemies which I have uttered"; wherefore, for fifteen days he continued to weep bitterly for his sins, beseeching mercy of God, and confessing himself wholly to a priest. And St. Francis beholding so clear a miracle, which God had wrought by his hands, gave thanks to God and gat him thence, going to countries very far away; because by reason of humility he desired to flee every glory, and in all his works sought only the honour and glory of God and not his own. Afterward, as it pleased God, the said leper, healed in body and soul, after his fifteen days of penance, fell sick of another sickness, and fortified with the sacraments of the Church, died a holy death; and, as his soul went into paradise, it appeared in the air to St. Francis, who was praying in a wood, and said unto him: "Knowest thou me?" "Who art thou?" said St. Francis. "I am that leper whom Christ the blessed healed through thy merits, and today I go to eternal life; wherefore I give thanks to God and to thee.

Blessed be thy soul and thy body, and blessed thy holy words and works; because through thee many souls shall be saved in the world; and know that there is no day in the world, whereon the holy angels and the other saints thank not God for the holy fruits which thou and thy Order bring forth in divers parts of the world; and therefore do thou take comfort and thank God, abiding alway in His benediction." And when he had said these words he went into heaven; and St. Francis remained much consoled.

26

How St. Francis converted three robbers which were murderers, and how they became friars; and of the very noble vision which one of them, who was a most holy friar, saw

ST. FRANCIS went upon a time through the desert of Borgo San Sepolcro, and as he passed through a walled place which is called Monte Casale, there came to him a young man, noble and luxurious, who said unto him: "Father, I would very willingly be one of your friars". St. Francis replied: "Son, thou art a luxurious youth and noble, perchance thou couldst not bear poverty and hardships". And he said: "Father, are ye not men even as I am? Wherefore, even as ye bear them, so shall I be able to do, through the grace of Jesus Christ." This answer pleased St. Francis much, and thereupon he blessed him and forthwith received him into the Order, and gave him the name of Friar Angelo; and so graciously did this youth bear himself that, a short time thereafter, St. Francis made him guardian in the Place which is called [the Hermitage] of Monte Casale. Now at that time three notorious robbers frequented the district, the which wrought many ill deeds therein; and upon a day they came to the said Place of the friars and besought the said Friar Angelo, the guardian, that he would give them to eat; whereupon the guardian answered them after this manner, rebuking them harshly: "Ye robbers and cruel murderers, not only are ye not ashamed to rob others of the fruits of their toil, but, presumptuous and impudent that ye are, ye would even devour the alms which are sent to the servants of God. Unworthy are ye that the earth should bear you up; for ye have no reverence for men or for the God who created you. Go, then, about your business, and never show yourselves here again." Therefore were they wrath and gat them thence in eat indignation. And lo! St. Francis returned from without, with his wallet of bread and a small vessel of wine, which he and his companion had begged; and, when the guardian had told him how he had driven those men away, St. Francis rebuked him severely, saying that he had borne himself cruelly, inasmuch as sinners are better led back to God by gentleness than by cruel reproofs;" For [said he] our Master Jesus Christ, whose Gospel we have promised to observe, saith *that they that are whole need not a physician but they that are sick, and that He was not come to call the righteous but sinners to repentance;* and therefore often did He eat with them. Seeing, then, that thou hast done contrary to charity and contrary to the Holy Gospel of Christ, I command thee, by holy obedience, that thou forthwith take this wallet of bread, which I have begged, and this vessel of wine, and seek them diligently, through mountains and valleys, until thou find them, and give them all this bread and wine in my name; and afterward do thou kneel down before them and humbly confess to them thy sin of cruelty; and then pray them in my name to do evil no longer, but to fear God and offend Him no more; and, if they will do this, I promise to provide for their needs, and to give them to eat and drink continually; and when thou shalt have told them this, return hither humbly." While the said guardian went to do his commandment, St. Francis betook himself to prayer and besought God that He would soften the hearts of those robbers and convert them to repentance. The obedient guardian came up with them and gave them the bread and wine, and did and said that which St. Francis had laid upon him. And, as it pleased God, while yet those robbers ate the alms of St. Francis, they began to say, one to the other: "Woe unto us, unhappy wretches that we are! how sore are the pains of hell which await us! for we not only go about robbing our neighbours and beating and wounding them, but also slaying them; and yet, notwithstanding all the enormous wrongs and wickednesses which we do, we have no remorse of conscience, nor fear of God; and lo! this holy friar, who hath come to us on account of a few words which he spake unto us justly by reason of our wickedness, hath humbly confessed his fault to us; and more than this, he hath brought us bread and wine, and so gracious a promise from the holy father. Verily these friars are saints of God, who merit the paradise of God; and we are children of eternal perdition, who merit the pains of hell, and every day we increase our damnation; nor do we know whether, from the sins which we have committed until now, we shall be able to turn to the mercy of God." And, when one of them had spoken these and like words, the others aid: "Verily thou speakest the truth, but what then ought we to do?" "Let us go," said one, "to St. Francis; and if he gives us hope that we may be able to turn from our sins to the mercy of God, let us do that which he commands us, if so be we may deliver our souls from the pains of hell." This counsel was pleasing to the others; and so, all three of them being agreed, they went in haste to St. Francis and spake unto him thus: "Father, by reason of the many horrible sins which we have committed, we do not believe that we can turn to the mercy of God; but if thou hast any hope that God will receive us to mercy, lo! we are ready to do that which thou shalt bid us, and to do penance with thee". Then St. Francis received them lovingly and with benignity, and consoled them with many ensamples, assuring them of the mercy of God, and promising them that of a surety he would obtain it for them from God, showing them that the mercy of God is infinite, and even if our sins were infinite the mercy of God is greater than our sins, according to the Gospel; and St. Paul the Apostle said: *Christ the blessed came into this world to redeem sinners.*

Through the which words and similar teachings, the said three robbers renounced the devil and his works; and St. Francis received them into the Order, and they began to do great penance; and two of them lived but a little while after their conversion, and went to paradise. But the third, surviving his companions, and bethinking him of his sins past, turned himself to the doing of such penance that for fifteen successive years, except during the common Lenten fasts, which he kept with the other friars, he fasted three days a week on bread and water, always going barefoot and with one sole habit on his back, and never did he sleep after matins. During this time, St. Francis passed from this miserable life; and when this man [*i.e.*, the converted robber] had for many years continued in such penance, lo! one night after matins, there came upon him so great a temptation to sleep that he might by no means resist it and keep watch as he was wont to do. Finally, being unable to resist his drowsiness or to pray, he went to his bed to sleep; and anon, as soon as he had laid down his head, he was rapt away and led in the spirit to a very high mountain, where was a chasm exceeding deep; and on this side and on that were rocks, broken and splintered, and uneven ledges which jutted out from the rocks, so that it was a dreadful sight to look into that chasm. And the angel that was leading this friar pushed him and flung him down that chasm; and rebounding and striking from ledge to ledge and rock to rock, at last he reached the bottom of the precipice, all dismembered and dashed to fragments, as it seemed to him; and as he lay thus upon the ground in evil case, he that led him said: "Get up, for thou must needs make a greater journey". The friar answered: "Thou seemest to me a very unreasonable and cruel man, who, when thou seest me at the point of death from this fall which hath thus broken me to pieces, biddest me rise up". And the angel drew nigh unto him and, touching him, perfectly healed all his limbs and made him whole. And thereafter he showed him a great plain, full of stones, sharp and cutting, and of thorns and briars, and told him that it behoved him to run across all that plain, and to go barefooted until he reached the end, where he beheld a burning fiery furnace, into the which he must needs enter. And when the friar had passed over all the plain with great anguish and pain, the angel said: "Enter into this furnace for it behoves thee so to do". The friar made answer: "Ah me! how cruel a guide art thou! who seest me well-nigh dead by reason of this grievous plain, and now tellest me to enter for repose into this fiery furnace". And as he looked, he saw, round about the furnace, many demons with forks of iron in their hands, wherewith, because he hesitated to enter, they forthwith thrust him inside. And, when he was come into the furnace, he looked and saw one who had been his godfather, who was all on fire; and he asked of him: "O unhappy godfather, how camest thou hither?" And he replied: "Go a little farther, and thou wilt find my wife, thy godmother, who will tell thee the reason of our damnation". When the friar had gone a little farther, behold! the said godmother appeared to him all ablaze, enclosed in a cornmeasure; and he asked of her: "O ill-fated and miserable godmother, wherefore earnest thou into such cruel torment?" And she replies: "Because, at the time of the great famine, which St. Francis foretold, my husband and I sold wheat and grain by false measure, and therefore do I burn shut up in this measure".

And, when she had spoken these words, the angel, who was leading the friar, thrust him out from the furnace, and thereafter said to him: "Prepare to make a horrible journey, which thou must needs go". And he, lamenting said: "O most cruel guide, who hast no compassion on me, thou seest that I am almost altogether burnt up in this furnace, and yet thou wouldest lead me upon a perilous and horrible journey". And then the angel touched him and made him whole and strong. Thereafter he led him to a bridge, whereover none might pass without great danger; inasmuch as it was very slight and narrow and exceeding slippery and without any railing on the side; and below there ran a terrible river, full of serpents and dragons and scorpions, and it sent forth a very great stench; and the angel said: "Pass over this bridge, for verily it behoveth thee to cross it". He made answer: "And how shall I be able to cross it without falling into that perilous river?" Said the angel: "Follow after me, and set thy foot where thou shalt see me set mine. So shalt thou cross safely." The friar followed the angel as he had told him, until he reached the middle of the bridge, and, when he had come thus to the middle thereof, the angel flew away, and departing from him, betook himself to the top of a very high mountain, a long way off, on the farther side of the bridge; and the friar noted well the place whither the angel had flown; but, being left without a guide, he looked down and saw those very terrible beasts, waiting with their heads out of the water and with their mouths open, ready to devour him, if he should fall; and he was so terrified that he knew not on anywise what to do or to say; because he could neither turn back nor go forward. Wherefore, finding himself in such dire straits, and having no other refuge save God alone, he laid him down and embraced the bridge with his arms, and with all his heart and with tears, recommended himself to God, beseeching Him that of His most holy pity He would vouchsafe to succour him. And when he had finished praying, it seemed to him that he began to put forth wings; wherefore he waited for them to grow, with great joy, so that he might be able to fly to the farther side of the bridge whither the angel had flown. But after some time, for the strong desire which he had to cross over this bridge, he set himself to fly; and because his wings were not yet sufficiently grown, he fell upon the bridge and all the feathers dropped out of them. Therefore, he once more embraced the bridge with his arms, and, as at the first, he recommended himself to God; and when he had prayed, it seemed to him that he put forth wings again, but as before he waited not until they were perfectly grown; so that, when he attempted to fly before the time, he fell back anew upon the bridge and the feathers dropped off. For the which cause, perceiving that his fall was due to his haste to fly before the time, he began to say within himself: "Of a surety, if I put forth wings a third time, I will wait until they shall be so large that I shall be able to fly without falling". And as he thus thought, he perceived that he was putting forth wings a third time; and, waiting a long while until they were grown large, it seemed to him that, what with the first and second and third putting forth of wings, he had waited 150 years or more. At last, he raised himself up this third time, and, with all his strength, took flight, and flew high up into the air, even to the place where the angel had flown; and when he knocked upon the gate of the palace, where the angel was, the porter asked him: "Who art thou that comest hither?" He made answer: "I am a minor friar". Said the porter: "Await me here, for I am minded to bring St. Francis to see whether he knows thee". And, while he went for St. Francis, the other began to regard the wonderful walls of this palace, and lo! these walls showed so transparent and so clear that he saw plainly the choirs of the saints and all that was being done therein.

And while he stood looking thereat, beside himself with wonder, behold! St. Francis came, and Friar Bernard and Friar Giles, and behind them so great a multitude of holy men and women who had followed in his footsteps, that they seemed well-nigh innumerable: and, when St. Francis arrived, he said to the porter: "Let him come in, for he is one of my friars". And no sooner had he entered than he felt such great consolation and such sweetness that he forgot all the tribulations which he had had even as though they had never been. And then St. Francis led him in and showed him many marvellous things and thereafter spake to him on this wise: "Son, thou must needs return to the world, and there thou wilt remain seven days, in the which do thou prepare thyself diligently and with great devotion; because, after seven days, I will come for thee and then thou shalt come with me to this place of the blessed". St. Francis was clad in a marvellous robe adorned with very beautiful stars, and his five stigmata were like five most beautiful stars, of such splendour that they illuminated all the palace with their rays.

And Friar Bernard had upon his head a crown of very beautiful stars; and Friar Giles was adorned with a marvellous light; and many other holy friars did he recognise among them whom in the world he had never seen. Then, having taken leave of St. Francis, he returned, albeit unwillingly, to the world. Now, although to him it seemed that his dream had lasted many years, yet when he awoke and returned to himself, and re- covered his senses, the friars were ringing for prime. And he told all this vision in order to his guardian, and, within the seven days, he fell sick of a fever; and, on the eighth day, St. Francis came for him as he had promised, with a very great multitude of glorious saints, and led away his soul to the kingdom of the blessed, to life eternal.

27

How St. Francis converted at Bologna two scholars, who became friars; and afterward delivered one of them from a great temptation

ST. FRANCIS arriving, on a time, at the city of, Bologna, all the people of the city ran to see him; and so great was the press that only with great difficulty might the folk come unto the piazza; and when the piazza was all full of men and of women and of scholars, St. Francis went up into an high place, in the midst thereof, and began to preach that which the Holy Spirit taught him; and he preached so marvellously that it seemed rather as if an angel were preaching than a man; his celestial words appeared like unto sharp arrows, which pierced the heart of them who heard him, so that, in that preaching, a great multitude of men and women were turned to repentance. Among whom were two noble students of the March of Ancona, whereof one was named Pellegrino and the other Rinieri; the which two, being touched in heart by Divine inspiration through the said preaching, came to St. Francis and told him that they were altogether minded to abandon the world, and to be his friars. Then St. Francis, knowing by revelation that they were sent by God, and that they would lead a holy life in the Order, and considering their great, fervour, received them gladly, saying: "Thou, Pellegrino, hold to the way of humility, in the Order; and thou, Friar Rinieri, serve the friars". And so it was; for Friar Pellegrino, albeit he was very learned and a great canonist, was never willing to become a clerk but lived as a lay brother, by which humility he came to great perfection of virtue, insomuch that Friar Bernard (the firstborn son of St. Francis) said of him, that he was one of the most perfect friars in this world. And finally, the said Friar Pellegrino, full of virtue, passed from this life to the blessed life, with many miracles both before his death and after. And the said Friar Rinieri devotedly and faithfully served the friars, living in great holiness and humility, and he became very intimate with St. Francis. Thereafter, being made Minister of the province of the March of Ancona, he ruled it long time in very great peace and with discretion. Then, after a certain time, God suffered him to be tempted in his soul with a very great temptation; and he, being troubled and tormented thereby, afflicted himself sore, with fasts and with flagellations, with tears and prayers, both day and night; yet was he not able to cast forth that temptation; wherefore, by reason thereof, he deemed himself abandoned of God. Thus despairing, for a last remedy, he resolved to go to St. Francis, thinking within himself: "If St. Francis shall make me welcome, and shall treat me as his familiar friend, even as he is wont to do, I believe that God will yet have pity on me; but, if not, it will be a sign that I shall be abandoned of God". Wherefore he departed and went to St. Francis, who at that time was lying grievously sick in the palace of the Bishop of Assisi; and God revealed to him all the manner of the temptation and the mind of the said Friar Rinieri, and his intent, and his coming. And forthwith St. Francis called Friar Leo and Friar Masseo, and said unto them: "Go quickly to meet my dearest son Friar Rinieri and embrace him in my name and salute him and tell him that, among all the friars which are in the world, I love him exceedingly". So they went and found Friar Rinieri on the way, and embraced him and said unto him that which St. Francis had bidden them. Whereby his soul was filled with such consolation and sweetness that he was well-nigh beside himself; and, giving thanks to God with all his heart, he went forward and came to the place where St. Francis lay sick. And, albeit St. Francis was grievously sick, nevertheless, when he heard Friar Rinieri coming, he rose up and went to meet him and embraced him most sweetly and spake unto him thus: "My dearest son, Friar Rinieri, among all the friars which are in the world, I love thee exceedingly". And, when he had said this, he made the sign of the most holy Cross upon his brow, and there he kissed him, and afterward said unto him: "Dearest son, God hath permitted thee to be thus tempted for thy great gain of merit; but, if thou wouldst not have this gain any more, have it not". O marvel! So soon as St. Francis had said these words, all the temptation departed from him, as if, never in his life, had he felt it at all; and he remained altogether comforted.

28

Of an ecstasy which came to Friar Bernard whereby he abode from morning even until nones without coming to himself

HOW much grace God ofttimes bestowed upon them who embraced gospel poverty, and who abandoned the world for love of Christ, is shown forth in Friar Bernard of Quintavalle, the which, after he had taken the habit of St. Francis, was very often rapt in God, by the contemplation of heavenly things. Among other times, it once befel that, being in church for the hearing of Mass, with all his mind fixed upon God, he became so absorbed and rapt in God that at the elevation of the Body of Christ he was nothing aware thereof, and neither kneeled him down nor drew back his cowl, as did the others, but without winking his eyes abode gazing fixedly, from morning even until nones, insensible; and after nones, when he had returned to himself, he went through the Place shouting, in enraptured tones: "O friars! O friars! O friars! there is no man in this country so great or so noble but that, if he were promised a most fair palace full of gold, he would lightly carry a sackful of dung, if thereby he might gain so noble a treasure". The mind of the said Friar Bernard was so uplifted to this celestial treasure, promised unto the lovers of God, that for fifteen successive years he ever went with mind and face raised toward heaven; and in all that time never did he satisfy his hunger at table, albeit he ate a little of that which was set before him; for he used to say that abstinence from that which a man tasteth not is not perfect abstinence, but that true abstinence lieth in being temperate in those things which taste good to the mouth; and thereby he attained unto such clearness and light of understanding that even great ecclesiastics had recourse unto him for the solving of hardest questions and obscure passages of Scripture; and he made plain unto them every difficulty. And because his mind was altogether loosed and abstracted from earthly things, he, after the fashion of the swallow, winged his way to very great heights, through contemplation; so that, sometimes for twenty days and sometimes for thirty, he abode alone on the tops of the highest mountains, contemplating celestial things. For the which cause Friar Giles said of him that this gift which was given unto Friar Bernard of Quintavalle was not given unto other men, to wit, that he should feed flying even as doth the swallow. And by reason of this excellent grace which God had given him, St. Francis willingly and ofttimes talked with him by day and by night; whence sometimes it came to pass that they were both found rapt in God all the night long, in the wood where they had met together to speak of God.

29

How the devil in the form of Christ Crucified appeared many times to Friar Ruffino, telling him that he was losing the good which he did, because he was not among those elected to eternal life. Whereof St. Francis knew by revelation of God, and made Friar Ruffino to perceive the error which he had believed

FRIAR RUFFINO, one of the most noble citizens of Assisi and a companion of St. Francis, a man of great sanctity, was once most violently assailed and tempted in his soul concerning predestination; whereby he became exceeding sad and melancholy, in that the demon put it into his heart that he was damned and was not among those predestined to eternal life, and that he was losing that which he did in the Order. And this temptation continuing for many many days, albeit he revealed it not to St. Francis for very shame, he nevertheless abandoned not the observance of the customary prayers and fasts; wherefore the enemy began to add grief to grief, over and above the battle within, assailing him also from without by false apparitions. Wherefore, on a time, he appeared to him in the form of Christ Crucified, and said unto him: "O Friar Ruffino, wherefore dost thou afflict thyself in penance and in prayer, when thou art not among those predestined to eternal life? And, believe me, I know whom I have elected and predestined; and believe thou not the son of Peter Bernardoni, if he tell thee the contrary, and also ask him not touching this matter, because neither he nor others know it, save I alone who am the Son of God; and, therefore, believe me for certain that thou art of the number of the damned; and the son of Peter Bernardoni, thy father, and his father, also are damned, and whosoever follows him is deceived."

And, when these words had been spoken, [the mind of] Friar Ruffino began to be so darkened by the Prince of Darkness, that he lost all the faith and love which he had had for St. Francis, and cared not to tell him anything thereof. But that which Friar Ruffino said not to the holy father the Holy Spirit revealed to him; wherefore St. Francis, seeing in spirit the exceeding peril of the said friar, sent Friar Masseo for him; to whom Friar Ruffino replied upbraidingly: "What have I to do with Friar Francis?" Then Friar Masseo, fulfilled with Divine wisdom and knowing the wiles of the devil, said: "O Friar Ruffino, knowest thou not that Friar Francis is as an angel of God, who hath illumined so many souls in the world, and from whom we have received the grace of God? Wherefore I will that by all means thou come with me to him; because I see clearly that thou art deceived by the devil." And when he had thus spoken, Friar Ruffino arose and went to St. Francis. And seeing him coming afar off, St. Francis began to shout: "O Friar Ruffino, thou poor wretch, whom hast thou believed?"

And when Friar Ruffino had come unto him, he told him in order all the temptation wherewith he had been tempted by the demon, both within and without; and he showed him clearly that he who had appeared unto him was the devil and not Christ, and that on nowise ought he to consent to his suggestions; "but when the devil shall say unto thee again: 'Thou art damned,' do thou answer him thus: 'Open thy mouth, for now I would void my dung therein'; and this shall be a sign unto thee that he is the devil and not Christ, that when thou shalt have thus answered him he will immediately flee away. Also by this token thou oughtest to have known that he was the devil, because he hardened thy heart to every good thing, the which is his proper office; but Christ the blessed never hardens the heart of the faithful man, but rather softens it, according as He saith by the mouth of the prophet: *I will take away from you the stony heart and will give you a heart of flesh.*"

Then Friar Ruffino, perceiving that St. Francis told him in order all the fashion of his temptation, was moved to repentance by his words and began to weep sore and to adore St. Francis as a saint, and to humbly acknowledge his fault in having concealed his temptation. Thus was he filled with consolation and comfort by the admonishments of the holy father, and altogether changed for the better. Thereafter, at the last, St. Francis said unto him: "Go, son, and confess thyself and forget not thy accustomed diligence in prayer; and know of a surety that this temptation will be to thee a great benefit and consolation, as in a little while thou shalt prove." Then Friar Ruffino returned to his cell in the wood, and lo! while he continued in prayer, with many tears, the enemy appeared to him in the person of Christ, according to all outward seeming, and said unto him: "O Friar Ruffino, have I not told thee not to believe the son of Peter Bernardoni and not to weary thyself in tears and prayers, because thou art damned? What doth it profit thee to afflict thyself while thou art alive, when afterward, when thou shalt die thou shalt be damned?" And forthwith Friar Ruffino replied to the demon: "Open thy mouth, for now would I void my dung therein"; and immediately, the devil departed, full of fierce anger, with such tempest and commotion of the rocks of Mount Subassio, which was there beside, that the shattering of the rocks which fell down lasted for a long time; and so mightily did they crash together that they shot forth horrible gleams of fire through all the valley; and, for the terrible din which they made, St. Francis and his companions came forth from the Place in great amazement, to see what new thing this might be; and even unto this day that exceeding great ruin of rocks may be seen there. Then Friar Ruffino perceived clearly that it was the devil who had deceived him; and he returned to St. Francis and anew flung himself upon the ground and acknowledged his fault, and St. Francis once more comforted him with sweet words and sent him back to his cell wholly consoled.

There, while he continued in prayer with exceeding great devotion, the blessed Christ appeared to him, and enkindled all his soul with Divine love, and said:

"Well hast thou done, son, that thou didst believe Friar Francis, in that he who afflicted thee was the demon; but I am Christ, thy master; and to make thee very sure thereof I give thee this sign: As long as thou shalt live, thou shalt never feel any sadness or melancholy".

And, when He had thus spoken, Christ departed leaving him so full of joy and sweetness of spirit and exaltation of soul, that day and night he was absorbed and rapt in God. And, from thenceforward, he was so confirmed in grace and in assurance of salvation that he became altogether changed into another man; and he would have continued day and night in prayer and in contemplation of Divine things, if the others would have let him alone.

Wherefore St. Francis used to say of him, that Friar Ruffino was in this life canonised by Christ, and that, except in his presence, he would not hesitate to call him St. Ruffino, albeit he was yet alive on earth.

30

Of the beautiful sermon which St. Francis and Friar Ruffino preached in Assisi, when they preached naked

THROUGH continual contemplation, the aforesaid Friar Ruffino was so absorbed in God that he had become well-nigh insensible and dumb, and exceeding rarely spoke; and moreover he had neither grace nor courage nor eloquence in preaching. Nevertheless St. Francis, one day, ordered him to go to Assisi and preach to the people that which God inspired him to preach. Whereto Friar Ruffino made answer: "Reverend father, I beseech thee that thou have me excused and send me not, because, as thou knowest, I have not the gift of preaching and am a simple man and ignorant". Then said St. Francis: "Inasmuch as thou hast not obeyed at once, I command thee by holy obedience that thou go to Assisi, naked as thou wast born, save only for thy breeches, and that thou enter into a church, thus naked, and preach to the people". At this command, the aforesaid Friar Ruffino stripped himself, and went to Assisi, and entered into a church; and, when he had bowed himself before the altar, he went up into the pulpit and began to preach; whereat children and men began to laugh, and said: "Behold, now, how these men do so much penance that they become fools and beside themselves". In the meantime, St. Francis, considering the prompt obedience of Friar Ruffino, who was of one of the noblest families of Assisi, and of the hard commandment which he had given him, began to blame himself, saying: "How hast thou such great presumption, son of Peter Bernardoni, vile manikin, as to command Friar Ruffino, one of the first gentlemen of Assisi, to go naked to preach to the people like a madman? By God, thou shalt prove in thine own person that which thou orderest others to do." And anon, in fervour of spirit, he stripped himself naked likewise, and so gat him up to Assisi, taking with him Friar Leo, that he might carry his habit and that of Friar Ruffino. And, when the men of Assisi beheld St. Francis likewise naked they made a mock at him, deeming that he and Friar Ruffino had gone mad through excessive penance. Then St. Francis entered into the church where Friar Ruffino was preaching these words: "Oh most dearly beloved, flee the world and cease from sin; render unto others that which is theirs, if ye would escape hell; keep the commandments of God, loving God and your neighbour if ye would go to heaven; do penance if ye would possess the kingdom of heaven". Thereupon St. Francis went up naked into the pulpit, and began to preach so marvellously of the contempt of the world, of holy repentance, of voluntary poverty and of the desire of the celestial kingdom, and of the nakedness and shame of the passion of our Lord Jesus Christ, that all they which were at the sermon, men and women in great numbers, began to weep very bitterly, with wonderful devotion and compunction of heart; and not there alone, but throughout the whole of Assisi, was there on that day so great weeping for the passion of Christ that never had there been the like; and, the people being thus edified and comforted by the work of St. Francis and Friar Ruffino, St. Francis reclothed Friar Ruffino and himself; and, thus reclothed, they returned to the Place of the Porziuncula praising and glorifying God who had given them grace to conquer themselves through contempt of self, and to edify the little sheep of Christ by their good example, and to show how much the world is to be despised. And on that day so greatly did the devotion of the people increase toward them, that he who might touch the hem of their garment deemed himself blessed.

31

How St. Francis knew, in their order, the secrets of the hearts of all his friars

EVEN as our Lord Jesus Christ saith in the Gospel: "I know My little sheep and they know Me," so the good father St. Francis, like a good shepherd, knew all the merits and virtues of his companions by Divine revelation, and so likewise he knew their imperfections also; whereby he was able to provide for all of them the best remedy; to wit, humbling the proud, exalting the humble, rebuking vice, and praising virtue; as may be read in the wonderful revelations which he had concerning that first family of his. Among the which we find that once, when St. Francis was with his said family in a Place, discoursing of God, Friar Ruffino was not with them, being in the wood in contemplation; but, while they continued to discourse of God, lo! Friar Ruffino [a noble citizen of Assisi, but a nobler servant of God, a most pure virgin, sublimated by the noble prerogative of Divine contemplation, and adorned before God and man with the flowers of odoriferous conversation] came forth from the wood and passed by at some distance from them. Thereupon, St. Francis, beholding him, turned to his companions and asked them, saying: "Tell me, which, think ye, is the holiest soul that God hath upon this earth?" Whereto they made answer and said that they believed it was his own. Then St. Francis said unto them: "Most dear friars, I am of myself the most unworthy and the vilest man that God hath in this world; but see ye that Friar Ruffino who is now coming forth from the wood? God hath revealed unto me that his soul is one of the three holiest souls in the world; and of a sooth I tell you that I would not fear to call him St. Ruffino while he is yet alive, inasmuch as his soul is confirmed in grace and sanctified and canonised in heaven by our Lord Jesus Christ;" but St. Francis never spake these words in the presence of the said Friar Ruffino. How St. Francis knew the imperfections of his friars was clearly seen in like manner in Friar Elias, whom he often rebuked for his pride; and in that Friar Giovanni della Cappella, unto whom he foretold that he would hang himself by the neck; and in that friar whose throat was held fast by the devil what time he was admonished for disobedience; and in many other friars whose secret defects and virtues he knew clearly by revelation of Christ.

32

How Friar Masseo obtained from Christ the virtue of his humility

THE first companions of St. Francis strove with all their might to be poor in earthly things and rich in those virtues, through the which we attain unto the true celestial and eternal riches. Now it befel upon a day that, while they were gathered together to speak of God, one of them told this ensample: "There was one who was a great friend of God, and had great grace in the active and contemplative life; and there-withal so extreme was his humility, that he deemed himself a very great sinner: the which humility sanctified him and confirmed him in grace, and made him to increase continually in virtue and in the gifts of God, and never suffered him to fall into sin". Friar Masseo hearing such marvellous things concerning Humility, and knowing that she was a treasure of life eternal, began to be so inflamed with love and desire of this virtue of humility, that with great fervour lifting up his face toward heaven, he made a vow and very firm resolve never again to take any joy in this world, until he should perfectly feel the said virtue in his soul; and from thenceforward he abode well-nigh continually shut up in his cell, afflicting himself with fasts, vigils, prayers and very bitter weepings before God, to the end that he might obtain from Him this virtue, wherewith that friend of God of whom he had heard was so abundantly dowered, and lacking which he deemed himself worthy of hell. And when Friar Masseo had continued for many days in this desire, it came to pass that one day he entered into the wood, and in fervour of spirit went therethrough, shedding tears and sending forth sighs and cries, demanding of God, with ardent desire, this Divine virtue; and, because God willingly giveth ear to the prayers of the humble and contrite, while yet Friar Masseo was praying, there came a voice from heaven which called him twice: "Friar Masseo! Friar Masseo!" And he, knowing through the Holy Spirit that it was the voice of Christ, made answer: "My Lord!" And Christ spake unto him saying: "What wouldest thou give to have this grace which thou beseechest?" Friar Masseo answered: "Lord, I would give the eyes out of my head". And Christ said unto him: "It is My will that thou have this grace and thine eyes also". And anon; with these words, the voice ceased; and Friar Masseo remained fulfilled with so much grace of the virtue of humility after which he had yearned, and of the light of God, that from thenceforward he was always glad; and oftentimes when he prayed he gave vent to his joy by making a soft low sound like the cooing of a gentle dove; and with happy face and joyful heart he abode on this wise in contemplation; and therewith having become most humble, he esteemed himself the least of all men upon earth. When Friar James of Fallerone asked him wherefore in his chant of joy he never changed his note, he replied with great gladness: that, when a man findeth every good in one thing, he needeth not to change his note.

33

How St. Clare, at the bidding of the Pope, blessed the bread which was upon the table: whereby the sign of the holy Cross appeared on every loaf

ST. CLARE, most devout disciple of the Cross of Christ and noble plant of Messer St. Francis, was of such great sanctity that not only bishops and cardinals, but also the Pope was filled with great longing to see her and to hear her, and oftentimes visited her in person. Among the other times was one when the holy father went to her convent to hear her speak of things celestial and Divine; and, while they thus reasoned together of divers matters, St. Clare caused the tables to be made ready and bread to be set thereon, that the holy father might bless it. Wherefore, when their spiritual discourse was ended, St. Clare kneeled down with great reverence and besought him to vouchsafe to bless the bread which was upon the table. The holy father made answer: "Most faithful Sister Clare, I desire that thou bless this bread and make thereover the sign of the most holy Cross of Christ, unto whom thou hast wholly given thyself". St.

Clare said: "Most holy father, I pray thee have me excused, for I should be deserving of great blame, if, before the Vicar of Christ, I, who am but a vile and worthless woman, should presume to give this blessing". And the Pope made answer: "To the end that this be not imputed to presumption but to merit of obedience, I command thee by holy obedience that thou make the sign of the most holy Cross over this bread and bless it in the name of God". Then St. Clare, as a true daughter of obedience, blessed those loaves most devoutly with the sign of the most holy Cross. O marvellous thing! On all those loaves there instantly appeared the sign of the holy Cross most fairly cut; thereafter of those loaves part were eaten and part were preserved in record of the miracle. And the holy father, when he had beheld the miracle, departed, taking some of the said bread with him, giving thanks to God and leaving St. Clare with his blessing. At that time there dwelt in the Convent Sister Ortolana, the mother of St. Clare, and Sister Agnes, her sister, both of them like St. Clare full of virtue and of the Holy Ghost, with many other holy nuns and brides of Christ; to whom St. Francis was wont to send much sick folk; and they by their prayers and by the sign of the most holy Cross restored health ' to them all.

34

How St. Louis, King of France, in the garb of a pilgrim, went in person to Perugia to visit the holy Friar Giles

ST. LOUIS, King of France, went on pilgrimage to visit the sanctuaries throughout the world; and hearing very great report of the sanctity of Friar Giles, who had been among the first companions of St. Francis, he resolved and was wholly determined to visit him in person; for the which cause he came to Perugia, where the said Friar Giles then dwelt. And coming to the gate of the Place of the friars, as a poor pilgrim and unknown, with but few companions, he asked very urgently for Friar Giles, saying naught to the doorkeeper who he was that asked for him. Then the doorkeeper went to Friar Giles and told him that there was a pilgrim at the gate who asked for him; and through inspiration and revelation of God, Friar Giles knew that it was the King of France. Wherefore, with great fervour, he straightway came forth from his cell and ran to the gate; and without further questioning, albeit they twain had never before seen one another, they kneeled them down together and embraced and kissed each other, with great familiarity, as though for a long time there had been fast friendship between them. Nevertheless, with all this, neither of them spake any word, but ever they embraced one another with those signs of love and affection, in silence. And, after they had continued on this wise for a long time without speaking any word, they departed the one from the other; and St. Louis gat him up and went on his journey and Friar Giles returned to his cell. Now, as the king was departing, a friar asked one of his companions who he was that for so long a time had embraced Friar Giles; and he made answer that it was Louis, King of France, who had come to see Friar Giles. Thereafter, when this friar had told it to his fellows, they were exceeding grieved that Friar Giles had spoken no word to the king; and they murmured against him and said unto him: "O Friar Giles, why hast thou shown thyself so churlish to so saintly a king, who hath come out of France to see thee and to hear thee speak some good word, and thou hast never spoken to him at all?" Friar Giles made answer: "Well-beloved friars, marvel not thereat; for neither was I able to say word to him nor he to me, since no sooner had we embraced one another than the light of Divine wisdom revealed and made manifest his heart to me and mine to him; and thus, by Divine operation, each of us looked into the heart of the other and knew those things which I desired to say to him and he to me far better than if we had spoken them with our lips, and we took more comfort thereof than if we had tried to explain with our voices that which we felt in our hearts. By reason of the deficiency of human speech, which may not clearly express the secret mysteries of God, we should have been rather saddened than comforted. Wherefore, know ye that the king departed from me marvellously contented and comforted in his soul."

35

How, on Christmas Eve, St. Clare being sick was miraculously carried to the Church of St. Francis and there heard the office

ONCE St. Clare was grievously sick, so that she could not go at all to say the office in church with the other nuns; and when the festival of the Nativity of Christ was come, all the other nuns went to matins, and she remained abed, sad at heart because she was not able to go with the others and partake of that spiritual consolation. But Jesus Christ, her spouse, willing not to leave her thus disconsolate, caused her to be miraculously carried to the church of St. Francis and to be present at the whole office of matins and of the midnight Mass, and, besides this, to receive the Holy Communion and afterward to be carried back to her bed again. Now the nuns returned to St. Clare, when the office in S. Damiano was over, and said unto her: "O our mother, Sister Clare, what great consolation have we had, this holy Christmas Day! Would that it had been God's will that you had been with us!" And St. Clare made answer: "Sisters mine and dearest daughters, I give thanks and praise to our blessed Lord Jesus Christ, because in every solemnity of this most holy night, and even more than you, have I had my part to the great comfort of my soul; because, by the intercessions of my father St. Francis and by the grace of our Lord Jesus Christ, I have been present in the church of my venerable father St. Francis, and with the ears of my body and of my mind have heard all the office and the music of the organs which was made there; and in the same place have I taken the most Holy Communion. Wherefore, for such a grace vouchsafed unto me do ye rejoice and give thanks unto our Lord Jesus Christ."

36

How St. Francis expounded unto Friar Leo a fair vision which he had seen

ONCE, when St. Francis was exceeding sick, Friar Leo waited on him; and it befel that, while the said Friar Leo was praying beside St. Francis, he was rapt in ecstasy and was carried in the spirit to a very great river, wide and rapid. And, as he waited to see who crossed over it, he beheld certain friars enter the river laden with burdens, and straightway they were overthrown by the force of the stream and were drowned; certain others went a third of the way across; others reached the middle of the river, and some almost gained the opposite bank; but, at the last, by reason of the force of the stream and of the burdens which they bore, all of them fell and were drowned. Now, when he saw this, Friar Leo had very great compassion for them; and anon, while yet he stood there, lo! a great multitude of friars drew nigh, all of them without any burden or load of any kind; resplendent with the light of holy Poverty. And they entered the river and crossed over it without any danger; and, when he had seen this, Friar Leo came to himself again. Then St. Francis, perceiving in spirit that Friar Leo had seen some vision, questioned him concerning that which he had seen: and, when Friar Leo had told him all his vision in order, St. Francis said: "That which thou hast seen is true. The great river is this world; the friars who were drowning in the river are those who follow not the Gospel profession and especially with regard to most high Poverty; but they who passed over without danger are those friars who neither seek nor possess in this world any earthly or carnal thing, but having food and raiment are therewith content, following Christ naked on the cross; and gladly and willingly do they bear the burden and sweet yoke of Christ and of most holy Obedience; whereby they pass without difficulty from the temporal life to the life eternal."

37

How Jesus Christ the blessed, at the prayer of St. Francis, caused a rich man to be converted and to become a friar, the which had shown great honour and liberality unto St. Francis

ST. FRANCIS, the servant of Christ, arrived one evening at the house of a great and powerful gentleman and was by him received to lodge there, he and his companion, as angels of God, with very great courtesy and devotion; for the which thing St. Francis loved him, considering how when he entered into his house he had embraced and kissed him as a friend, and had humbly washed his feet and wiped and kissed them; and afterward, a great fire having been lighted and a table spread with many excellent viands had waited on him continually, with joyful countenance, while he ate. Now, when St. Francis and his companion had eaten, this gentleman said: "Behold, my father, I offer you myself and my goods. As often as ye have need of habit or mantle or of any other thing, buy them and I will pay for them; and remember that I am ready to provide for you in all your needs, because by God's grace I am able so to do, in that I abound in temporal goods; and therefore for love of God, who hath given them unto me, I willingly do good therewith to His poor." Wherefore St. Francis, seeing in him such great courtesy and loving-kindness, and hearing the large offers which he made, conceived for him so great a love, that thereafter, departing thence, he spake unto his companion, as they went upon their way, and said: "Of a truth this gentleman, who is so grateful to God and so mindful of His benefits, and so loving and courteous to his neighbour and to the poor, would be good for our religion and company. Know, beloved friar, that courtesy is one of the attributes of God, who giveth His sun and His rain to the just and to the unjust, through courtesy; and Courtesy is own sister to Charity, the which extinguisheth hate and keepeth love alive. Now, because I have known so much Divine virtue in this good man, I would gladly have him for a companion; and therefore I am minded some day to return to him, if peradventure God should have touched his heart to desire to accompany us in the service of God, and meanwhile, we will pray God to put this desire in his heart and to give him grace to bring the same to good effect." O marvellous thing! a few days after St. Francis had made this prayer, God put this desire into the heart of that gentleman; and St. Francis said to his companion: "Brother mine, let us go to the house of the courteous man, for I have sure hope in God that he with the same courtesy which he hath shown in things temporal will give himself to us and will become our companion." And they went. And when they drew nigh unto his house, St. Francis said to his companion: "Wait for me a little while, because I would first pray God that He may prosper our journey, and that it may please Jesus Christ, through the virtue of His most holy passion, to grant to us, though poor and weak, this noble prey which we think to snatch from the world". And having thus spoken, he betook himself to prayer in a place where he could be seen of the said courteous man. Whereby, as it pleased God, while he was looking hither and thither, he saw St. Francis most devoutly praying before Christ, who, in great splendour, appeared unto him in the said prayer and stood before him; and therewith he saw St. Francis lifted bodily from the ground, for a good space. Through the which sight he was so touched of God and inspired to leave the world that, anon, he came forth from his palace and, in fervour of spirit, ran toward St. Francis; and coming unto him while he was yet praying, he kneeled down at his feet and, with great earnestness and devotion, besought him that he would be pleased to receive him and to do penance together with him. Then St. Francis, perceiving that God had heard his prayer, and that that gentleman was urgently begging for that which he himself desired, rose up and, in fervour and gladness of spirit, embraced and kissed him, very devoutly thanking God who had added so gallant a knight to his company. And the gentleman said to St. Francis: "My father, what dost thou bid me do? Lo! I am ready to obey thy commandments and to give all I possess to the poor and to follow Christ with thee, having thus disburdened myself of every temporal thing." And thus did he, according to the counsel of St. Francis; for he distributed all his possessions among the poor and entered the Order, and lived in great penitence and holiness of life and honest conversation.

38

How St. Francis knew in spirit that Friar Elias was damned and would die out of the Order; wherefore, at the entreaty of Friar Elias, he prayed to Christ for him, and was heard

ONCE when St. Francis and Friar Elias were sojourning in a Place together, it was revealed of God to St. Francis, that Friar Elias was damned, and would apostatise from the Order and finally die out of the Order. For which cause St. Francis conceived so great a distaste for Friar Elias that he never spake nor conversed with him; and, if it came to pass at any time that Friar Elias came towards him, he turned aside and went by another way so as not to meet him; whereby Friar Elias began to perceive and to understand that St. Francis was displeased with him. Wherefore, desiring to know the reason thereof, he one day drew nigh unto St. Francis to speak with him, and, when St. Francis avoided him, detained him by force but courteously, humbly beseeching him that he would be pleased to tell him the reason why he thus avoided his company and would not speak with him. And St. Francis answered him: "The reason is this: that it hath been revealed to me of God that thou, through thy sins, wilt apostatise from the Order and wilt die out of the Order, and also God hath revealed unto me that thou art damned". Now when he had heard this, Friar Elias spake thus: "My reverend father, I beseech thee for love of Jesus Christ that for this thou avoid me not, neither drive me away from thee; but like a good shepherd, after the example of Christ, seek and save the sheep which must perish if thou help it not; and pray God for me that, if it be possible, He may revoke the sentence of my damnation; for it is written that God will change His sentence if the sinner amend his fault: and so great faith have I in thy prayers that, if I were in the midst of hell and thou shouldst pray unto God for me, I should feel some relief. Wherefore again do I beseech thee that thou recommend me, a sinner, to the God who came to save sinners, that He may receive me to His mercy." And this Friar Elias said with great devotion and with many tears. Thereupon St. Francis, as a pitiful father, promised him to pray God for him; and he did so. And, praying God most devoutly for him, he knew by revelation, that his prayer was heard by God, touching the revocation of the sentence of damnation against Friar Elias, and that his soul would not be finally damned; but that he would certainly leave the Order and die out of the Order. And so it came to pass; because, when Frederick, King of Sicily, rebelled against the Church and was excommunicated by the Pope (he and all who gave him aid or counsel), the said Friar Elias, who was reputed one of the wisest men in all the world, at the request of the said King Frederick, adhered unto him, and became a rebel against the Church and an apostate from the Order, for the which thing he was excommunicated by the Pope and deprived of the habit of St. Francis. And, while he was thus excommunicate, he fell grievously sick; and one of his brethren hearing of his said sickness, the same being a lay-brother who had remained in the Order and was a man of good and honest life, went to visit him; and among other things he said unto him: "My dearest brother, much doth it grieve me that thou art excommunicate and out of thy Order and so must die; but if thou shouldst perceive any way or manner whereby I can deliver thee from this danger, I would willingly take any pains for thy sake". Friar Elias made answer: "Brother mine, I see no other way but that thou go to the Pope, and beseech him, for the love of God and of St. Francis, his servant, through whose teachings I abandoned the world, that he absolve me from his excommunication and restore to me the habit of the Religion". His brother told him that he would gladly labour for his salvation; and so, departing from him, he gat him to the feet of the holy Pope, humbly beseeching him to pardon his brother for the love of Christ and of St. Francis, his servant. And, as God willed it, the Pope granted his prayer that he should return, and if he found Friar Elias alive, should absolve him from the excommunication and should restore his habit to him: wherefore he departed full of joy, and, returning to Friar Elias with all speed, found him alive though almost at the point of death; and so he absolved him from the excommunication; and once more putting on him the habit, Friar Elias passed from this life and his soul was saved by the merits of St. Francis and by his prayer in which Friar Elias had had such great hope.

39

Of the marvellous sermon which St. Antony of Padua, a minor friar, preached in the Consistory

THE marvellous vessel of the Holy Ghost, Messer St. Antony of Padua, one of the chosen disciples and companions of St. Francis, whom St. Francis called his vicar, preached upon a time in the Consistory before the Pope and the cardinals; in the which Consistory were men of divers nations, to wit, Greeks, Latins, French, Germans, Slavonians and English, and of other diverse languages of the world. And, being inflamed by the Holy Ghost, he set forth the word of God so efficaciously, so devoutly, so subtly, so sweetly, so clearly and so learnedly, that all those who were in the Consistory, albeit they spoke different languages, understood all his words as clearly and distinctly as if he had spoken in the dialect of each of them; and they were all amazed; and it seemed that the ancient miracle of the Apostles had been renewed, when, at the Feast of Pentecost, they spake in every language by the virtue of the Holy Ghost; and they marvelled and said one to another: "Is not this man who preacheth a Spaniard? How, then, do we all hear in his speech the language of our own countries?" The Pope likewise considering, and marvelling within himself at the deep wisdom of his words, said: "Of a truth this man is the Ark of the Covenant and a repository of Holy Writ".

40

Of the miracle which God wrought, when St. Antony, being at Rimini, preached to the fishes of the sea

CHRIST the blessed (willing to show forth the great sanctity of His most faithful servant Messer St. Antony, and to teach with what devotion men ought to give ear to His preaching and to His holy doctrine) one time among the rest, rebuked the folly of infidel heretics through the instrumentality of unreasoning animals, to wit of the fishes, even as, long ago, in the Old Testament, he had rebuked the ignorance of Balaam through the mouth of the ass. For St. Antony being once in Rimini, where was a great multitude of heretics, and wishing to bring them back to the light of the true faith and to the way of virtue, he preached unto them for many days and disputed with them of the faith of Christ and of the Holy Scriptures; but they, as men hard of heart and obstinate, would not even listen to him. Wherefore St. Antony gat himself one day by Divine inspiration to the bank of the river hard by the sea, and standing thus upon the shore between the sea and the river he began to speak unto the fishes, as a preacher sent unto them of God: "Hear the word of God, ye fishes of the sea and of the river, since the infidel heretics refuse to hear it". And anon, when he had thus spoken, there came to him to the bank so vast a multitude of fishes, big, little and of middling size, that never in that sea or in that river had there been seen so great a multitude. And all of them held their heads out of the water, and all gazed attentively on the face of St. Antony, abiding there in very great peace and gentleness and order; for in the front rank and nearest to the shore were the little tiny fish, behind them were the moderately large fish, and farther out, where was deeper water, the biggest fish. The fish, then, being arranged in this order and disposition, St. Antony commenced solemnly to preach unto them, and spake after this manner: "My brethren the fish, much are ye bounden, as far as in you lies, to give thanks to our Creator, who hath given you so noble an element for your dwelling-place, wherein according to your pleasure ye may have fresh water or salt; He hath given you many places of refuge to escape from the tempest; He hath also given you a clear and transparent element, and food whereby ye may live. God, your Creator, courteous and kind, when He made you, commanded you to increase and multiply and gave you His blessing. Thereafter, when, in the universal deluge, all other creatures died God preserved you alone uninjured. Moreover He hath given you fins wherewith ye may roam wheresoever ye will. To you it was granted, through the commandment of God, to preserve Jonah the prophet, and after the third day to cast him up upon dry land, safe and sound. Ye offered the tribute-money to our Lord Jesus Christ, which He, by reason of His poverty, could not pay. By a singular mystery, ye were the food of the Eternal King, Jesus Christ, both before and after His resurrection; for all which things much are ye bounden to praise and bless

God who hath loaded you with so great benefits more than other creatures." At these and other like words and admonishments of St. Antony, the fishes began to open their mouths and to bow their heads, and with these and other signs of reverence, on such wise as they were able, gave praise to God. Then St. Antony, seeing the great reverence of the fishes toward God, their Creator, rejoiced in spirit and cried with a loud voice: "Blessed be the Eternal God because the fishes of the waters honour Him more than heretic men; and creatures which have not reason hear His word more willingly than unbelieving men". And the longer St. Antony preached the more did the multitude of fish increase; and not one of them left the place which he had taken. To see this miracle the people of the city began to run thither, and among them came also the heretics aforesaid; who, beholding so marvellous and clear a miracle, were pricked in their hearts, and all cast themselves at the feet of St. Antony to hear his words. Then St. Antony began to preach of the Catholic faith; and so nobly did he preach it that he converted all those heretics and they turned to the true faith of Christ; and all the faithful were comforted thereby, being filled with very great joy, and stablished in the faith. And, when the preaching was over, St. Antony dismissed the fishes with the blessing of God, and they all departed with marvellous signs of joy, and likewise also the people. Thereafter, St. Antony abode in Rimini for many days, preaching and gathering much spiritual fruit of souls.

41

How the venerable Friar Simon delivered from a great temptation a friar, who for this cause was minded to depart out of the Order

ABOUT the time of the commencement of the Order of St. Francis, and while he was yet alive, a young man of Assisi, who was called Friar Simon, entered the Order; the which was adorned and dowered of God with such grace, and with such contemplation and elevation of mind that his whole life was a mirror of holiness, according as I have heard from those who were with him for a long time. Very rarely was he seen out of his cell; and if, at any time, he was in the company of the friars, he always spake of God. Never had he learned grammar; yet such profound and high things did he speak of God and of the love of Christ that his words appeared supernatural words; whence it came to pass that one evening, having gone into the wood with Friar James of Massa, to speak of God, he talked so sweetly of the Divine love that they passed the whole night in that discourse; and, in the morning, it seemed to them that it had been but a very little while, according to that which the said Friar James told me. And, when the said Friar Simon received the illuminations of God's love, he was filled in spirit with such exceeding sweetness and peace, that ofttimes, when he felt them coming upon him, he laid himself down upon his bed; because the tranquil sweetness of the Holy Ghost demanded of him not only repose of soul, but also of body; and in such Divine visitations he was often rapt in God, and became altogether insensible to corporal things. Wherefore, once while he was thus rapt in God and insensible to the world, burning inwardly with Divine love and with his bodily senses feeling nothing at all of external things, a certain friar, wishing to prove if this were really so, and to see if he was as he appeared to be, went and took a coal of fire and laid it on his naked foot; and Friar Simon felt nothing, neither did it make any mark upon his foot, albeit it remained thereon for so long a time that it went out of itself. The said Friar Simon, when he sat him down at table, or ever he took bodily food, took spiritual food for himself and gave it to others, speaking of God. By his devout speech he once converted a youth of San Severino, the which in the world was a very vain and worldly youth, of noble blood and very dainty of body; and Friar Simon, having received the said youth into the Order, kept his secular garments by him; and he abode with Friar Simon to be instructed in the rules of the Order. Wherefore, the devil, who seeketh to bring to naught every good thing, vexed him with so sore a temptation and with such burning lust of the flesh that on no wise might he resist it; for the which cause he betook himself to Friar Simon and said unto him: "Give me back my garments which I wore in the world, for I can no longer resist this carnal temptation". Then, Friar Simon, having great compassion for him, said unto him: "Sit thou here with me, my son, a little while"; and he began to speak to him of God, after such a manner that every temptation left him; and thereafter what time the temptation returned and he asked for his garments, Friar Simon drove it away by speaking of God. And when this had been done divers times, finally, one night, the said temptation assailed him so much more violently than usual that, for nothing in the world, might he resist it; and he went to Friar Simon to demand of him, once for all, his secular garments, in that by no means might he any longer stay. Then Friar Simon, according to his wont, made him sit by his side, and, as he spake of God, the young man bowed his head upon the bosom of Friar Simon for grief and sorrow of heart. Thereupon Friar Simon, for the great compassion that he had, lifted up his eyes to heaven and prayed God most devoutly for him; and he was rapt in God and his prayer was answered; so that, when he returned unto himself, the young man was wholly freed from that temptation, as if he had never felt it at all. Moreover the fire of the temptation was changed into the fire of the Holy Ghost; and, because he had drawn nigh unto the burning coal, to wit unto Friar Simon, he was all inflamed with love of God and of his neighbour; so much so that, once, when a malefactor had been taken and condemned to have both his eyes torn out, he, to wit, the aforesaid young man, was so filled with pity that he went boldly to the Rector and in full Council, with many tears and devout prayers, begged that one of his own eyes might be put out, and one only of the malefactor's, to the end that he might not lose them both. But the Rector and his Council, beholding the great fervour of the charity of this friar, pardoned both the one and the other. Now one day, the said Friar Simon being in prayer in the wood and feeling great consolation in his soul, a flock of crows began to annoy him with their cries; wherefore he commanded them in the name of Jesus to depart thence, and to return no more; and, thereupon, the said birds gat them thence and thereafter were never more seen or heard, neither there nor in all the district round about. And this miracle was evident in all the territory of Fermo, wherein was the said place.

42

Of beautiful miracles which God wrought through the holy friars, Friar Bentivoglia, Friar Peter of Monticello and Friar Conrad of Offida; and how Friar Bentivoglia carried a leper fifteen miles in a very short time; and how to the other St. Michael spoke; and to the third the Virgin Mary came and placed her Son in his arms

OF old, the province of the March of Ancona was adorned, even as is the sky with stars, by holy and exemplary friars; who, like the lights of heaven, have illuminated and adorned the Order of St. Francis and the world by example and by doctrine. Among the others was, firstly, Friar Lucidus, the elder, who was truly resplendent with sanctity, and burning with Divine charity; whose glorious tongue, informed by the Holy Ghost, reaped marvellous fruits in his preachings. Another was Friar Bentivoglia of San Severino, who was seen of Friar Masseo, lifted up into the air for a great space, what time he was in prayer in the wood; by reason of which miracle Friar Masseo, being then a parish priest, left his parish and became a minor friar; and was of such great sanctity that he wrought many miracles both in his life and after his death; and his body is buried at Murro. Once, while the aforesaid Friar Bentivoglia was sojourning alone at Trave Bonanti to care for and serve a leper, he received orders from the Bishop to depart thence, and go to another place; the which place was fifteen miles distant; and, not wishing to abandon that leper, with great fervour of charity, he took him and set him upon his back and carried him, between daybreak and the rising of the sun, the whole of that fifteen miles, even to the place whither he was sent, which is called Monte Suncino; the which journey, had he been an eagle, he could not have flown in so short a time; and at this Divine miracle there it was great wonder and amazement in all that country. Another was Friar Peter of Monticello, who was seen by Friar Servodio of Urbino (being then the guardian of the old Place of Ancona) bodily raised from the ground, five or six cubits, even unto the foot of the Crucifix of the Church, before which he was praying. And this Friar Peter, once when he was fasting with great devotion during the forty days' fast of St. Michael the Archangel, and on the last day of that fast was in the church in prayer, was heard by a young friar (who lay hidden beneath the high altar, to the end that he might behold some manifestation of his sanctity) speaking with St. Michael the Archangel; and the words which they spake were these: St. Michael said: "Friar Peter, thou hast laboured faithfully for me, and in many ways hast thou afflicted thy body. Behold, I am come to console thee, and that thou mayest ask whatsoever grace thou wilt, and I am willing to obtain it for thee from God." Friar Peter made answer: "Most holy Prince of the celestial armies, most faithful zealot of the Divine honour, pitiful protector of souls, I ask of thee this grace, that thou obtain for me from God the pardon of my sins". St. Michael replied: "Ask another grace, for this I shall most easily obtain for thee"; and, when Friar Peter asked him nothing else, the Archangel concluded:

"For the faith and devotion which thou hast toward me, I will obtain for thee this grace which thou demandest, and many others". And when their speaking was ended, the which lasted for a long time, the Archangel St. Michael gat him thence, leaving Friar Peter full of consolation. Now, in the days of this holy Friar Peter, there lived also the holy Friar Conrad of Offida; and, while these two dwelt together in the Place of Forano in the territory of Ancona, the said Friar Conrad betook himself, one day, to the wood to meditate on God; and Friar Peter went after him secretly to see that which should befal him; and Friar Conrad began to pray and most devoutly to beseech the Virgin Mary with great piety that she would obtain for him this grace of her blessed Son, that he might experience a little of that sweetness which St. Simeon felt, on the day of the Purification, when he carried in his arms Jesus, the blessed Saviour.

And, when he had thus prayed, the ever-pitiful Virgin Mary gave ear unto him; and lo! the Queen of Heaven appeared with her blessed Son in her arms, with very great splendour of light; and, drawing nigh unto Friar Conrad, she placed that blessed Son in his arms; whom he received most devoutly, and, embracing and kissing Him and clasping Him to his heart, was altogether melted and dissolved in Divine love and inexplicable consolation; and Friar Peter, likewise, who saw everything from his hiding-place, felt very great sweetness and consolation in his soul. And, when the Virgin Mary had departed from Friar Conrad, Friar Peter returned in haste to the Place, that he might not be seen of him; but afterward, when Friar Conrad returned all merry and jocund, Friar Peter said unto him: "O heavenly man, great consolation hast thou had to-day!" Said Friar Conrad: "What sayest thou, Friar Peter? and what knowest thou of that which I have had?" "Well do I know," said Friar Peter. "Well do I know how the Virgin Mary with her blessed

Son hath visited thee." Then Friar Conrad, who, as a truly humble man, desired to keep secret the graces which he received of God, besought him that he would not tell any one thereof; and so great was the love, which, from thenceforward, was between them, that it seemed as if they were of one heart and of one soul in everything. And, once, the said Friar Conrad, in the Place of Siruolo, liberated by his prayers a damsel who was possessed by the devil, praying for her all one night, and appearing to her mother; and, in the morning he fled, that he might not be found and honoured by the people.

43

How Friar Conrad of Offida converted a young friar, who annoyed the other friars. And how the said young friar, after his death, appeared to the said Friar Conrad, beseeching him to pray for him; and how by his prayer he delivered him from the very grievous pains of purgatory

THE said Friar Conrad of Offida, wonderful zealot of evangelical poverty and of the rule of St. Francis, was of so religious a life and of so great merit before God, that Christ the blessed honoured him, both in life and in death, with many miracles; among the which was this: he having come, upon a time, as a guest to the Place of Offida, the friars besought him, for the love of God and of charity, that he would admonish a young friar who was in that Place, and who behaved himself so childishly and disordinately and dissolutely that he interrupted both the old and young of that community in the Divine office, and little or nothing did he care for the other observances of the Rule. Wherefore, Friar Conrad, for compassion of that young man and at the prayers of the friars, one day called the said young man aside, and, in fervour of charity, spake unto him such efficacious and devout words of admonishment that, by operation of Divine grace, he forthwith became an aged man in his behaviour, instead of a child, and so obedient and obliging and diligent and devout, and therewithal so gentle and serviceable and so studious of every virtuous thing, that, as formerly all the community had been disturbed by him, so now by him were they all contented and consoled; and they loved him much. Now it came to pass, as God willed it, that, a little while after this his conversion, the said young man died; and the friars went mourning for him. And, a few days after his death, his soul appeared to Friar Conrad, while he was devoutly praying before the altar of the said convent, and saluted him devoutly, as a father. And Friar Conrad asked him: "Who art thou?" He made answer and said: "I am the soul of that young friar that died in these days". And Friar Conrad said: "O my dearest son, how is it with thee?" And he answered: "Through God's grace and through your teaching it is well with me, seeing that I am not damned; but for certain sins of mine, whereof I had not time to purge me sufficiently, I endure very great torments in purgatory: but I pray thee, father, that, as through thy pity thou didst?' succour me when I was alive, so now thou wilt vouchsafe to succour me in my torments, saying some Paternoster for me; for thy prayer is very acceptable in the sight of God". Then Friar Conrad, courteously consenting unto his request, said the Paternoster once for him, together with the *Requiem æternam;* whereupon that soul said: "O dearest father, what benefit and what relief I feel! Now I beseech thee that thou say it a second time." And Friar Conrad said it; and, when he had said it, the soul said: "Holy father, when thou prayest for me I feel myself greatly eased; wherefore I beseech thee that thou cease not to pray for me". Then Friar Conrad, perceiving that that soul was much aided by his prayers, said a hundred Paternosters for him; and, when he had said them, that soul said: "I thank thee, most dear father, in the name of God and of the charity which thou hast shown toward me; because by thy prayers I am delivered from all my torments, and now am I going to the heavenly kingdom". And, when he had thus spoken, that soul departed. Then Friar Conrad, to give joy and comfort to the friars, related to them in order all his vision. And on this wise the soul of that youth went to paradise, through the merits of Friar Conrad.

44

How the Mother of Christ and St. John the Evangelist appeared to Friar Conrad, and told him which of them suffered the greater grief for the Passion of Christ

AT the time when there dwelt together, in the territory of Ancona in the Place of Forano, Friar Conrad and Friar Peter aforesaid, the which were two brilliant stars in the Province of the March, and two heavenly men; forasmuch as there was between them such love and charity that they seemed to be of one self-same heart and of one soul, they bound themselves together by this compact: that every consolation, which the mercy of God should grant them, they would reveal each to the other in love. Now, after they had made this compact together, it befel that, one day, while Friar Peter was praying and meditating most devoutly of the Passion of Christ, and how the most blessed Mother of Christ and St. John the Evangelist, the well-beloved disciple, and St. Francis were depicted at the foot of the Cross, as being, by grief of mind, crucified with Christ; there came upon him a desire to know which of those three had had greater grief for the Passion of Christ; whether the Mother which had borne Him, or the disciple which had slept upon His bosom, or St. Francis who was crucified with Christ. And as he thus devoutly meditated, the Virgin Mary appeared to him with St. John, the Evangelist, and with St. Francis, clad in most noble garments of beatific glory; but St. Francis appeared clad in more beautiful vesture than St. John. And at this vision Peter was sore afraid; but St. John comforted him and said: "Fear not, most dear friar, seeing that we are come to console thee touching thy doubt. Know, then, that the Mother of Christ and I, above all other creatures, were grieved at the Passion of Christ; but after us St. Francis had greater grief than any other; and therefore dost thou behold him in so great glory." And Friar Peter asked him: "Most holy Apostle of Christ, wherefore doth the vesture of St. Francis show more beautiful than thine?" St. John made answer: "The reason is this: because, when he was in this world, he wore viler garments than I". And, when he had thus spoken, St. John gave Friar Peter a glorious garment, which he carried in his hand, and said unto him: "Take this garment which I have brought for thee"; and, when St. John would have clad him therewith, Friar Peter fell to the ground in terror and amaze, and began to cry: "Friar Conrad, dearest Friar Conrad, aid me quickly; come hither and behold marvellous things". And, as he spake these words, that holy vision vanished away. Thereafter, when Friar Conrad came he told him everything in order; and they gave thanks to God.

45

Of the conversion, life, miracles and death of the holy Friar John of Penna

WHEN Friar John of Penna was still a boy and a scholar in the Province of the March, one night there appeared unto him a very beautiful Child and called him, saying: "John, go to [the church of] Santo Stefano, where one of My minor friars is preaching; believe his doctrine, and give ear unto his words, for I have sent him thither; and, when thou hast so done, thou hast a long journey to make; and thereafter thou shalt come to Me". Thereupon, he rose up at once, and he felt a great change in his heart; and going to Santo Stefano, he found a great multitude of men and women there, who were waiting to hear the preaching. And he who was to preach was a friar whose name was Philip, the same being one of the first friars who had come to the March of Ancona; for as yet but few Places were taken in the March. Now this Friar Philip rose up to preach, and he preached most devoutly, not with words of human wisdom but by virtue of the Spirit of Christ, proclaiming the Kingdom of Life Eternal. And, when the sermon was ended, the said boy went to the said Friar Philip and said unto him: "Father, if you would vouchsafe to receive me into the Order, I would willingly do penance and serve our Lord Jesus Christ". Friar Philip, perceiving and knowing the marvellous innocence of the boy, and his ready will to serve God, said unto him: "Thou shalt come to me on such a day at Recanati, and I will cause thee to be received". (Now in that place the Provincial Chapter was about to be held.) Wherefore the boy, who was very simple, thought within himself that this was the long journey which he must make, according to the revelation which he had had, and that thereafter he must go to paradise; and this he believed that he must do as soon as he had been received into the Order. He went, therefore, and was received; and, perceiving that his expectations were not fulfilled at once, when the minister said in the Chapter that whosoever desired to go into the Province of Provence, for the merit of holy obedience, would be freely given leave so to do, there came upon him a great desire to go thither; for he thought in his heart that this was the long journey which he must make before he went to paradise; but, being ashamed to say so, at the last, having great trust in the aforesaid Friar Philip who had received him into the Order, he besought him earnestly that he would obtain for him this favour, that he might have leave to go into the Province of Provence. Then Friar Philip, seeing his simplicity of heart and holy purpose, obtained for him that leave; whereupon Friar John set out with great rejoicing, having this opinion, that, when he had finished that journey, he would go to paradise. But, as God willed it, he abode in the said province twenty-five years, in this expectation and desire; living in very great honesty and sanctity, ever setting a good example and growing in favour with God and man; and he was greatly beloved by the friars and by the laity. Now, one day, while Friar John was praying devoutly, and weeping and lamenting because his desire was not fulfilled and his earthly pilgrimage was too much prolonged, Christ the Blessed appeared unto him; at the sight of Whom his soul was altogether melted. And He said unto him: "My son, Friar John, ask Me what thou wilt"; and he replied: "My Lord, I know not what to ask of Thee save Thyself alone, for I desire nothing else; but this only do I beseech Thee that Thou pardon all my sins, and give me grace to see Thee another time, when I have greater need thereof". Jesus said: "Thy prayer is heard".

And when He had thus spoken He departed and Friar John remained full of consolation. At last, the friars of the March, hearing report of his sanctity, so wrought with the General that he sent him his commandment to return to the March; and, when he had received the said commandment, he set out on his way with joy, thinking that, when he had finished that journey, he would go to heaven according to the promise of Christ. But, after he had returned to the Province of the March, he lived therein thirty years; and there was not one of his kinsmen who knew him again; and every day he awaited the mercy of God, that He should fulfil His promise to him. And in those days, he divers times filled the office of guardian with great discretion; and through him God wrought many miracles. And among the other gifts which he had of God, was the spirit of prophecy; whereby it came to pass that, on a time, when he was away from the Place, a certain novice of his was assailed by the devil, and so grievously tempted that he, consenting unto the temptation, resolved within himself to leave the Order, as soon as Friar John should have returned; the which thing, to wit his temptation and resolve, having been made known unto Friar John through the spirit of prophecy, he forthwith returned home, and called unto him the said novice, and said that he desired that he should confess; but, before he confessed, he recounted to him in order all his temptation, even as God had revealed it unto him, and concluded thus: "Son, because thou didst await me, and desiredst not to depart without my blessing, God hath granted thee this grace that never shalt thou leave the Order, but shalt die therein with the Divine blessing". Then was the said novice stablished in good resolve, and, continuing in the Order, became a holy friar; and all these things Friar Hugolin told me.

The said Friar John was a man of cheerful and quiet mind, and rarely spake; he was constant in prayer and in devotion, and especially after matins he never returned to his cell, but abode in the church in prayer even until day. And one night, while he continued in prayer after matins, the angel of the Lord appeared unto him and said: "Friar John, thy journey hath reached its end, the which thou hast so long awaited; and therefore I announce unto thee, in the name of God, that thou mayest choose what grace thou wilt. And further I announce unto thee that thou mayest choose which thou wilt, either one day in purgatory, or seven days of suffering in this world." And, Friar John choosing rather the seven days of suffering in this world, he straightway sickened of divers sicknesses; for he was sore smitten with a fever, and with gout in his hands and feet, and with colic and many other ills; but that which vexed him worse than all was this: that a demon ever stood before him, holding in his hand a great scroll, whereon were written all the sins that he had ever done or thought, and spake unto him continually, saying: "For these sins which thou hast committed in thought, word and deed, thou art condemned to the depths of hell". And he remembered not any good thing that he had ever done, nor that he was in the Order, nor that he had ever been therein; and so he verily believed that he was damned, even as the demon said unto him. Wherefore, whenever he was asked how he fared, he made answer: "Ill, for I am damned". Now, when the friars saw this, they sent for an aged friar, who was called Friar Matthew of Monte Rubbiano, the same being a holy man and a great friend of this Friar John; and the said Friar Matthew came unto him on the seventh day of his affliction, and saluted him and asked him how he fared; whereto he replied that he fared ill because he was damned. Then Friar Matthew said: "Dost thou not remember that thou hast ofttimes been confessed by me, and that I have wholly absolved thee of all thy sins? Dost thou not remember that thou hast ever served God in this holy Order for many years? Further, dost thou not remember that the mercy of God is greater than all the sins of the world, and that Christ the blessed, our Saviour, paid to redeem us an infinite price? Wherefore be thou of good hope that of a surety thou art saved." And while he thus spake, inasmuch as the period of Friar John's purgation was ended, the temptation left him, and consolation came unto him. Then spake Friar John to Friar Matthew, with great joy, saying: "Because thou art weary and the hour is late, I pray thee go and take some rest": and albeit Friar Matthew desired not to leave him, at the last, by reason of his much urging, he departed from him and went to lie down; and Friar John remained alone with the friar which waited on him. And lo! Christ the Blessed came with very great splendour and with an exceeding sweet fragrance, even as He had promised him that He would appear to him a second time when he should have greater need thereof: and so He healed him thoroughly from all his sickness. Then Friar John, with clasped hands, gave thanks to God, because He had brought the long journey of the present miserable life to so fair an ending; and, commending his soul into the hands of Christ and yielding it up to God, he passed from this mortal life to the life eternal with Christ the blessed, whom He had so long waited for and desired to behold. And the said Friar John was buried in the Place of Penna San Giovanni.

46

How Friar Pacificus, while he was praying, beheld the soul of Friar Humilis, his brother, going up to heaven

IN the said Province of the March, after the death of St. Francis, there were two brothers in the Order; the name of the one was Friar Humilis, and the name of the other was Friar Pacificus, the which were men of exceeding great sanctity and perfection. Now one of them, to wit Friar Humilis, abode in the Place of Soffiano, and there he died; and the other dwelt in a community in another place at a great distance from him. As God willed it, Friar Pacificus, while praying one day in a solitary place, was rapt in ecstasy and beheld the soul of his brother Friar Humilis depart out of his body and go straight to heaven without any let or impediment whatsoever. Thereafter, it came to pass that, many years later, Friar Pacificus, being still alive, dwelt with the other friars in the said Place of Soffiano, where his brother had died. At this time the friars, at the request of the Lords of Bruforte, exchanged the said Place for another; wherefore, among other things, they carried away with them the relics of the holy friars who had died in that Place; and, coming to the tomb of Friar Humilis, Friar Pacificus, his brother, took his bones and washed them with good wine and, thereafter, wrapped them in a white cloth, and with great reverence and devotion kissed them and wept over them; whereupon the other friars marvelled and deemed that his example was not good; in that it seemed that he, albeit a man of great sanctity, bewailed his brother with a carnal and worldly love, and showed more devotion to his relics than to those of the other friars whose sanctity had not been less than that of Friar Humilis, and whose relics were as worthy of reverence as his. And Friar Pacificus, knowing the perverse imaginings of the friars, and being willing to give them satisfaction, humbly spake unto them and said: "Well-beloved friars, marvel ye not that I have done to the bones of my brother that which I have not done to the other bones; for, blessed be God, carnal love hath not moved me as ye believe; but thus have I done because, when my brother departed from this life, as I was praying in a desolate place and far from him, I beheld his soul ascend up into heaven by a straight path; and, therefore, am I certain that his bones are holy, and that they ought to be in Paradise. And, if God had granted me the same certainty touching the other friars, I would have shown the same reverence to their bones." For the which cause, the friars, seeing his holy and devout intent, were greatly edified by him, and gave praise to God, who Both such marvellous things unto the saints, His friars.

47

Of that holy friar to whom the Mother of Christ appeared, when he was sick, and brought him three boxes of electuary

IN the above-mentioned Place of Soffiano, there was of old a Minor Friar of such great sanctity and grace, that he seemed quite Divine, and ofttimes was he rapt in God. Now, on a certain time, this friar being all absorbed in God and lifted up (for he had in a marked degree the grace of contemplation), there came unto him birds of divers sorts, and familiarly perched upon his shoulders, and upon his head, and upon his arms, and upon his hands; and marvellously did they sing. He was a man who loved solitude and rarely spoke; but, when anything was asked of him, he answered so courteously and wisely that he seemed rather an angel than a man; and very greatly was he given to prayer and to contemplation; and the friars held him in great reverence. Now this friar, having finished the course of his virtuous life, according to the Divine disposition, fell sick unto death, so that he could take no food; and therewithal he desired not to use any earthly medicine, but all his trust was in the heavenly

Physician, Jesus Christ the Blessed, and in His Blessed Mother; by whom, through the Divine clemency, he merited to be mercifully visited and tended. Wherefore, on a time, as he lay upon his bed and prepared himself for death with all his heart and with entire devotion, the glorious Virgin Mary, the Mother of Christ, appeared unto him, with marvellous splendour, in the midst of a very great multitude of angels and of holy virgins, and drew nigh unto his bed. And, as he looked upon her, he took therefrom exceeding great comfort and delight, both in soul and body, and began humbly to pray her that she would make intercession with her beloved Son that, through His merits, He would draw him forth from the prison-house of this miserable flesh. And, while yet he continued in this prayer, with many tears, the Virgin answered him, calling him by name, and said: "Doubt not, my son, for thy prayer is heard, and I am come to comfort thee a little before thou departest out of this life". Now there were, beside the Virgin Mary, three holy maidens, who carried in their hands three boxes of electuary of surpassing fragrance and sweetness. Then the glorious Virgin took one of those boxes and opened it, and all the house was filled with the perfume thereof; and, taking some of that electuary in a spoon, she gave it to the sick man, who, as soon as he had tasted it, felt such consolation and such sweetness that it seemed as if his soul could no longer remain within his body; wherefore he began to say: "No more, O blessed Virgin Mother most holy, O blessed physician and saviour of the human race, no more; for I may not endure such sweetness." But the kind and pitiful Mother continued to offer that electuary to the sick man, and to compel him to take it, until she had emptied all the box. Thereafter, when the first box was emptied, the Blessed Virgin took the second box, and put the spoon therein to give him that also: whereupon he lamented, saying: "O most blessed Mother of

God, if, by reason of the warmth and sweetness of the first electuary, my soul is well-nigh melted altogether, how then shall I be able to endure the second? I pray thee, who art blessed above all the saints and all the angels, be pleased to give me no more thereof." Thereto the glorious Virgin Mary made answer: "Son, taste also a little of this second box"; and having given him a little of it she said: "To-day, son, thou hast taken as much as may suffice thee. Be of good cheer, son, for I will soon come back for thee and will take thee to the kingdom of my Son, which thou hast alway sought and desired." And, when she had thus spoken, she took leave of him and departed thence; and he remained so consoled and comforted through the sweetness of this confection, that he lived for divers days, satiated and strong, without any bodily food. And, after certain days, while he was merrily talking with the friars, he passed from this wretched life with great joy and gladness.

48

How Friar James of Massa saw in a vision all the minor friars of the world, in a vision of a tree, and knew the virtue and the merits and the faults of each of them

FRIAR JAMES of Massa (to whom God opened the door of His secrets, and gave perfect knowledge and understanding of the Holy Scriptures and of things to come) was of so great sanctity that Friar Giles of Assisi, and Friar Mark of Montino, and Friar Juniper, and Friar Lucidus said of him; that they knew no one in the world greater in the sight of God than this Friar James. I had great desire to see him, because, while I was praying Friar John, the companion of the said Friar Giles, to explain to me certain spiritual things, he said unto me: "If thou wouldst be well informed in the spiritual life, endeavour to have speech with Friar James of Massa; for Friar Giles himself desired to be instructed by him, and to his words no man may add or take away anything, in that his mind hath penetrated celestial secrets and his words are words of the Holy Ghost; and there is no man on this earth whom I so much desire to see". This Friar

James, in the beginning of the ministry of Friar John of Parma, was once rapt in God as he prayed; and he remained three days in this ecstasy, with every bodily feeling suspended, and so complete was his insensibility that the friars doubted whether he were not dead; and, while he was in this rapture, that which shall hereafter come to pass touching our Religion was revealed to him of God; for the which cause, when I heard thereof, my desire to hear and to speak with him increased. And when it pleased God that I had leisure to talk with him, I besought him after this manner: "If that which I have heard tell of thee be true, I beseech thee that thou keep it not hidden from me. I have heard that among the other things which God revealed unto thee, when thou wast for three days as one dead, was that which must befal this our Religion; and Friar Matthew, minister of the March, unto whom thou didst reveal it for obedience' sake, hath said so." Then Friar James confessed with great humility that that which Friar Matthew said was true. Now the words which he (to wit, Friar Matthew, minister of the March) spake, were these: "I know a friar, to whom God hath revealed that which shall come to pass in our Religion; in that Friar James of Massa hath manifested and said unto me that, after God had revealed to him many things touching the state of the Church militant, he beheld in a vision a passing great and beautiful tree, whereof the root was gold and its fruits men; and all of them were Minor friars. Its main branches were distinct and separate, according to the number of the provinces of the Order, and each branch bore as many fruits as there were friars in the province represented by that branch; and then he knew the number of all the friars of the Order and of every province, as also their names and ages and condition, and the great offices, dignities and graces of all of them, and their faults. And he saw Friar John of Parma on the highest point of the central branch of this tree; and on the tops of the branches, which were round about the central branch, were the ministers of all the provinces. And, thereafter, he saw Christ sitting upon a very great white throne; and Christ called St. Francis up thither and gave him a chalice full of the spirit of life, and sent him forth, saying: 'Go and visit thy Friars, and give them to drink of this chalice of the spirit of life; for the spirit of Satan will rise up against them and smite them; and many of them will fall and will not rise up again'. And Christ gave to St. Francis two angels that they might bear him company. Then St. Francis came to offer the chalice of life to his friars; and first he offered it to Friar John of Parma; who took it and drank it all, in haste, and devoutly; and anon he became luminous as the sun. And after him St. Francis offered it to all the others in turn; and few there were of them which took it with becoming reverence and devotion and drank it all. Those who took it devoutly, and drank it all, forthwith became resplendent as the sun; and those who spilled it all and did not take it with devotion, became black, dark, and deformed and horrible to see: those who drank part of it and spilled part of it became partly shining and partly dark, and more or less, according to the quantity drunk or spilled; but the aforesaid Friar John was resplendent above all the others, inasmuch as he had more completely drunk the chalice of life, and had thereby gazed more deeply into the abyss of the infinite light divine; and, in that light, had discerned the adversity and the tempest which must arise against the said tree and shake and agitate its branches. For the which cause the said Friar John departed from the top of the branch whereon he had been; and descending below all the branches, hid himself in the solid part of the trunk of the tree, and remained there full of gloomy thoughts; and a friar who had drunk part of the chalice and had spilled part, climbed up to that branch and to that place whence Friar

John had descended. And, being in the said place, the nails of his hands became iron, sharp and keen as razors; whereupon he departed from that place, whereto he had climbed up, and with impetuosity and fury sought to fling himself upon the said Friar John to harm him; but Friar John, beholding this, cried aloud and commended himself to Christ which sat upon the throne; and, at his cry, Christ called St. Francis and gave him a sharp flint and said unto him: 'Go thou with this flint and cut the nails of that friar wherewith he is seeking to tear Friar John, so that he may not be able to harm him'; then St. Francis came and did as Christ had commanded him. And, when he had so done, a great storm of wind arose and smote the tree so strongly that the friars thereof fell to the ground; and the first to fall were they which had spilled the whole of the chalice of the spirit of life; and they were carried away by demons into places of darkness and pain. But Friar John, together with the others which had drunk all the chalice, were borne by the angels into the place of life and light eternal and of beatific splendour. And the aforesaid Friar James understood and discerned particularly and distinctly that which he saw in the vision, touching the name and condition and estate of each one of them clearly. And so long did that tempest continue to rage against the tree that it fell, and the wind carried it away. And afterward, as soon as the tempest had ceased, from the root of this tree, which was of gold, there sprang another tree which was all gold, and which brought forth leaves and flowers and golden fruit. Touching which tree and how it spread abroad its branches and struck deep its roots, and of its beauty and fragrance and virtue, it is better to be silent than to speak thereof at this present."

49

How Christ appeared to Friar John of Alvernia

AMONG other wise and holy friars, sons of St. Francis, who, according to the saying of Solomon, are the glory of their father, there was in our days, in the said Province of the March, the venerable and holy friar, John of Fermo, who, by reason of the long time which he dwelt in the holy place of Alvernia where too he passed from this life, was also called Friar John of Alvernia; for he was a man of excellent life and of great sanctity. This Friar John, while he was yet a boy and living in the world, desired with all his heart to follow the life of penance, which preserves the purity of both body and soul; wherefore, even as a very little child, he began to wear the mail-shirt and the iron ring next his flesh, and to use great abstinence, and, especially when he sojourned with the Canons of San Pietro of Fermo, who lived sumptuously, he shunned fleshly delights and mortified his body with exceeding rigid abstinence; but, inasmuch as he had in that place companions who were much opposed thereto and who despoiled him of his mail-shirt and thwarted his abstinence in divers manners; he, being inspired of God, resolved to leave the world and its lovers and to offer himself wholly to the arms of the Crucified, assuming the habit of the crucified St. Francis; and so he did. And having been received into the Order so young and committed to the care of the master of the novices, he became so spiritual and devout that, whenever he heard the said master speak of God, his heart melted like wax before the fire; and he was enkindled with such sweetness and grace by the Divine love, that, being unable to endure such sweetness sitting still, he would rise up and, as one drunken with the spirit, would run hither and thither, now through the garden, now through the wood, and now through the church, even as the flame and impetus of the Spirit drove him. Thereafter, in process of time, the Divine grace caused this angelic man to increase continually from virtue to virtue, and in celestial gifts and Divine ecstasies and raptures; insomuch so that anon his mind was uplifted to the splendours of the Cherubim, anon to the ardours of the Seraphim, anon to the joys of the Blessed, anon to amorous and immoderate embracings of Christ, not only with inward spiritual delights, but also with manifest external indications and corporal pleasure. And, once in particular, was his heart inflamed beyond measure by the fire of Divine love; and this fire lasted in him for three full years; during which period he received marvellous consolations and visitations Divine, and ofttimes was he rapt in God; and, in a word, during the said period, he seemed all on fire and burning with the love of Christ; and this was on the holy mountain of Alvernia. But, because God hath singular care for His children, giving them, at divers times, now consolation now tribulation, now prosperity and now adversity, as He seeth that their need is, to preserve them in humility or to enkindle in them a greater desire for heavenly things; it pleased the

Divine goodness, after those three years, to withdraw from the said Friar John this light and fire of Divine love, and to deprive him of every spiritual consolation. Wherefore Friar John, being left without light and without love of God, was wholly disconsolate and afflicted and sorrowful; for the which cause, being in such anguish, he went through the wood, running hither and thither, calling with voice and tears and sighs the beloved Spouse of his soul, who had hidden Himself and departed from him, and without whose presence his soul found no quiet nor repose; but in no place nor in any manner might he find again his sweet Jesus, or renew that sweet spiritual consolation of the love of Christ, which he had enjoyed aforetime.

And this tribulation lasted for many days, in the which he persevered in continual weeping and sighing, ever beseeching God that of His pity He would give back to him the well-beloved Spouse of his soul. At last, when it pleased God to have sufficiently proved his patience and enkindled his desire, upon a day, while Friar John went through the aforesaid wood, thus afflicted and troubled, he sat him down for weariness and leaned against a beech-tree and there abode, with his face all bathed with tears, gazing toward heaven; and lo! on a sudden Jesus Christ appeared before him in the pathway whereby Friar John had come; but He spake no word. Then, Friar John, beholding Him and knowing full well that it was Christ, forthwith cast himself down at His feet, and with infinite weeping very humbly besought Him and said: "Help me, O my Lord, for without Thee, my sweetest Saviour, I abide in darkness and in woe; without Thee, most gentle Lamb, I am full of anguish and pain and terror; without Thee, Son of God, most high, I am fulfilled with confusion and shame; without Thee I am despoiled of every good and am blinded; for Thou art Jesus Christ, the true light of souls; without Thee I am lost and damned, because Thou art the life of souls, the life of lives; without Thee I am barren and dry, because Thou art the fountain of every gift and of every grace; without Thee I am altogether disconsolate, because Thou art Jesus our redemption, love and desire, the bread which giveth strength, and the wine which maketh glad the hearts of the angels and the hearts of all the saints; enlighten me, Master most gracious, and Shepherd most pitiful, for I am Thy little sheep, albeit all unworthy".

But because the desire of holy men, when God delays to hear, enkindles them to greater love and merit, Christ the blessed departed without giving ear unto his prayer and without answering him a word, and gat Him thence by the aforesaid pathway. Then Friar John rose up and ran after Him, and anew cast himself at His feet, and, with holy importunity, laid hold upon Him and held Him, and with most devout tears besought Him, saying: "O most sweet Jesus Christ, have mercy upon me in my affliction; hear me out of the abundance of Thy mercy and for the truth of Thy salvation, and give me back again the joy of Thy countenance and of Thy pitiful regard, for the whole earth is full of Thy mercy". And, yet again, Christ departed and spake no word unto him, nor gave him any consolation; and He did even as doth the mother to her child, when she makes him desire the breast and follow after her weeping, to the end that he may thereafter take it the more eagerly. Wherefore Friar John, with yet greater fervour and desire, followed Christ, and, when he had overtaken Him, Christ the blessed turned toward him and looked upon him with glad and gracious countenance; and, opening His most holy and most merciful arms, embraced him very tenderly; and as He opened His arms, Friar John beheld resplendent rays of light issue from the most holy bosom of the Saviour, which illuminated all the wood, and him also, both in soul and body. Then Friar John kneeled down at the feet of Christ, and the Blessed Jesus, even as He had done to the Magdalene, graciously offered him His foot to kiss; and Friar John, holding it with extreme reverence, bathed it with so many tears that, of a truth, he seemed another Magdalene; and he said, devoutly: "I pray Thee, my Lord, that Thou look not on my sins, but, by the shedding of Thy most holy blood, revivify my soul in the grace of Thy love; for Thou hast commanded us to love Thee with all our heart and with all our soul; and this commandment may no man fulfil without Thy aid. Aid me, then, most loving Son of God, that I may love Thee with all my heart and with all my strength." And while Friar John thus spoke, lying at the feet of Christ, his prayer was answered, and he received from Him once again the first grace, to wit the fire of Divine love, and felt himself wholly renewed and comforted; and, knowing that the gift of Divine grace had returned to him, he began to thank the Blessed Christ and to devoutly kiss His feet.

And, thereafter, having risen up to look upon the face of Christ, Jesus Christ held out His most holy hands and offered them to him to kiss; and, when Friar John had kissed them, he drew nigh and leaned upon the breast of Jesus and embraced and kissed Him; and Christ, in like manner, embraced and kissed him. And in this embracing and kissing Friar John perceived so Divine a fragrance that, if all the odoriferous graces and all the fragrant things of the world had been gathered together, the odour thereof would have seemed a stench in comparison with that fragrance; and therein Friar John was rapt and consoled and illuminated; and that fragrance endured within his soul for many months. And from thenceforward, out of his mouth, which had drunk of th e fountain of Divine wisdom in the sacred breast of the Saviour, there came marvellous and celestial words, which changed men's hearts and brought forth much fruit in the souls of them who gave ear unto him; and in that woodland pathway where stood the blessed feet of Christ, and for some distance round about, Friar John, for a long time thereafter, smelled that fragrance and saw that splendour, whenever he went thither. Now, when Friar John had come to himself after that rapture, and the corporal presence of Christ had disappeared, he remained so illuminated in soul, in the abyss of his divinity, that, albeit he was not a man learned through human study, yet he marvellously solved and explained the most subtle and lofty questions concerning the Divine Trinity, and the profound mysteries of the Holy Scriptures. And ofttimes, thereafter, when speaking before the Pope and the cardinals, and kings, and barons, and masters, and doctors, he greatly amazed them all by the sublime words which he spake and by his profound judgments.

50

How, as he said Mass on the day of the dead, Friar John of Alvernia saw many souls liberated from purgatory

ONCE, while the aforesaid Friar John was saying Mass, the day after All Saints' Day, for all the souls of the dead, according as the Church has ordained, with such fervour of charity and with such anguish of compassion did he offer that most sublime sacrament (which, for its efficacy, the souls of the dead desire above all other things which can be done on their behalf) that it seemed as if he were all melted with tender pity and brotherly love. For which cause, during that Mass, while he was devoutly elevating the body of Christ and offering it to God the Father, and praying that, for love of His Blessed Son Jesus Christ, who had hung upon the cross to redeem men's souls, it would please Him to liberate from the pains of purgatory the souls of the dead by Him created and redeemed, — immediately he beheld an almost infinite multitude of souls coming forth from purgatory, like the sparks of fire innumerable, which fly from a blazing furnace; and he saw them rise up to heaven, through the merits of the passion of Christ, who every day is offered for the living and the dead in that most sacred Host, the which is worthy to be adored in *sæcula sæculorum*.

51

Of the holy Friar James of Fallerone; and how after his death he appeared to Friar John of Alvernia

WHAT time Friar James of Fallerone, a man of great sanctity, lay grievously sick in the Place of Moliano in the district of Fermo, Friar John of Alvernia, who was then sojourning at the Place of Massa, heard of his sickness, and, in that he loved him as his dear father, he betook himself to prayer for him, beseeching God devoutly with heartfelt prayers that He would give Friar James health of body if it were good for his soul; and, as he prayed thus devoutly, he was rapt in ecstasy and beheld, in the air, a great army of saints and angels, above his cell which was in the wood; and so great was the brightness of them that all the district round about was illuminated thereby; and among those angels he saw that sick Friar James, for whom he was praying, clad in white and shining raiment. Also he saw among them the blessed father St. Francis, adorned with the holy stigmata of Christ and with great glory. Also he saw there and recognised the holy Friar Lucidus, and ancient Friar

Matthew of Monte Rubbiano and many other friars, whom he had never seen or known in this life. And while Friar John thus gazed with great delight upon that blessed company of saints, the salvation of the soul of the said sick friar was certainly revealed to him; and that he must die of that sickness, but that he might not go to paradise immediately after his death, since it was first necessary that he should cleanse himself a little while in purgatory. At which revelation Friar John had such great joy, by reason of the salvation of his soul, that he recked nothing at all of the death of his body; but, with great sweetness of spirit, called unto him within himself, saying: "Friar James, sweet father mine; Friar James, sweet brother; Friar James, most faithful servant and friend of God; Friar James, companion of angels and associate of the blessed". And so, in this certainty and joy he returned to himself, and went to visit the said Friar James at Moliano; and finding him so weighed down with sickness, that scarcely was he able to speak, he announced to him the death of his body and the salvation and glory of his soul, according to the certainty which he had thereof, through the Divine revelation; whereat Friar James, all joyful in heart and face, received him with great gladness and with jocund laughter, thanking him for the good news which he had brought him, and devoutly commending himself to him. Then Friar John besought him tenderly that, after his death he would return to him and tell him of his state; and Friar James promised him so to do, if it should be God's will. And, when he had thus spoken, the hour of his passing drew nigh; and Friar James began to recite devoutly the verse of the Psalm: *In pace in idipsum dormiam et resquiescam;* which is to say: "In peace shall I sleep and take my rest in the life eternal"; and when he had recited this verse, with glad and happy face he passed from this life. And, after he was buried, Friar John returned to the Place of Massa, and awaited the fulfilment of the promise of Friar James that he would return to him on the day that he had said. But, on the said day, as he was praying, Christ appeared to him with a great company of angels and saints; and Friar James was not among them: wherefore Friar John marvelled greatly and commended him devoutly to Christ. Thereafter, on the following day, while Friar John was praying in the wood, Friar James appeared to him, accompanied by angels, all glorious and all glad; and Friar John said unto him: "O dearest father, why didst thou not return to me on the day that thou didst promise me?" Friar James made answer: "Because I had need of some purgation; but in that same hour wherein Christ appeared to thee, and thou didst commend me to Him, Christ gave ear unto thy prayer and delivered me from all pain, and at that time I appeared to Friar James of Massa, that holy lay-brother, who was serving the Mass and saw the consecrated Host, when the priest elevated it, transmuted and changed into the likeness of a very beautiful living Child: and to him I said: 'To-day I go with this Child to the kingdom of life eternal, whereunto none may go without him'". And, when he had said these words Friar James vanished away, and departed into heaven with all that blessed company of angels; and Friar John remained much consoled. The said Friar James of Fallerone died on the Vigil of St. James the Apostle, in the month of July, in the aforesaid Place of Moliano; wherein, after his death, the Divine Goodness wrought many miracles, through his merits.

52

Of the vision of Friar John of Alvernia whereby he understood all the order of the Holy Trinity

THE aforesaid Friar John of Alvernia, in that he had perfectly suffocated every worldly and temporal delight and consolation, and had set all his joy and all his hope in God, was given marvellous consolations and revelations by the Divine Goodness, and especially on the festivals of Christ; wherefore, on a time when the Festival of the Nativity of Christ drew nigh, whereon he looked with confidence to receive from God consolation of the sweet humanity of Jesus, the Holy Ghost put in his heart such great and exceeding love and fervour for the charity of Christ, whereby He humbled Himself to take upon Him our humanity, that of a verity it seemed to him that his soul was drawn forth from his body and that it burned like a furnace. Whereupon, not being able to endure such ardours, he was in agony and altogether melting away, and cried out with a loud voice; because, through the violent impulse of the Holy Ghost and through the too great fervour of love, he could not restrain himself from crying out. And in that hour wherein this measureless fervour came upon him, there came therewith so sure and certain a hope of salvation that, for nothing in the world, could he believe that, if he were then to die, he must pass through the pains of purgatory; and this love endured with him for six full months, albeit he felt not that excessive fervour continually, but it came upon him at certain hours of the day. And during this time he received marvellous visitations and consolations from God; and oftentimes he was rapt in ecstasy, even as that friar, who first wrote of these things, saw. Among the which times, he was one night so elevated and rapt in God that he beheld in Him, the Creator, all created things, both celestial and terrestrial, and all their perfections and grades and separate orders. And then he clearly understood how every created thing represented its Creator, and how God is above, and within, and outside, and beside all created things. Thereafter, he discerned one God in Three Persons, and Three Persons in one God, and the infinite charity which caused the Son of God to become incarnate in obedience to the Father. And, finally, he perceived, in that vision, how that there was no other way whereby the soul could go to God and have eternal life, save only through Christ the blessed, who is the Way, the Truth and the Life of the soul.

53

How, while he was saying Mass, Friar John of Alvernia fell down as if he were dead

TO the said Friar John in the aforesaid Place of Moliano, according to that which the friars who were there present related, there befel on a time this marvellous case: On the first night after the octave of St. Laurence and within the octave of the Assumption of Our Lady, having said matins in the church with the other friars, the unction of the Divine grace fell upon him and he betook himself to the garden to meditate on the Passion of Christ, and to prepare himself with all devotion to celebrate the Mass which, that morning, it fell to his turn to sing; and, while he meditated on the words of the consecration of the body of Christ, considering the infinite love of Christ, by reason whereof He not only willed to redeem us with His precious blood, but also to leave us, for spiritual food, His body and most excellent blood, the love of the sweet Jesus began to increase in him, with so great fervour and with such tenderness, that his soul might no more endure for the great sweetness which he felt; but he cried aloud and, as one drunken in spirit, never ceased to say within himself: *Hoc est corpus meum;* for, as he said these words, it seemed to him that he beheld the blessed Christ, with the Virgin Mary and with a multitude of angels, and, in thus speaking, he was illuminated by the Holy Spirit touching all the profound and lofty mysteries of that most exalted sacrament. And, when day broke, he entered into the church, in that fervour of spirit and with that anxiety and with those words upon his lips, not thinking to be heard or seen by any one; but there was in the choir a certain friar, who was praying; and who saw and heard all. And, not being able to restrain himself in that fervour, through the abundance of the Divine grace, he cried with a loud voice, and continued after this manner until it was time to say the Mass; and thereupon he went to make himself ready for the altar. And, when he began the Mass, the farther he proceeded the more did there increase in him the love of Christ, and that fervour of devotion, wherewith there was given unto him an ineffable sense of God's presence, the which he himself knew not, nor was afterward able to express with his tongue. Wherefore, fearing that that fervour and sense of God's presence would increase so much that he would be compelled to leave the Mass, he stood in great perplexity, knowing not what to do, whether to proceed further with the Mass or to stop and wait. But, because, once before, a like case had befallen him, and the Lord had so tempered that fervour that he had not been obliged to leave the Mass, he trusted, at this time also, to he able to do the like, and, with great fear, set himself to continue the Mass until he came to the Preface of Our Lady, when the Divine illumination and the gracious sweetness of the love of God increased so much within him, that, reaching the *Qui pridie,* scarcely might he endure such joy and sweetness. Finally, coming to the act of consecration, and having spoken half of the words over the Host, to wit *Hoc est;* on nowise might he proceed farther, but continued to repeat these same words, to wit *Hoc est enim;* and the reason wherefore he could not proceed farther was that he felt and saw the presence of Christ with a multitude of angels, whose majesty he might not endure; and he saw that Christ entered not into the Host, neither was the Host transformed into the body of Christ, because he could not utter the other half of the words, to wit *corpus meum*. Wherefore, while he abode in this anxiety and could proceed no farther, the Guardian and the other friars, and also many lay folk, which were in the church to hear Mass, drew nigh unto the altar, and there stood, terrified to behold and to consider the action of Friar John; and many of them wept for devotion. At the last, after a long time, to wit when God willed it, Friar John pronounced the *enim corpus meum* with a loud voice; and straightway the form of the bread vanished away, and on the Host appeared Jesus Christ the blessed, incarnate and glorified, and manifested unto him the humility and charity which caused Him to become incarnate of the Virgin Mary, and which causes Him to come every day into the hands of the priest when he consecrates the Host; for the which cause he was yet more lifted up in sweetness of contemplation. Thereafter, when he had elevated the Host and the consecrated chalice, he was rapt out of himself and, his soul being raised above corporal feelings, his body fell backwards, and, if he had not been held up by the guardian, who stood behind him, he had fallen supine to the ground. Wherefore there ran thither the friars and the lay folk who were in the church, both men and women, and he was carried by them into the sacristy, as one dead, for his body was all cold and the fingers of his hands were clenched so tightly that scarcely could they be unclosed or moved at all. And on this wise he lay swooning or rapt even until Terce; and it was summer-time. And because I, who was there present, desired greatly to know that which God had wrought upon him, as soon as he had returned to himself, I went to him, and besought him, for the love of God, that he would tell me everything; wherefore, because he trusted me much, he narrated everything to me in order; and, among other things, he told me that, while he was considering the body and blood of Jesus Christ there present, his heart became even as wax which is melted in a great heat, and his flesh appeared to be without bones, on such wise that scarcely might he raise his arms and his hands to make the sign of the cross over the Host and over the chalice. Also he told me that, or ever he became a priest, it had been revealed to him by God that he must swoon during the Mass; but, because he had already said many Masses and this had not befallen him, he deemed that the revelation had not been of God. Nevertheless, perhaps fifty days before the Assumption of Our Lady, whereon the aforesaid case befel him, it had been again revealed unto him of God that this thing would befal him about the said feast of the Assumption; but thereafter he remembered not the said vision, or revelation, made to him by our Lord.

OF THE MOST HOLY STIGMATA OF ST. FRANCIS

INTRODUCTION

OF THE MOST HOLY STIGMATA OF ST. FRANCIS AND OF THEIR CONSIDERATIONS

IN THIS PART WE SHALL BEHOLD WITH DEVOUT CONSIDERATION THE GLORIOUS, SACRED AND HOLY STIGMATA OF OUR BLESSED FATHER, MESSER SAINT FRANCIS, THE WHICH HE RECEIVED OF CHRIST UPON THE HOLY MOUNTAIN OF ALVERNIA

Because the said stigmata were five, even as the wounds of our Lord Jesus Christ were five, therefore this treatise will have five considerations.

The first consideration will be touching the manner in which St. Francis came to the holy mountain of Alvernia.

The second consideration will be touching the life which he lived, and the conversation which he held with his companions on the said holy mountain.

The third consideration will be touching the seraphic vision and the imprinting of the most sacred stigmata.

The fourth consideration will be how St. Francis descended from the mountain of Alvernia, after he had received the sacred stigmata, and returned to Santa Maria degli Angeli.

The fifth consideration will be touching certain Divine visions and revelations made after the death of St. Francis to holy friars and to other devout persons concerning the said sacred and glorious stigmata.

OF THE FIRST CONSIDERATION
OF THE MOST HOLY STIGMATA

AS to the first consideration, it must be known that, in 1224, St. Francis, being then forty-three years old, was inspired of God to depart from the Val di Spoleto and to go into Romagna, with Friar Leo his companion; and as he went, he passed at the foot of the Castello di Montefeltro; in the which town there was then being held a great banquet and festival for the knighting of one of those Counts of Montefeltro; and St. Francis, hearing of this festival, and that many gentlefolk were gathered there from divers lands, said unto Friar Leo: "Let us go up thither unto this feast, since by God's help we shall gather some good spiritual fruit". Now among the other gentlemen, who had come thither from that district to that ceremonial, was a great and rich gentleman of Tuscany, by name Messer Orlando of Chiusi in Casentino, the which, by reason of the marvellous things which he had heard touching the sanctity and miracles of St. Francis, bore him great devotion and had very great desire to see him and to hear him preach. St. Francis then, having arrived at this town, entered in and gat him to the piazza, where were assembled all the multitude of those gentlemen; and, in fervour of spirit, he climbed upon a little wall and began to preach, taking as the text of his sermon these words in the vulgar tongue:

> So great the bliss I hope to see,
> That every pain delighteth me.

And from this text, by the inspiration of the Holy Ghost, he preached so devoutly and so profoundly, proving the truth thereof by divers sufferings and torments of holy apostles and of holy martyrs, by the severe penances of holy confessors, and by the many tribulations and temptations of holy virgins and of other saints, that every man stood with eyes and mind fixed upon him, and hearkened unto hint as if it were an angel of God that spoke; among whom, the said Messer Orlando, being touched in the heart by God, through the marvellous preaching of St. Francis, was minded to consult and speak with him after the sermon concerning the affairs of his soul. Wherefore, when the preaching was done, he drew St. Francis aside and said unto him: "O father, I would take counsel with thee touching the salvation of my soul". St. Francis made answer: "Well content am I; but go thou this morning and do honour to thy friends who have invited thee to this festival, and dine with them; [and, after thou hast dined, we will talk together as long as thou shalt please". Messer Orlando, therefore, went to dinner;] and, after dinner, he returned to St. Francis and laid before him fully all the affairs of his soul and took counsel with him concerning the same. And finally this Messer Orlando said to St. Francis: "I have in Tuscany a mountain most apt for devotion, the which is called the mountain of Alvernia, exceeding solitary, and passing well fitted for such as would do penance in a place remote from men, and desire a life of solitude. If it pleases thee, gladly would I give it to thee and to thy companions for the salvation of my soul." St. Francis, hearing so liberal an offer of a thing which he much desired, was exceeding joyful thereat; and praising and thanking first God, and then Messer Orlando, he spake unto him thus: "Messer Orlando, when you shall have returned to your home, I will send unto you some of my companions, and you shall show them that mountain; and, if it shall seem to them fitted for prayer and for the doing of penance, even from this moment do I accept your charitable offer".

And, when he had thus spoken, St. Francis departed; and after he had finished his journey he returned to Santa Maria degli Angeli; and Messer Orlando likewise, when the festivities for the making of that knight were ended, returned to his castle, which was called Chiusi, and which was distant a mile from Alvernia. St. Francis, then, having returned to Santa Maria degli Angeli, sent two of his companions to the said Messer Orlando, who, when they were come unto him, welcomed them with very great joy and charity: and, desiring to show them the mountain of Alvernia, he sent with them fully fifty armed men, to the end that they might defend them from the wild beasts; and thus accompanied those friars went up into the mountain and explored it diligently; and at last they came unto a part of the mountain exceeding well fitted for devotion and for contemplation; in the which part there was some level ground; and that place they chose for their habitation and for that of St. Francis; and with the aid of those armed men which were in their company they made a little cell with the boughs of trees, and on this wise, in the name of God, they accepted and took possession of the mountain of Alvernia and of the Place of the friars in that mountain, and departed and returned to St. Francis. And, when they had come unto him, they told him how and in what manner they had taken the said Place upon the mountain of Alvernia, well fitted for prayer and contemplation. Now, when St. Francis heard this news, he rejoiced greatly, and, giving praise and thanks to God, spake unto those friars with happy face, and said: "My sons, we are drawing nigh to our forty days' fast of St. Michael the Archangel; and I firmly believe that it is the will of God that we keep this fast in the mountain of Alvernia, the which by Divine dispensation hath been made ready for us, to the end that we may, through penance, merit from Christ the consolation of consecrating that blessed mountain to the honour and glory of God and of His glorious mother, the Virgin Mary, and of the holy angels". And then, having said these words, St. Francis took with him Friar Masseo da Marignano of Assisi, the which was a man of great wisdom and eloquence, and Friar Angelo Tancredi da Rieti, who was a man of very noble birth, and who in the world had been a knight, and Friar Leo, who was a man of very great simplicity and purity; for the which cause St. Francis loved him much.

And with these three friars St. Francis betook himself to prayer, and commended himself and his companions aforesaid to the prayers of the friars which remained behind, and set out with those three in the name of Jesus Christ the Crucified, to go to the mountain of Alvernia; and, as he went, St. Francis called unto him one of those three companions, to wit Friar Masseo, and spake unto him thus: "Thou, Friar Masseo, shalt be our Guardian and Superior on this journey; to wit while we shall be going and abiding together, and we will observe our custom: that either we will say the office, or we will speak of God, or we will keep silence; and we will take no thought beforehand, neither of eating, nor of drinking, nor of sleeping; but when the time to rest for the night shall be come, we will beg a little bread, and will lodge and repose ourselves in that place which God shall make ready for us." Then those three companions bowed their heads, and, signing themselves with the sign of the cross, went forward; and the first evening they came to a Place of friars, and there they lodged. The second evening, by reason of the bad weather and because they were weary, they were not able to reach any Place of friars, or any walled town, nor any hamlet; and when night and the bad weather overtook them, they sought shelter in an abandoned and disused church, and there they laid them down to rest, and, while his companions slept, St. Francis gave himself to prayer; and lo! in the first watch of the night, there came a great multitude of most ferocious demons with very great noise and tumult, and began vehemently to give him battle and annoy; for one plucked him on this side and another on that; one pulled him down and another up; one menaced him with one thing and another accused him of another; and thus in divers manners did they seek to disturb him in his prayer; but they were not able, because God was with him. Wherefore, when St. Francis had borne these assaults of the demons for some time, he began to cry with a loud voice: "O damned spirits, ye can do nothing save that which the hand of God permitteth you; and therefore, in the name of God Omnipotent I tell you that ye may do unto my body whatsoever is permitted you by God, and I will bear it willingly; for I have no greater enemy than this body of mine. Wherefore, if ye take vengeance for me upon mine enemy, ye do me very great service."

Thereupon the demons, with very great impetus and fury, laid hold of him and began to hale him about the church and to do him much greater injury and annoy than at first. And then St. Francis commenced to cry aloud and said: "My Lord Jesus Christ, I thank Thee for the great honour and charity which Thou showest me; for it is a token of much love when the Lord thoroughly punisheth His servant for all his faults in this world, to the end that he may not be punished in the next. And I am ready to endure joyfully every pain and every adversity which Thou, my God, mayest vouchsafe to send me for my sins." Then the demons, being put to confusion and conquered by his constancy and patience, left him, and St. Francis, in fervour of spirit, went forth from the church into a wood which was thereby, and there he gave himself to prayer; and, with supplications and tears and beatings of his breast, sought to find Jesus Christ, the Spouse and delight of his soul. And when, at last, he found Him in the secret places of his soul, he now spake reverently unto Him as his Lord; now answered Him as his Judge; now besought Him as his Father; and now talked with Him as to a Friend. On that night and in that wood, his companions, after they were awakened and had come thither to hear and to consider that which he was doing, saw and heard him, with tears and cries, devoutly beseeching the Divine mercy for sinners.

Then too he was heard and seen to bewail the Passion of Christ with a loud voice as if he saw the same with his bodily eyes. On that same night they beheld him praying, with his arms held in the form of a cross, uplifted for a great space and raised from the ground, surrounded by a resplendent cloud. And on this wise, in these holy exercises, he passed the whole of that night without sleeping; and thereafter, in the morning, because they knew that, by reason of the fatigues of the night which he had passed without sleep, St. Francis was very weak in body and could ill have travelled on foot, his companions went to a poor labourer of that district, and besought him for the love of God to lend his little ass to St. Francis, their father, who could not go on foot. Now, when this man heard them make mention of Friar Francis, he asked them: "Are ye some of the friars of that friar of Assisi whereof so much good is spoken?" The friars answered: "Yes"; and that it was in truth for him that they asked the beast of burden. Then that good man made ready the little ass, with great devotion and diligence, and led it to St. Francis with great reverence and made him mount thereon; and they continued their journey; and he with them, behind his little ass. And, when they had gone some distance, that villain said to St. Francis: "Tell me, art thou Friar Francis of Assisi?" And St. Francis answered him, "Yea." "Strive thou, then (said the villain), to be as good as all folk hold thee to be, for there are many which have great faith in thee; and therefore I admonish thee, that thou fall not short of that which men hope to find thee." Hearing these words, St. Francis did not disdain to be admonished by a villain, and said not within himself: "What beast is this that admonisheth me?" even as many many proud fellows who wear the friar's habit would say to-day; but forthwith he cast himself to earth from off the ass, and kneeled him down before that villain and kissed his feet, and thanked him humbly, because he had deigned to admonish him so charitably. Then the villain, together with the companions of St. Francis, raised him up from off the ground with great devotion, and set him upon the ass again, and continued their journey. And when they had gone perhaps half way up the mountain; because the heat was very great and the ascent difficult, this villain became exceeding thirsty, so that he began to cry aloud behind St. Francis, saying: "Alas! I am dying of thirst; if I have not something to drink I shall presently swoon away."

For the which cause St. Francis dismounted from his ass and betook himself to prayer; and he remained upon his knees with his hands raised to heaven until he knew by revelation that God had heard him. And then St. Francis said to the villain: "Run, go quickly to yonder rock, and there thou shalt find living water, which Jesus Christ, in this hour, hath of His mercy made to issue forth from that rock". So he went to the place which St. Francis had shown him, and found there a fair spring which had come forth from the hard rock at the prayer of St. Francis, and he drank copiously thereof, and was comforted. And it was clearly seen that that fountain was miraculously produced by God through the prayers of St. Francis, because neither before nor after was there ever found, in that place, a spring of water, nor any living water near that place for a great distance round about. When he had thus done, St. Francis, with his companions and with the villain, gave thanks to God for the miracle vouchsafed, and thereafter they continued their journey. And when they drew nigh to the foot of the peak of Alvernia itself, it pleased St. Francis to rest himself a little beneath an oak which was in that place and which is there yet; and, as he sat beneath it, St. Francis began to consider the situation of the place and of the country thereabout; and, while he was thus considering, lo! a great multitude of birds came thither from divers parts, the which, with singing and beating of wings, all showed very great joy and gladness; and they surrounded St. Francis on such wise that some alighted upon his head, and some upon his shoulders, and some upon his arms, some in his bosom, and some about his feet. Now when his companions and the villain saw this they marvelled greatly; whereupon St. Francis, all joyful in spirit, spake unto them thus: "I believe, most dear brethren, that it is the will of our Lord Jesus Christ that we dwell in this solitary mountain, because out sisters and brothers the birds show such joy of out coming". And when he had said these words, they rose up and continued their journey; and finally came unto the place which his companions had chosen at the first. And this sufficeth for the first consideration, to wit how St. Francis came to the holy mountain of Alvernia.

OF THE SECOND CONSIDERATION OF THE MOST HOLY STIGMATA

THE second consideration is touching the conversation of St. Francis with his companions upon the said mountain of Alvernia. And as to this it is to be known; that, when Messer Orlando had heard that St. Francis with three companions had gone up into the mountain of Alvernia to dwell there, he had very great joy thereof; and, on the following day, he set out with many of his retainers and came to visit St. Francis, bearing bread and wine and other victuals for him and for his companions; and, coming to the place where they were, he found them in prayer; and drawing nigh unto them he saluted them. Then St. Francis rose up and with very great charity and joy welcomed Messer Orlando and his company; and, when he had thus done, he entered into conversation with him; and, after they had talked together and St. Francis had thanked him for the holy mountain which he had given him and for his coming thither, he besought him that he would cause a poor little cell to be made at the foot of a very beautiful beech-tree, which was distant a stone's throw from the Place of the friars, because that spot seemed to him most apt and dedicate to prayer. And straightway Messer Orlando caused it to be built; and, when it was finished, because the evening drew nigh and it was time for them to depart, St. Francis, before they went, preached unto them a little: and, after that he had preached and given them his blessing, Messer Orlando, since he could no longer stay, called St. Francis and his companions aside and said unto them: "My most dear friars, I would not that, in this savage mountain, ye suffered any bodily want, whereby ye might be let and hindered from spiritual things; and therefore I desire (and this I tell you once for all) that ye fail not to send to my house for all that ye need; and, if ye do not do so, I shall take it very ill of you". And, having thus spoken, he departed with his company and returned to his castle.

Then St. Francis made his companions sit down and instructed them concerning the manner of life which they, and whosoever desireth to live religiously in hermitages, must lead. And, among other things, he especially laid upon them the observance of holy poverty, saying: "Regard not overmuch the charitable offer of Messer Orlando, that in naught may ye offend our lady and mistress, holy Poverty. Be ye sure that the more we shun Poverty the more the world will shun us; but, if we shall closely embrace holy Poverty, the world will follow after us and will abundantly supply all our needs. God hath called us to this holy religion for the salvation of the world, and hath made this covenant between us and the world; that we should give unto the world a good ensample and the world should provide for us in our necessities. Let us continue, therefore, in holy poverty, because that is the way of perfection and the pledge and earnest of eternal riches. And, after many beautiful and devout words and admonishments touching this matter, he concluded, saying: "This is the manner of life which I lay upon myself and upon you; for I perceive that I draw nigh unto my death, and I am minded to be solitary, and to turn all my thoughts to God and to bewail my sins before Him; and Friar Leo, when it shall seem good to him, shall bring me a little bread and a little water; and on nowise do ye permit any layman to come unto me; but do ye answer them for me". And when he had said these words he gave them his blessing, and gat him to the cell beneath the beech-tree; and his companions abode in the Place, firmly resolved to observe the commandments of St. Francis. A few days thereafter, as St. Francis was standing beside the said cell, considering the conformation of the mountain, and marvelling at the huge chasms and clefts in those tremendous rocks, he betook himself to prayer; and then was it revealed to him of God that those wondrous fissures had been made miraculously in the hour of Christ's Passion, when, even as saith the evangelist, "the rocks were rent". And this, as God willed it, was singularly manifested in that mountain of Alvernia because it was foreordained that, in that place, St. Francis must renew the Passion of our Lord Jesus Christ, in his soul through love and pity, and in his body through the imprinting of the most holy stigmata. Now, when he had received this revelation, St. Francis straightway shut himself up in his cell, and, closing his mind to all earthly things, disposed himself to await the mystery of this revelation. And from thenceforward, because he continued alway in prayer, St. Francis began, more often than heretofore, to taste the sweetness of Divine contemplation; whereby he was ofttimes so rapt in God that he was seen by his companions uplifted from the ground and rapt from out himself.

In these raptures of contemplation, not only were things present and future revealed unto him by God, but also the secret thoughts and desires of the friars, even as Friar Leo, his companion, on that day, proved in his own person. For the said Friar Leo being vexed of the devil with a very grievous temptation, not carnal but spiritual, there came upon him a great desire to have some holy thing written by the hand of St. Francis; for he thought that, if he had it, that temptation would leave him, either altogether or in part; nevertheless, albeit he had this desire, for shame and reverence he lacked the courage to speak thereof to St. Francis; but that which Friar Leo told him not, was revealed to him by the Holy Ghost. Wherefore St. Francis called him unto him and made him bring inkhorn and pen and paper, and with his own hand wrote a laud of Christ, according to the desire of the friar, and at the end thereof made the sign of the *Tau*, and gave it unto him saying: "Take this paper, dearest friar, and keep it diligently until thy death. God bless thee and preserve thee from every temptation. Be not dismayed that thou hast temptations, for then do I hold thee more my friend and a truer servant of God; and I love thee the more the more thou hast fought against thy temptations. Verily I say unto thee that no man may call himself a perfect friend of God until he hath passed through many temptations and tribulations." And when Friar Leo had received this writing with very great devotion and faith, anon every temptation left him; and, returning to the Place, he related to his companions, with great joy, what grace God had done him as he received that writing from St. Francis; and he put it in a safe place and preserved it diligently; and therewith, in after-time, the friars wrought many miracles.

And from that hour the said Friar Leo commenced to scrutinise and to consider the life of St. Francis, with great purity and goodwill; and, by reason of his purity, he merited to behold how many a time and oft St. Francis was rapt in God and uplifted from the ground, sometimes for the space of three cubits, sometimes of four, and sometimes even to the height of the beech-tree; and sometimes he beheld him raised so high in the air, and surrounded by such radiance, that scarcely could he see him. And what did this simple friar do when St. Francis was so little raised above the ground that he could reach him? He went softly and embraced his feet and kissed them with tears, saying: "My God, have mercy upon me a sinner; and, for the merits of this holy man, grant me to find Thy grace." And, one time among the rest, while he stood thus beneath the feet of St. Francis, when he was so far uplifted from the ground, that he could not touch him, he beheld a scroll inscribed with letters of gold descend from heaven and rest above the head of St. Francis, upon the which scroll these words were written: "QVI È LA GRAZIA DI DIO—*Here is the grace of God*"; and, after that he had read it, he saw it return again to heaven. By reason of this grace of God which was in him, not only was St. Francis rapt in God through ecstatic contemplation, but also he was sometimes comforted by angelic visitations. Thus, one day, while St. Francis was thinking of his death and of the state of his Religion after his life should be ended, and was saying: "Lord God, what after my death shall become of Thy mendicant family, the which through Thy goodness Thou hast entrusted to me a sinner? Who shall console them? Who shall correct them? Who shall pray to Thee for them?" While he spake these and such-like words, there appeared unto him the angel sent by God, which comforted him, saying: "I tell thee in God's name that the profession of thy Order shall not fail until the Day of Judgment; and there shall be no sinner so great that, if he shall love thy Order from his heart, he shall not find mercy with God; and no one who persecuteth thy Order maliciously shall live long.

Moreover no one, in thy Order, who is very wicked and who doth not amend his life will be able to remain long in the Order. Therefore grieve not thyself if thou see in thy Religion certain friars who are not good, and who observe not the Rule as they ought to do; neither think thou that for this thy Religion languisheth; for there will always be very many therein who will perfectly follow the life of the gospel of Christ and the purity of the Rule; and such as these, as soon as ever their earthly life is done, will go to the life eternal, without passing through purgatory at all; some will follow it, but not perfectly; and these, before they go to paradise, will be in purgatory: but the time of their purgation will be remitted unto thee by God. But for those who observe not the Rule at all, care thou not, saith God, because He careth not for them." And when the angel had spoken these words he departed, leaving St. Francis consoled and comforted. Thereafter, when the feast of the Assumption of Our Lady drew nigh, St. Francis sought to find a fitting spot, more secret and remote, wherein in greater solitude he might keep the forty days' fast of St. Michael the Archangel, the which commenceth on the said feast of the Assumption. Wherefore he called Friar Leo and spake unto him thus: "Go and stand at the doorway of the oratory of the Place of the friars; and, when I shall call thee, do thou return to me". Friar Leo went and stood in the said doorway; and St. Francis gat him thence a space and called loudly. Friar Leo, hearing him call, returned unto him; and St. Francis said: "Son, search we out another more secret spot whence thou shalt not be able thus to hear me when I shall call thee"; and, as they searched, they saw, on the southern side of the mountain, a lonely place exceeding well fitted for his purpose; but it was impossible to reach it, because there was in front of it a rocky chasm, horrible and fearful, and very great. Wherefore, with much labour they laid a tree across the same, after the fashion of a bridge, and passed over to the other side.

Then St. Francis sent for the other friars and told them how he purposed to keep the forty days' fast of St.

Michael in that solitary place; and therefore he besought them that they would make him a little cell there, so that for no crying of his might he be heard of them; and, when the little cell of St. Francis was finished, he said unto them: "Go ye to your own Place and leave me here alone; for, with the help of God, I mean to keep this fast in this place without any trouble or disturbance of mind; and therefore let none of you come nigh me, nor suffer any layman to come unto me. But thou, Friar Leo, alone shalt come unto me, once a day, with a little bread and water, and at night once again, at the hour of matins; and then shalt thou come unto me in silence; and, when thou art at the head of the bridge, thou shalt say unto me: *Domine, labia mea aperies;* and, if I answer thee, pass over and come to the cell and we will say matins together; but if I answer thee not, get thee gone immediately." And this St. Francis said because he was sometimes so rapt in God that he heard not nor perceived anything with the bodily senses; and, when he had thus spoken, St. Francis gave them his blessing; and they returned to the Place. Now, the feast of the Assumption being come, St. Francis began the holy fast with very great abstinence and severity, mortifying his body and comforting his spirit with fervent prayers, vigils and flagellations; and in these prayers, ever growing from virtue to virtue, he prepared his mind to receive the Divine mysteries and the Divine splendours, and his body to endure the cruel assaults of the fiends, with whom oftentimes he fought bodily. And among the other times was one when, on a day, as St. Francis came forth from his cell in fervour of spirit, and went to a place hard by, to pray in the cavity of a hollow rock, wherefrom down to the ground there is a very great height, and a horrible and fearful precipice; suddenly the devil came in terrible shape, with tempest and with very great uproar, and smote him to cast him down from thence. Wherefore, St.

Francis, not having any place to flee unto, and being unable to endure the passing cruel aspect of the demon, forthwith turned himself round, with his hands and face and with all his body against the rock, commending himself to God, and groping with his hands if, perchance, he might find something to lay hold of.

But, as it pleased God, who never allows His servants to be tempted beyond that which they can bear, on a sudden the rock whereto he clung miraculously hollowed itself to the form of his body and so received him into itself; and even as if he had put his hands and face into liquid wax, so was the shape of the face and hands of St. Francis imprinted upon the said rock; and, on this wise, being helped of God, he escaped from the devil. But that which the devil could not then do to St. Francis, namely to cast him down from thence, he did a good while thereafter, when St. Francis was dead, to a dear and devout friar of his, the which, in that same place, was adjusting certain pieces of wood to the end that it might be possible to go thither without peril, for devotion toward St. Francis and toward the miracle which was wrought there; and one day the devil pushed him, when he had a great log on his head which he wished to set there, and caused him to fall down thence with that log on his head; but God, who had saved and preserved St. Francis from falling, through his merits saved and preserved that devout friar of his from the peril of the fall; for, as the friar fell, he commended himself with very great devotion and with a loud voice to St. Francis, who straightway appeared to him and took him and set him on the rocks below, without permitting him to suffer any shuck or hurt. Then, the friars, having heard his cry as he fell, and believing that he was dead and dashed to pieces, by reason of the great height wherefrom he had fallen upon the sharp rocks, with great sorrow and weeping took the bier and went from the other side of the mountain to search for the fragments of his body and to bury them. Now, when they had already come down from the mountain, the friar who had fallen met them, with the log wherewith he had fallen upon his head; and he was singing the *Te Deum laudamus*, in a loud voice. And, because the friars marvelled greatly, he related unto them in order all the manner of his falling, and how St. Francis had rescued him from every peril. Then all the friars accompanied him to the place, singing most devoutly the aforesaid psalm, *Te Deum laudamus*, and praising and thanking God together with St. Francis for the miracle which he had wrought in his friar. St. Francis, then, continuing (as hath been said) the aforesaid fast, albeit he sustained many assaults of the devil, nevertheless received many consolations from God, not only through angelic visitations but also through the birds of the air; for, during all the time of that fast, a hawk, which was building its nest hard by his cell, awakened him every night a little before matins, with its cry, and by beating itself against his cell, and departed not until he rose up to say matins; and, when St. Francis was more weary than usual, or weak or sick, this hawk, after the manner of a discreet and compassionate person, uttered its cry later than it was wont to do.

And so St. Francis took great joy of this clock, because the great diligence of the hawk drove away from him all sloth, and urged him to prayer: and besides this, sometimes, in the daytime, it would familiarly sit with him. Finally, touching this second consideration, St. Francis, being much weakened in body, both by reason of his great abstinence, and of the assaults of the devil, and desiring to comfort his body with the spiritual food of the soul, began to meditate on the immeasurable glory and joy of the blessed in the life eternal, and therewith he began -to pray God that He would grant him to taste a little of that joy. And, as he continued in this thought, anon there appeared unto him an angel, with very great splendour, bearing a viol in his left hand and in his right a bow; and, while yet St. Francis was all amazed at the sight of him, the angel drew his bow once across the viol; and straightway St. Francis heard so sweet a melody that it filled all his soul with rapture and rendered it insensible to every bodily feeling; insomuch that, according to that which he afterward told his companions, he doubted whether, if the angel had drawn the bow back again across the viol, his soul must not have departed out of his body by reason of the intolerable sweetness. And this sufficeth for the second consideration.

OF THE THIRD CONSIDERATION OF THE MOST HOLY STIGMATA

COMING to the third consideration, to wit the seraphic vision and the imprinting of the most holy stigmata, it is to be considered that when the festival of the most Holy Cross of the month of September was drawing nigh, Friar Leo went one night, at the accustomed hour, to say matins with St. Francis, and calling, as he was wont, from the head of the bridge: Domine, labia mea aperies, and St. Francis making no answer, Friar Leo turned not back again as St. Francis had commanded him; but, with good and holy purpose, he crossed over the bridge and softly entered the cell; and, finding him not, he thought that he was somewhere in the wood in prayer; wherefore he came forth and, by the light of the moon, went searching softly through the wood; and finally he heard the voice of St Francis; and, drawing nigh, he saw him on his knees in prayer, with face and hands raised to heaven; and in fervour of spirit he was speaking thus: "Who art Thou, my most sweet God? What am I, most vile worm and Thine unprofitable servant?" And these same words alone did he repeat, and said no other thing. For the which cause, Friar Leo, marvelling thereat, raised his eyes and gazed toward heaven; and, as he looked, he beheld, coming down from heaven, a torch of fire, most beautiful and bright, which descended and lighted upon the head of St. Francis; and from out the said flame he heard a voice come which spake with St. Francis; but Friar Leo understood not the words. Hearing this, and deeming himself unworthy to abide so near to that holy place, where was that marvellous apparition, and fearing also to offend St. Francis, or to disturb him in his contemplation, if he should be perceived by him, he softly drew back, and, standing afar off, waited to see the end; and, gazing fixedly, he saw St. Francis stretch out his hands three times to the flame; and finally, after a long time, he saw the flame return to heaven.

Wherefore he gat him thence, deeming himself unseen and glad of the vision, and was returning to his cell. And, as he went confidently, St. Francis perceived him by the rustling which his feet made upon the leaves, and commanded him to wait for him and not to move. Then Friar Leo, obedient, stood still and waited for him, with such fear that, as he afterwards told his companions, he would rather, at that moment, that the earth had swallowed him up than wait for St. Francis, who he thought was angered with him; because with very great diligence he took heed not to offend his fatherhood, lest, through fault of his, St. Francis should deprive him of his company. Then, when he had come up to him, St Francis asked him: "Who art thou?" and Friar Leo, all trembling, replied: "My father, I am Friar Leo"; and St. Francis said unto him: "Wherefore didst thou come hither, friar little sheep? Did I not tell thee not to come and watch me? For holy obedience, tell me whether thou sawest or heardest aught." Friar Leo replied: "Father, I heard thee speak and say many times: 'Who art Thou, my most sweet God? What am I, most vile worm and Thine unprofitable servant?'" And then Friar Leo, kneeling down before St. Francis, confessed himself guilty of disobedience, in that he had done contrary to his commandment, and besought his pardon with many tears. And thereafter he prayed him devoutly that he would explain those words which he had heard, and would tell him those which he had not understood.

Then, seeing that to the humble Friar Leo God had revealed or granted to hear and to see certain things, by reason of his simplicity and purity, St. Francis condescended to reveal and to explain unto him that which he asked; and he spake as follows: "Know, friar little sheep of Jesus Christ, that when I was saying those words which thou heardest, then were shown unto me two lights for my soul; the one of knowledge and understanding of my own self, the other of knowledge and understanding of the Creator. When I said: 'Who art thou, O my most sweet God?' then I was in a light of contemplation wherein I saw the abyss of the infinite goodness and wisdom and power of God; and when I said: 'What am I?' I was in a light of contemplation in the which I beheld the depth of my baseness and misery; and therefore I said: 'Who art Thou, Lord of infinite goodness and wisdom, that deignest to visit me, that am a vile worm and abominable?' And in that flame which thou sawest was God; who in that form spake with me, even as of old He spake unto Moses. And, among other things which He said unto me, He asked me to give Him three gifts; and I made answer: 'Lord, I am all Thine; Thou knowest well that I have nothing beside the habit and the cord and the breeches, and even these three things are Thine; what then can I offer or give unto Thy majesty?' Then God said unto me: 'Search in thy bosom, and give Me that which thou findest therein'. I searched and found a ball of gold; and I offered it to God; and thus did I three times, even as God three times commanded me; and thereafter I kneeled me down three times and blessed and thanked God who had given me wherewith to offer Him.

And straightway, it was given me to understand that these three offerings signified holy obedience, highest poverty and most resplendent chastity; the which God, through His grace, hath permitted me to observe so perfectly that my conscience accuseth me of nothing. And as thou sawest me put my hands in my bosom and offer to God those three virtues symbolised by those three balls of gold, which God had placed in my bosom; so hath God given me such virtue in my soul that, for all the benefits and all the graces which He hath granted me of His most holy goodness, I ever praise and magnify Him with heart and mouth. These are the words which thou heardest when I thrice lifted up my hands, as thou sawest. But look to it, friar little sheep, that thou watch me no more; but return to thy cell with the blessing of God, and do thou have diligent care of me; because, a few days from now, God will do such great and marvellous things upon this mountain that all the world shall wonder thereat; for He will do certain new things, the which He hath never done unto any creature in this world." And, when he had spoken these words, he caused the book of the Gospels to be brought unto him; for God had put it in his mind that, by the opening of the book of the Gospels three times, that which it was the will of God to do unto him should be revealed. And, when the book was brought unto him, St. Francis betook himself to prayer; and, when he had finished his prayer, he caused the book to be opened three times by the hand of Friar Leo, in the name of the Most Holy Trinity; and, as it pleased the Divine Providence, in those three times ever there appeared before him the Passion of Christ. By the which thing it was given him to understand that, even as he had followed Christ in the actions of his life, so he must follow Him, and be conformed to Him in afflictions and sorrows and in his passion, before he departed from this life. And from that moment St. Francis began to taste and to feel more abundantly the sweetness of Divine contemplation and of the Divine visitations. Among the which he had one which was an immediate preparative for the imprinting of the most holy stigmata; and it was upon this wise: On the day before the festival of the most Holy Cross of the month of September, while St. Francis was secretly praying in his cell, the angel of God appeared unto him, and said unto him in God's name: "I exhort thee and admonish thee that thou prepare and dispose thyself, humbly and with all patience, to receive that which God willeth to give thee, and to work in thee". St. Francis made answer: "I am ready to bear patiently everything that my Lord willeth to do unto me"; and, when he had said this, the angel departed. The next day came, to wit the day of the most Holy Cross, and St. Francis, betimes in the morning, or ever it was day, betook himself to prayer before the entrance of his cell, and turning his face towards the East, prayed after this manner: "O my Lord Jesus Christ, two graces do I beseech Thee to grant me before I die: the first, that, during my lifetime, I may feel in my soul and in my body, so far as may be possible, that pain which Thou, sweet Lord, didst suffer in the hour of Thy most bitter passion; the second is that I may feel in my heart, so far as may be possible, that exceeding love, whereby Thou, Son of God, wast enkindled to willingly bear such passion for us sinners".

And, when he had continued long time in this prayer, he knew that God would hear him, and that, as far as was possible for a mere creature, so far would it be granted to him to feel the aforesaid things. Having this promise, St. Francis began to contemplate with very great devotion the Passion of Christ and His infinite charity; and so much did the fervour of devotion increase in him that he altogether transformed himself into Jesus through love and pity. And, being thus self-inflamed in this contemplation, on that same morning, he saw, coming from heaven, a Seraph, with six wings resplendent and ablaze; the which Seraph, flying swiftly, drew near unto St. Francis, so that he was able to discern Him clearly, and he perceived that He bore the likeness to a crucified Man; and His wings were so disposed that two wings extended above His head, two were spread out to fly, and the other two covered all His body. Seeing this, St. Francis was sore afraid, and, at the same time, was filled with joy and grief and wonder. He had passing great joy of the gracious aspect of Christ, who appeared to him so familiarly and regarded him so kindly; but, on the other hand, seeing Him crucified upon the cross, he felt immeasurable grief for pity's sake. Next, he marvelled much at so strange and stupendous a vision, knowing well that the infirmity of suffering agreeth not with the immortality of the seraphic spirit. And, while he thus marvelled, it was revealed unto him by Him who appeared to him: that that vision had been shown unto him in that form, by the Divine providence, to the end that he might understand that, not by corporal suffering but by enkindling of the mind, he must be altogether transformed into the express image of Christ crucified, in that marvellous vision. Then all the mountain of Alvernia seemed to burn with brightest flame, which shone forth and lighted up all the mountains and the valleys round about, even as if the sun had risen upon the earth; wherefore the shepherds, who kept watch in those regions, beholding the mountain all on fire and so great a light round about it, were very much afraid, according as they afterward related to the friars, declaring that that flame continued upon the mountain of Alvernia for the space of an hour or more.

In like manner, by reason of the brightness of this light, which shone through the windows into the hostelries of the countryside, certain muleteers, who were journeying into Romagna, rose up, believing that the sun had risen, and saddled and loaded their beasts; and, as they went upon their way, they beheld the said light die out, and the material sun arise. In the said seraphic vision, Christ, who appeared to St. Francis, spake unto him certain high and secret things, the which St. Francis was never willing to reveal to any one during his life; but, after his death, he revealed it, even as is set forth below; and the words were these: "Knowest thou," said Christ, "that which I have done unto thee? I have given thee the stigmata, which are the tokens of My Passion, so that thou mayest be My standard-bearer. And even as I, on the day of My death, descended into Limbo, and, in virtue of these My stigmata, drew out thence all the souls which I found there; so to thee do I grant that, every year on the day of thy death, thou shalt go to purgatory, and in virtue of thy stigmata, shalt draw out thence all the souls of thy three Orders, to wit minors, sisters and continents, and also those others who have borne great devotion unto thee, and shalt lead them unto the glory of paradise, to the end that thou mayest be conformed to Me in death as thou art in life." Now when, after long and secret converse, this marvellous vision vanished away, it left an exceeding ardour and flame of Divine love in the heart of St. Francis, and in his flesh a marvellous image and imprint of the Passion of Christ. For anon, in the hands and in the feet of St. Francis the marks of nails began to appear after the same fashion as he had just seen in the body of Jesus Christ crucified, the which had appeared unto him in the form of a seraph; and even so were his hands and his feet pierced through the midst with nails, the heads whereof were in the palms of the hands and in the soles of the feet, outside the flesh; and the points came out through the back of the hands and of the feet, where they showed bent back and clinched on such wise that, under the clinching and the bend, which all stood out above the flesh, it would have been easy to put a finger of the hand, as in a ring; and the heads of the nails were round and black. In like manner, in his right side appeared the likeness of a lance wound, open, red and bloody; the which oftentimes thereafter spouted blood from the holy breast of St. Francis, and covered his habit and breeches with blood.

Wherefore his companions, before they knew thereof from him, perceiving nevertheless that he uncovered neither his hands nor his feet, and that he could not put the soles of his feet to the ground; and therewithal finding his habit and breeches all bloody, when they washed them, knew certainly that he bore, imprinted on his hands and feet and likewise on his side, the express image and likeness of our Lord Jesus Christ crucified. And although he very earnestly endeavoured to conceal and to hide those most holy and glorious stigmata which were so clearly imprinted on his flesh, he perceived that he could but ill conceal them from his familiar companions; and therefore he stood in very great doubt, fearing to make public the secrets of God, and knowing not whether he ought to reveal the seraphic vision and the imprinting of the most holy stigmata. At the last, being goaded thereunto by his conscience, he called to him certain of his most intimate friends among the friars, and, setting before them his doubt in general terms, yet without explaining the actual fact, he asked their advice; and among the said friars was one of great sanctity, who was called Friar Illuminatus. Now this man, being of a truth illuminate by God, and understanding that St. Francis must have seen marvellous things, answered him after this manner: "Friar Francis, know thou that, not for thy sake only but also for the sake of others, God manifesteth unto thee at divers times His mysteries; and therefore thou hast good reason to fear that, if thou keepest secret that which God hath shown thee for the benefit of others, thou wilt be worthy of blame". Then St. Francis, being moved by these words, with great dread related unto them all the manner and form of the aforesaid vision; adding that Christ, who had appeared unto him, had spoken certain things unto him which he would never repeat as long as he lived. And, albeit those most holy wounds, inasmuch as they were imprinted by Christ, gave very great joy to his heart; nevertheless to his flesh and to his corporal senses they gave intolerable pain. Wherefore, being compelled thereunto by necessity, he chose Friar Leo, as more simple and more pure than the others, and to him he revealed everything; permitting him to see and to touch those sacred wounds and to bind them with certain handkerchiefs, for the allaying of the pain, and to catch the blood which issued and flowed from the said wounds; the which bandages, in time of sickness, he permitted him to change frequently, and even daily, except from Thursday evening to Saturday morning, during which time our Saviour Jesus Christ was taken for our sakes and crucified, slain and buried; and therefore, during that time, St. Francis would not suffer that the pain of the Passion of Christ, which he bore in his body, should be assuaged in anywise by any human remedy or medicine whatsoever. It befel, sometimes, that, as Friar Leo was changing the bandage of the wound in his side, St. Francis, for the pain which he felt when that blood-soaked bandage was plucked away, laid his hand upon the breast of Friar Leo; whereby, from the touch of those sacred hands, Friar Leo felt such sweetness of devotion in his heart, that he well-nigh fell swooning to the ground. And finally, as touching this third consideration, St. Francis having finished the fast of St. Michael the Archangel, prepared himself, by Divine revelation, to return to Santa Maria degli Angeli. Wherefore he called unto him Friar Masseo and Friar Agnolo, and, after many words and holy admonishments, he commended unto them that holy mountain with all possible earnestness, telling them that it behoved him, together with Friar Leo, to return to Santa Maria degli Angeli. And when he had said this, he took leave of them and blessed them in the name of Jesus crucified; and, yielding to their entreaties, he gave them his most holy hands, adorned with those glorious and sacred stigmata, to see, to touch and to kiss; and so leaving them consoled, he departed from them and descended the holy mountain.

OF THE FOURTH CONSIDERATION OF THE MOST HOLY STIGMATA

AS touching the fourth consideration, it must be that, after the true love of Christ had perfectly transformed St. Francis into God and into the true image of Christ crucified; having finished the fast of forty days in honour of St. Michael the Archangel upon the holy mountain of Alvernia; after the festival of St. Michael, the angelical man, St. Francis, descended from the mountain with Friar Leo and with a devout villain, upon whose ass he sat, because by reason of the nails in his feet he could not well go afoot. Now, when St. Francis had come down from the mountain, the fame of his sanctity was already noised abroad throughout the land; for it had been reported by the shepherds how they had seen the mountain of Alvernia all ablaze, and that this was the token of some great miracle which God had wrought upon St. Francis; wherefore, when the people of the district heard that he was passing, they all flocked to see him, both men and women, small and great, and all of them with much devotion and desire sought to touch him and to kiss his hands; and not being able to resist the devotion of the people, albeit he had bandaged the palms of his hands, nevertheless, the better to hide the most holy stigmata, he bandaged them yet more and covered them with his sleeves, and only gave them his fingers to kiss. But albeit he endeavoured to conceal and to hide the mystery of the most holy stigmata, to avoid every occasion of worldly glory, it pleased God for His own glory to show forth many miracles by virtue of the said most holy stigmata, and singularly in that journey from Vernia to Santa Maria degli Angeli, and very many thereafter in divers parts of the world, both during his life and after his glorious death; to the end that their occult and marvellous virtue, and the extreme charity and mercy of Christ, towards him to whom He had so marvellously given them, might be manifested to the world by clear and evident miracles; whereof we will set forth some in this place.

Thus, when St. Francis was drawing nigh unto a village which was upon the borders of the county of Arezzo, a woman came before him, weeping sore and holding her child in her arms; the which child was eight years old and had been dropsical for four years; and his belly was so terribly swollen that, when he stood upright, he could not see his feet; and this woman laid that son of hers before him, and besought him to pray God for him; and St. Francis first betook himself to prayer and then, when he had prayed, laid his holy hands upon the belly of the child; and anon, all the swelling disappeared, and he was made perfectly whole, and he gave him back to his mother, who received him with very great joy, and led him home, thanking God and St. Francis; and she willingly showed her son that was healed to all those of the district who came to her house to see him. On the same day St. Francis passed through Borgo San Sepolcro, and or ever he drew nigh unto the walls, the inhabitants of the town and of the villages came forth to meet him, and many of them went before him with boughs of olive in their hands, crying aloud: "Behold the saint! behold the saint!" And, for devotion and the desire which the folk had to touch him, they thronged and pressed upon him; but ever he went on his way with his mind uplifted and rapt in God through contemplation, and, albeit he was touched and held and plucked at by the people, he, even as one insensible, knew nothing at all of that which was done or said around him; neither did he perceive that he was passing through that town or through that district. For, when he had passed through Borgo and the crowd had returned to their homes, that contemplator of celestial things, having arrived at a house for lepers, a full mile beyond Borgo, returned to himself, and, as one who had come from another world, inquired of his companion: "When shall we be near Borgo?" Of a truth his soul, being fixed and rapt in contemplation of heavenly things, had been unconscious of anything earthly, whether of change of place, or of time, or of the people who thronged about him; and this befel many other times, as his companions proved by evident experience. That evening St. Francis reached the Place of the friars of Monte Casale, in the which place a friar was so cruelly sick and so horribly tormented by sickness that his disease seemed rather some affliction and torment of the devil than a natural infirmity; for sometimes he cast himself upon the ground trembling violently and foaming at the mouth; anon all the sinews of his body were contracted, then stretched, then bent, then twisted, and anon his heels were drawn up to the nape of his neck, and he flung himself into the air, and straightway fell flat on his back. Now, while St. Francis sat at table, he heard from the friars of this friar, so miserably sick and without remedy; and he had compassion on him, and took a piece of bread which he was eating, and, with his holy hands imprinted with the stigmata, made over it the sign of the most holy Cross, and sent it to the sick friar; who, as soon as he had eaten it, was made perfectly whole, and never felt that sickness any more. When the following morning was come, St. Francis sent two of those friars who were in that Place to dwell at Alvernia; and he sent back with them the villain, who had come with him behind the ass, which he had lent him, desiring that he should return with them to his home. The friars went with the said villain, and, as they entered the county of Arezzo, certain men of the district saw them afar off, and had great joy thereof, thinking that it was St. Francis, who had passed that way two days before; for one of their women, which had been three days in travail and could not bring to the birth was dying; and they thought to have her back sound and well, if St. Francis laid his holy hands upon her. But, when the said friars drew near, they perceived that St. Francis was not with them; and they were very sad.

Nevertheless, albeit the saint was not there in the flesh, his, virtue lacked not, because they lacked not faith. O marvellous thing! the woman was dying and was already in her death agony, when they asked the friars if they had anything which the most holy hands of St. Francis had touched. The friars thought and searched diligently, but could find nothing which St, Francis had touched with his hands save only the halter of the ass upon which he had come. With great reverence and devotion those men took that halter and laid it upon the belly of the pregnant woman, calling devoutly on the name of St. Francis and faithfully commending themselves to him. And what more? No sooner had the aforesaid halter been laid upon the woman than, anon, she was freed from all peril, and gave birth joyfully, with ease and safety. Now St. Francis, after he had been some days in the said place, departed and went to Città di Castello; and behold, many of the citizens brought to him a woman, who had been possessed of a devil for a long time, and humbly besought him for her deliverance; because, with her dolorous howlings and cruel shrieks and dog-like barkings, she disturbed all the neighbourhood. Then St. Francis, having first prayed and made over her the sign of the most holy Cross, commanded the demon to depart from her; and he straightway departed, leaving her sane in body and in mind. And, when this miracle was noised abroad among the people, another woman with great faith brought to him her sick child, who was afflicted with a cruel sore, and besought him devoutly that he would be pleased to make the sign of the Cross upon him with his hands. Then St. Francis gave ear unto her prayer, and took the child and loosed the bandage from off his sore and blessed him, making the sign of the most holy Cross over the sore three times, and thereafter with his own hands he replaced the bandage, and gave him back to his mother; and, because it was evening, she forthwith laid him on the bed to sleep. Thereafter, in the morning, she went to take her child from the bed, and found the bandage unloosed, and looked and saw that he was as perfectly whole as if he had never had any sickness at all; save only that, in the place where the sore had been, the flesh had grown over after the manner of a red rose; and that rather in testimony of the miracle than as a scar left by the sore; because the said rose, remaining during the whole of his lifetime, often moved him to devotion toward St. Francis who had healed him.

In that city, then, St. Francis sojourned for a month, at the prayer of the devout citizens, in the which time he wrought many other miracles; and thereafter he departed thence, to go unto Santa Maria degli Angeli with Friar Leo, and with a good man, who lent him his little ass, whereupon St. Francis rode. Now, it came to pass that, by reason of the bad roads and the great cold, they journeyed all day without being able to reach any place where they might lodge; for the which cause, being constrained by the darkness and by the bad weather, they took shelter beneath the brow of a hollow rock, to avoid the snow and the night which was coming on. And, being in this evil case And also badly clad, the good man, to whom the ass belonged, could not sleep by reason of the cold; wherefore he began to murmur gently within himself and to weep; and almost did he blame St. Francis, who had brought him into such a place. Then St. Francis, perceiving this, had compassion upon him, and, in fervour of spirit, stretched out his hand toward him and touched him. O marvellous thing! as soon as he had touched him with that hand of his, enkindled and pierced by the fire of the Seraph, all the cold left him; and so much heat entered into him, both within and without, that he seemed to be hard by the mouth of a burning furnace; whence being presently comforted in soul and body he fell asleep; and, according to that which he said, he slept more sweetly that night, among rocks and snow until morning, than he had ever slept in his own bed. Thereafter, on the next day, they continued their journey and came to Santa Maria degli Angeli; and, when they were nigh thereunto, Friar Leo lifted up his eyes and looked toward the said Place of Santa Maria degli Angeli, and saw an exceeding beautiful Cross, whereon was the figure of the Crucified, going before St. Francis, even as St. Francis was going before Him; and on such wise did the said Cross go before the face of St. Francis that when he stopped it stopped too, and when he went on it went on; and that Cross was of such brightness that, not only did it shine in the face of, St. Francis, but all the road about him also was lighted up; and it lasted until St. Francis entered into the Place of Santa Maria degli Angeli. St. Francis, then, having arrived with Friar Leo, they were welcomed by the friars with very great joy and charity. And from thenceforward, until his death, St. Francis dwelt for the greater part of his time in that Place of Santa Maria degli Angeli.

And the fame of his sanctity and of his miracles spread continually more and more through the Order and through the world, although, by reason of his profound humility, he concealed as much as he might the gifts and graces of God, and ever called himself the greatest of sinners. Wherefore, on a time, Friar Leo, marvelling within himself and thinking foolishly, said in his heart: "Lo, this man calleth himself a very great sinner in public, and becometh great in the Order, and is so much honoured of God, yet, in secret, he never confesseth any carnal sin. Can it be that he is a virgin?" And therewith he began to desire very earnestly to know the truth; and, fearing to ask St. Francis touching this matter, he betook himself to God; and urgently beseeching Him that He would certify him of that which he desired to know, through the much praying and merit of St. Francis, he was answered and certified, through this vision, that St. Francis was verily a virgin in body. For he saw, in a vision, St. Francis standing in a high and excellent place, whereunto none might go up nor attain to bear him company; and it was told him in spirit that this so high and excellent place signified that perfection of virginal chastity in St. Francis which was reasonable and fitting in the flesh that was to be adorned with the most holy Stigmata of Christ. St. Francis, seeing that, by reason of the stigmata of Christ, his bodily strength grew gradually less and that he was not able any more to take charge of the government of the Order, hastened forward the General Chapter of the Order; and, when it was assembled, he humbly excused himself to the friars for the weakness which prevented him from attending any more to the care of the Order, as touching the duties of General; albeit he renounced not that office of General because he was not able to do so, inasmuch as he had been made

General by the Pope; and therefore he could neither resign his office nor appoint a successor without the express leave of the Pope. Nevertheless he appointed as his Vicar Friar Peter Cattani, and commended the Order unto him and unto the Ministers of the Provinces with all possible affection.

And, when he had thus done, St. Francis, being comforted in spirit, lifted up his eyes and hands to heaven and spake thus: "To Thee, my Lord God, to Thee I commend this Thy family, which unto this hour Thou has committed unto me; and now, by reason of my infirmities, which Thou my most sweet Lord knowest, I am no longer able to take charge thereof. Also do I commend it to the Ministers of the Provinces; and if, through their negligence or through their bad example or through their too harsh correction, any friar shall perish, may they be held to give account thereof to Thee on the Day of Judgment." And in these words, as it pleased God, all the friars of the Chapter understood that he spake of the most holy Stigmata, to wit in that which he said excusing himself by reason of his infirmity: and for devotion none of them was able to refrain from weeping. And from thenceforward he left all the care and government of the Order in the hands of his Vicar and of the Ministers of the Provinces; and he was wont to say: "Now that, by reason of my infirmities, I have given up the charge of the Order, I have no other duty than to pray God for our Religion and to set a good ensample to the friars. And of a truth, I know well that, if my infirmity should leave me, the greatest help which I could render to the Religion would be to pray continually to God for it, that He would defend and govern and preserve it." Now, as hath been said above, albeit St. Francis, as much as in him lay, strove to hide the most holy Stigmata, and, from the time when he received then, always went with his hands bandaged and with stockings on his feet, yet, for all that he could do, he could not prevent many of the friars from seeing and touching them in divers manners, and particularly the wound in his side, the which he endeavoured with special diligence to hide.

Thus a friar, who waited on him, induced him, by a pious fraud, to take off his habit, that the dust might be shaken out of it; and, since he removed it in his presence, that friar saw clearly the wound in his side; and, swiftly putting his hand upon his breast, he touched it with three fingers and thus learned its extent and size; and in like manner his Vicar saw it at that time. But more clearly was Friar Ruffino certified thereof; the which was a man of very great contemplation, of whom St. Francis sometimes said that in all the world there was no more holy man than he; and by reason of his holiness he loved him as a familiar friend, and was wont to grant him all that he desired. In three ways did this Friar Ruffino certify himself and others of the said most holy Stigmata. The first was this: that, it being his duty to wash the breeches of St. Francis, which he wore so large that, by pulling them well up, he covered therewith the wound in his right side, the said Friar Ruffino examined them and considered them diligently, and found that they were always bloody on the right side; whereby he perceived of a surety that that was blood which came from the said wound; but for this St. Francis rebuked him when he saw that he spread out the clothes which he took off in order to look for the said token. The second way was this: that once, while the said Friar Ruffino was scratching St. Francis' back, he deliberately let his hand slip and put his fingers into the wound in his side; whereat, for the pain that he felt, St. Francis cried aloud: "God forgive thee, O Friar Ruffino, that thou hast done this".

The third way was that he once begged St. Francis very urgently, as an exceeding great favour, to give him his habit and to take his in exchange, for love of charity.

Whereupon the charitable father, albeit unwillingly, yielded to his prayer, and drew off his habit and gave it to him and took his; and then, in that taking off and putting on, Friar Ruffino clearly saw the said wound. Friar Leo likewise, and many other friars, saw the said most holy stigmata of St. Francis while yet he lived; the which friars, although by reason of their sanctity they were worthy of credence and men whose simple word might be believed, nevertheless, to remove doubt from every heart, sware upon the Holy Book that they had clearly seen them. Moreover, certain cardinals, who were intimate friends of St. Francis, saw them; and, in reverence for the aforesaid most holy Stigmata, they composed and made beautiful and devout hymns and psalms and prose treatises. The highest pontiff, Pope Alexander, while preaching to the people in the presence of all the cardinals (among whom was the holy Friar Buonaventura, who was a cardinal) said and affirmed that he had seen with his own eyes the most holy Stigmata of St. Francis, when he was yet alive. And Madonna Jacopa di Settensoli of Rome, who was the greatest lady of her time in Rome and was most devoted to St. Francis, saw them before he died, and, after his death, saw and kissed them many times with great reverence; for she came from Rome to Assisi, by Divine revelation, to the deathbed of St. Francis; and her coming was after this manner. For some days before his death, St. Francis lay sick at Assisi in the palace of the Bishop, with some of his companions; and, notwithstanding his sickness, he often sang certain lauds of Christ.

One day, one of his companions said unto him: "Father, thou knowest that these citizens have great faith in thee, and hold thee for a saintly man, and therefore they may think that, if thou art that which that they believe thee to be, thou shouldest, in this thine infirmity, think upon thy death, and rather weep than sing, in that thou art so exceeding sick; and know that thy singing and ours, which thou makest us to sing, is heard of many, both within and without the palace; for this palace is guarded on thy account by many armed men, who perchance may take bad ensample therefrom. Wherefore I believe (said this friar) that thou wouldest do well to depart hence, and that we should all of us return to Santa Maria degli Angeli; for this is no place for us, among seculars." St. Francis answered him: "Dearest friar, thou knowest that two years ago, when we abode at Foligno, God revealed unto thee the term of my life; and in like manner also He revealed unto me that, a few days hence, the said term shall end, in this sickness; and in that revelation God made me certain of the remission of all my sins, and of the bliss of paradise. Until I had that revelation I bewailed death and my sins; but, since I have had that revelation, I am so full of gladness that I can weep no more; and therefore do I sing, yea, and will sing unto God, who hath given me the blessing of His grace and hath made me sure of the blessings of the glory of paradise. As touching our departure hence, I consent thereunto and it pleaseth me; but do ye find means to carry me, because, by reason of mine infirmity, I cannot walk." Then the friars took him up in their arms and so carried him; and many of the citizens accompanied them. And, coming to a hospice, which was by the way, St. Francis said unto those who carried him: "Set me down on the ground, and turn me toward the city".

And, when he was set with his face toward Assisi, he blessed the city with many blessings, saying: "Blessed be thou of God, O holy city, for through thee many souls shall be saved, and in thee shall dwell many servants of God, and from thee many shall be chosen unto the Kingdom of Life Eternal". And, when he had said these words, he caused them to carry him on to Santa Maria degli Angeli. And, when they arrived at Santa Maria degli Angeli, they bore him to the infirmary and there laid him down to rest. Then St. Francis called unto him one of the companions and spake unto him thus: "Dearest friar, God hath revealed unto me that, of this sickness, on such a day, I shall depart from this life; and thou knowest that the well-beloved Madonna Jacopa di Settensoli, who is devoted to our Order, if she knew of my death and had not been present thereat, would be sore grieved; and therefore do thou send her word that, if she would see me alive, she come hither at once". The friar made answer: "Father, thou sayest rightly; for in truth, by reason of the great love which she beareth thee, it would be most unseemly if she were not present at thy death". "Go, then," said St. Francis, "and bring me inkhorn and paper and pen, and write as I bid thee." And, when he had brought them, St. Francis dictated the letter on this wise:

"To Madonna Jacopa, the servant of God, Friar Francis, the mendicant of Christ, greeting and the fellowship of the Holy Ghost in our Lord Jesus Christ. Know, well beloved, that Christ the blessed hath, of His grace, revealed unto me that the end of my life is at hand. Therefore, if thou wouldst find me alive, when thou hast seen this letter, arise and come to Santa Maria degli Angell; for, if thou art not come by such a day, thou wilt not find me alive; and bring with thee hair-cloth to wrap my body in, and the wax which is needed for my burial. Also I beseech thee to bring me some of that food which thou wast wont to give me to eat, when I was sick in Rome."

And, while this letter was being written, it was revealed of God to St. Francis that Madonna Jacopa was coming to him and was already nigh unto the place, and brought with her all those things which he was sending to ask for by the letter. Wherefore, when he had had this revelation, St. Francis told the friar who was writing the letter, not to write further, because there was no need thereof, but to lay aside the letter; whereat the friars marvelled greatly, because he finished not the letter and would not have it sent. And, while they continued thus, lo, after a little while, there was a great knocking at the door of the Place, and St. Francis sent the doorkeeper to open it; and, when he had opened the door, behold, there was Madonna Jacopa, the noblest lady of Rome, with two of her sons, Senators of Rome, and with a great company of men on horseback; and they entered in; and Madonna Jacopa gat her straight to the infirmary, and came unto St. Francis. Of whose coming St Francis had great joy and consolation, and she likewise, seeing him alive and speaking with him. Then she told him how God had revealed unto her in Rome, while she was praying, the short span of his life, and how he would send for her, and ask for those things, all of which she said that she had brought; and she caused them to be brought to St. Francis and gave him to eat thereof; and, when he had eaten and was much comforted, this Madonna Jacopa kneeled down at the feet of St. Francis, and took those most holy feet, marked and adorned with the wounds of Christ, and kissed and bathed them with her tears, with such limitless devotion that to the friars which were standing by it seemed that they verily beheld the Magdalene at the feet of Jesus Christ; and on nowise might they draw her away from them. And finally, after a long time, they raised her up and drew her aside, and asked her how she had come so duly and so well provided with all those things which were necessary for St. Francis while yet he was alive, and for his burial. Madonna Jacopa replied that, while she was praying one night in Rome, she heard a voice from heaven, which said: "If thou wouldest find St. Francis alive, get thee to Assisi without delay, and take with thee those things which thou art wont to give him when he is sick, and those things which will be necessary for his burial; and I (said she) have done so". So the said Madonna Jacopa abode there until St. Francis passed from this life and was buried; and at his burial she did him very great honour, she and all her company; and she bore all the cost of whatsoever was needed. And thereafter, this noble lady returned to Rome; and there, within a little while, she died a holy death; and for devotion to St. Francis she commanded that her body should be borne to Santa Maria degli Angeli and buried there; and so was it done.

HOW MESSER JEROME TOUCHED AND SAW THE MOST HOLY STIGMATA OF ST. FRANCIS, WHEREIN AT FIRST HE DID NOT BELIEVE

AT the death of St. Francis, not only did the said Madonna Jacopa and her sons together with all her company see and kiss his glorious and holy Stigmata, but also many citizens of Assisi; among whom was a knight of wide renown and a great man, who was named Messer Jerome, the which doubted much thereof and was incredulous concerning them, even as was St. Thomas concerning those of Christ; and to certify himself and others, in the presence of all the friars and the lay folk, he boldly moved the nails in the hands and feet, and touched the wound in the side before them all. Whereby he was thereafter a constant witness of that verity, swearing upon the Book that so it was, and so he had seen and touched. St. Clare, likewise, beheld and kissed the glorious and sacred Stigmata of St. Francis, together with her nuns, which were present at his burying.

OF THE DAY AND OF THE YEAR OF THE DEATH OF ST. FRANCIS

THE glorious confessor of Christ, Messer St. Francis, passed from this life in the year of our Lord M.C-C.XXVI., (1226) on the fourth day of October, on Saturday, and was buried on Sunday. That year was the twentieth year of his conversion, to wit when he began to do penance, and was the second year after the imprinting of the most holy Stigmata; and it was in the forty-fifth year from his birth.

OF THE CANONISATION OF ST. FRANCIS

THEREAFTER was St. Francis canonised in M.CC.XXVIII., (1228) by Pope Gregory IX., who came in person to Assisi to canonise him. And this sufficeth touching the fourth consideration.

OF THE FIFTH AND LAST CONSIDERATION OF THE MOST HOLY STIGMATA

THE fifth and last consideration is touching certain visions and revelations and miracles which God wrought and showed forth after the death of St. Francis, in confirmation of his most holy Stigmata, and for a declaration of the day and the hour whereon Christ gave them unto him. And as touching this matter, it is to be considered that, in the year of our Lord M.C-C.LXXXII., (1282) on the . . . day of the month of October, Friar Philip, Minister of Tuscany, at the commandment of Friar John Buonagrazia, Minister-General, in the name of holy obedience, asked Friar Matthew of Castiglione Aretino, a man of great devotion and sanctity, to tell that which he knew concerning the day and the hour whereon the most holy Stigmata were imprinted by Christ on the body of St. Francis; because he heard that he had had a revelation touching the same. Whereupon Friar Matthew, constrained by holy obedience, answered him after this manner: "While I was in the community of Alvernia, last year in the month of May, I one day betook myself to prayer in my cell, which is on the spot where it is believed that that seraphic vision took place. And in my prayer I besought God most devoutly that He would vouchsafe to reveal unto some person the day and the hour and the place wherein the most holy Stigmata were imprinted upon the body of St. Francis; and, when I had continued in prayer and i in this petition beyond the first watch, St. Francis appeared to me with very great radiance, and said unto me: 'Son, for what dost thou pray to God?'

And I said unto him: 'Father, I pray for such and such a thing'. And he said unto me: 'I am thy Father Francis. Dost thou know me well?' 'Father,' I said, 'yes.' Then he showed me the most holy Stigmata in his hands and feet and side, and said: 'The time hath come when God wills that that, which afore-time the friars have not been curious to know, shall be made manifest for His glory. Know thou then that He which appeared unto me was not an angel, but was Jesus Christ, in the form of a Seraph, who, with his own hands, imprinted on my body these wounds, even as He received them in His body on the Cross. And it was after this manner: On the day before the Exaltation of the Holy Cross, an angel came unto me, and, in God's name, bade me make me ready unto patience and to receive that which God might will to send me. And I made answer that I was ready to receive and to endure everything which might be God's good pleasure. Thereafter, on the following morning, to wit the morning of [the festival of the] Holy Cross, the which that year fell upon a Friday; at daybreak I came forth from my cell, in very great fervour of spirit, and went to pray in this place where thou now art and where I ofttimes prayed, and, as I prayed, lo, through the air, there came down from heaven, with great swiftness, a young man crucified, in the form of a Seraph with six wings; at which marvellous sight I humbly kneeled me down and began to contemplate devoutly the boundless love of Jesus Christ crucified, and the boundless pain of His passion; and the sight of Him engendered in me such pity that I verily seemed to feel His passion in my own body; and, at His presence, all this mountain shone as doth the sun; and, so descending, He came nigh unto me. And, standing before me, He said certain secret words unto me, the which I have not yet revealed unto any man; but the time draweth nigh when they shall be revealed. Then, after a while, Christ departed, and returned into heaven, and I found myself thus marked with these wounds. Go then,' said St. Francis, 'and tell these things to thy minister nothing doubting; for this is the operation not of man but of God.' And, when he had said these words, St. Francis blessed me and went back to heaven with a great multitude of youths, exceeding bright." All these things the said Friar Matthew said that he had seen and heard, not sleeping but awake. And he sware that he had of a truth told these things to the said minister in his cell at Florence, when he inquired of him concerning the same for obedience' sake.

HOW A HOLY FRIAR, READING THE LEGEND OF ST. FRANCIS IN THE CHAPTER OF THE MOST HOLY STIGMATA, PRAYED SO MUCH TO GOD CONCERNING THE SECRET WORDS, WHICH THE SERAPH SPAKE TO ST. FRANCIS. WHEN HE APPEARED UNTO HIM, THAT ST. FRANCIS REVEALED THEM UNTO THE SAID FRIAR

UPON another time, a devout and holy friar, while reading the legend of St. Francis in the chapter of the most holy Stigmata, began with great travail of spirit to consider what those so secret words could have been, which St. Francis said that he would not reveal to any one while he lived; the which the Seraph had spoken to him when He appeared unto him. And this friar said within himself: "St. Francis willed not to speak those words to any one during his lifetime; but now, after his bodily death, perchance he would tell them, if he were prayed devoutly so to do".

And from thenceforward, the devout friar began to pray God and St. Francis that they would vouchsafe to reveal those words; and this friar continuing eight years in this prayer, in the eighth year he merited to be heard on this wise: One day, after eating, thanks having been given in the church, he was in prayer in a certain part of the church, and was praying to God and St. Francis touching this matter, more devoutly than he was wont, and with many tears; when he was called by another friar, who commanded him in the name of the Guardian to bear him company to the town for the good of the Place. For the which cause, he, doubting not that obedience is more meritorious than prayer, as soon as he had heard the commandment of his superior, humbly left off praying and went with that friar that called him. And, as God willed it, he, by this act of ready obedience, merited that which he had not merited by his long praying. Whence, as soon as they had gone forth from the gate of the Place, they met two strange friars, who appeared to have come from a far country; and one of them seemed a young man and the other old and lean; and, by reason of the bad weather, they were all muddy and wet. Wherefore that obedient friar had great compassion for them, and said unto the companion, with whom he was going: "O dearest brother mine, if the business whereon we are going may wait a little, inasmuch as these strange friars have great need to be charitably received, I beseech thee to permit me first to go and wash their feet, and especially those of this aged friar, who hath the greater need thereof; and you will be able to wash those of this younger one; and thereafter we will go about the business of the convent".

Then this friar consenting unto the charitable desire of his companion, they went back and received those strange friars very charitably, and took them into the kitchen to the fire to warm and dry themselves; at the which fire eight other friars of the Place were warming themselves. And, after they had been a little while at the fire, they took them aside to wash their feet, even as they had agreed together. And while that obedient and devout friar was washing the feet of the older friar, and removing the mud therefrom, for they were very muddy, he looked and saw that his feet were marked with the most holy Stigmata; and anon, for joy and wonder he embraced them closely, and began to cry aloud: "Either thou art Christ, or thou art St. Francis". At that cry and at those words, the friars, which were at the fire, arose and came thither with great fear and reverence to see those glorious stigmata. And then, at their prayer, this ancient friar permitted them clearly to see and touch and kiss them. And, while they marvelled yet more for joy, he said unto them: "Doubt not and fear not, dearest friars and sons; I am your father Friar Francis, who, according to the will of God, founded three Orders. And seeing that, for eight years, I have been entreated by this friar, who is washing my feet, and to-day more fervently than ever before, that I would reveal unto him those secret words which the Seraph spake unto me when He gave me the stigmata, the which words I resolved never to reveal in my lifetime, to-day, by the commandment of God, by reason of his perseverance and the ready obedience with which he left the sweetness of contemplation, I am sent by God to reveal unto him, before you all, that which he asks."

And then, turning unto that friar, St. Francis spake thus: "Know, dearest friar, that, when I was upon the mountain of Alvernia, wholly absorbed in the remembrance of the passion of Christ in that seraphic apparition, I was by Christ thus marked on my body with the Stigmata, and then Christ said unto me: 'Knowest thou what I have done unto thee? I have given thee the tokens of My passion, so that thou mayest be My standard-bearer. And even as I, on the day of My death, descended into Limbo, and, in virtue of these My Stigmata, drew out thence all the souls which I found there, and took them to Paradise; so to thee do I grant even from this hour, to the end that thou mayest be conformed to Me in death as thou hast been in life, that, after thou shalt have passed from this life, every year on the day of thy death, thou shalt go to Purgatory, and, in virtue of thy Stigmata which I have given thee, shalt draw out thence all the souls of thy three Orders, to wit minors, sisters and continents, and, beyond this, those others whom thou shalt find there, who have borne devotion unto thee, and shalt lead them into Paradise.' And these words I never spake while I lived in the world." And, when he had said these words, St. Francis and his companion suddenly vanished away. Many friars afterwards heard this from those eight friars, who were present at this vision and at these words of St. Francis.

HOW ST. FRANCIS, AFTER HIS DEATH, APPEARED TO FRIAR JOHN OF ALVERNIA, WHILE HE WAS PRAYING

ONCE, upon the mountain of Alvernia, St. Francis appeared to Friar John of Alvernia, a man of great sanctity, while he was praying, and abode and talked with him for a very long time; and, at the last, desiring to depart, he spake thus: "Ask of me what thou wilt". Said Friar John: "Father, I pray thee to tell me that which I have long desired to know, to wit what you were doing, and where you were, when the Seraph appeared unto you". St. Francis made answer: "I was praying in that place where is now the chapel of Count Simon da Battifolle, and I was entreating two graces of my Lord Jesus Christ. The first was that He would grant me to feel, in this life, in my soul and in my body, as far as might be possible, all that pain which He had Himself felt at the time of His most bitter passion. The second grace which I asked of Him was in like manner that I might feel in my heart that intense love wherewith He was enkindled to bear so great passion for us sinners. And then God put it in my heart that He would grant me to feel both the one and the other, as much as was possible for a mere creature; the which thing was abundantly fulfilled in me at the imprinting of the Stigmata." Then Friar John asked him whether those secret words which the Seraph had spoken unto him had been even such as were rehearsed by that holy friar aforesaid, who declared that he had heard them from St. Francis in the presence of eight friars. St. Francis replied that the truth was even as that friar had said.

Thereupon, Friar John, encouraged by the liberality of the granter, took heart to ask yet more, and said thus: "O father, I beseech thee most earnestly that thou wilt suffer me to behold and to kiss thy most holy and glorious Stigmata; not because I doubt thereof at all, but only for my consolation; for for this have I alway yearned". And, St. Francis freely showing them and offering them unto him, Friar John clearly saw and touched and kissed them. And, at the last, he asked of him: "Father, how great consolation had your soul, beholding Christ the Blessed coming unto you to give you the marks of His most holy Passion? Now would to God that I might feel a little of that sweetness!" Then St. Francis made answer: "Seest thou these nails?" Said Friar John: "Father, yes". "Touch yet again," said St. Francis, "this nail which is in my hand." Then Friar John, with great reverence and fear, touched that nail, and immediately, as he touched it, so great a perfume issued therefrom, as it were a thin spiral of smoke after the fashion of incense, and, entering through the nose of Friar John, filled his soul and body with so much sweetness, that forthwith he was rapt in God in ecstasy, and became insensible; and he remained thus rapt from that hour, which was the hour of Terce, even until Vespers. And of this vision and familiar conversation with St. Francis Friar John never spake unto any man, save only to his confessor, until he came unto his death; but, being nigh to his death, he revealed it to many friars.

OF A HOLY FRIAR WHO SAW A WONDERFUL VISION OF ONE OF HIS COMPANIONS WHO WAS DEAD

IN the Province of Rome, a very devout and holy friar saw this marvellous vision. A certain friar, a very dear companion of his, having died one night, was buried, in the morning, before the entrance of the, chapter-house; and, on the same day, after dinner, that friar betook himself into a corner of the chapter-house, to pray God and St. Francis devoutly for the soul of that dead friar his companion. And, as he persevered in prayer with supplications and tears, at noon, when all the others were gone away to sleep, he heard a great noise as of one being dragged through the cloister; whereat immediately with great fear he turned his eyes toward the grave of his companion, and saw St. Francis standing there at the entrance of the chapter-house, and behind him a great multitude of friars round about the said grave. He looked beyond, and saw in the midst of the cloister a very great flaming fire, and in the flames was the soul of his companion who was dead. He looked round the cloister and he saw Jesus Christ walking round the cloister with a great company of angels and of saints. And, while he gazed upon these things and marvelled much, he saw that, when Christ passed before the chapter-house, St. Francis kneeled down with all those friars and spake thus: "I beseech Thee, my dearest Father and Lord, that, through the inestimable charity which Thou didst show to the human race in Thy incarnation, Thou wilt have mercy on the soul of this my friar, who burneth in yonder flame"; and Christ answered him never a word but passed on.

And, when He returned, the second time, and passed before the chapter-house, St. Francis again kneeled him down with his friars, as at the first, and besought Him on this wise: "I pray Thee, merciful Father and Lord, through the boundless charity which Thou didst show to the human race when Thou didst die upon the wood of the cross, that Thou wilt have mercy on the soul of this my friar"; and Christ passed on as before and answered him not. And going round the cloister He returned the third time and passed before the chapter-house, and then St. Francis, kneeling down as before, showed unto Him his hands and his feet and his side and spake thus: "I beseech Thee, merciful Father and Lord, by that great pain and great consolation which I endured when Thou didst set these Stigmata in my flesh, that Thou wilt have pity on the soul of this my friar that is in that fire of purgatory". O wonderful thing! No sooner was Christ prayed that third time by St. Francis in the name of his Stigmata, than He forthwith stayed His steps and, looking upon the stigmata, gave ear unto his prayer and spake thus: "To thee, Francis, I grant the soul of thy friar". And in this, of a surety, He willed to honour and confirm the glorious Stigmata of St. Francis, and openly to signify that the souls of his friars, which go to Purgatory, can in no way be more easily delivered from their pains and brought to the glory of Paradise, than by virtue of his Stigmata, according unto the words which Christ spake unto St. Francis when He imprinted them upon him. Wherefore, as soon as these words had been spoken, that fire in the cloister vanished, and the dead friar came to St. Francis: and, together with him and with Christ, all that blessed company went up into heaven with their glorious King. For the which cause, this friar his companion, who had prayed for him, was exceeding glad when he saw him delivered from his pains and taken to paradise; and thereafter he told all that vision in order to the other friars, and together with them gave praise and thanks to God.

HOW A NOBLE KNIGHT, WHICH WAS DEVOTED UNTO ST. FRANCIS, WAS CERTIFIED OF THE DEATH OF ST. FRANCIS AND OF HIS MOST HOLY STIGMATA

A NOBLE knight of Massa di Santa Piero, by name Messer Landolfo, who bare unto St. Francis very great devotion, and finally received the habit of the Third Order at his hands, was certified upon this wise of the death of St. Francis and of his most holy Stigmata: When St. Francis was nigh unto death, the devil entered into a woman of the said town, and cruelly tormented her; and therewith he caused her to speak with such subtlety of learning that she put to silence all the wise and learned men who came to dispute with her. It befel that the devil departed from her and, for two days, left her free; and, on the third day, returning unto her again, he afflicted her far more cruelly than before. Whereupon, Messer Landolfo, hearing thereof, gat himself to this woman and asked of the devil who dwelt in her, what was the reason that he had left her for two days, and thereafter returning, tormented her more grievously than before. The devil made answer: "When I left her the reason was this, that I, and all my fellows which are in these parts, gathered ourselves together and went in great force to the death-bed of the mendicant Francis, to dispute with him and to take his soul; but because it was surrounded and defended by a multitude of angels, more numerous than we, and was by them carried straight to heaven, we departed in confusion; wherefore do I requite and render unto this wretched woman that which in those two days I left undone". And then Messer Landolfo conjured him in the name of God to speak the truth concerning the sanctity of St. Francis, who he said was dead, and of St. Clare, who was alive. The demon made answer: "Whether I would or no, I will tell thee thereof that which is true. God the Father was so wrath against the sins of the world that it seemed that ere long He would pronounce the final sentence against men and women, and utterly destroy them from the earth if they amended not themselves.

But Christ, His Son, praying for sinners, promised to renew His life and His passion in a man, to wit in Francis, mendicant and destitute: by whose life and doctrine He would lead back many, throughout all the world, to the way of truth, and many also to penitence. And now, to make manifest unto the world that which He had wrought in St. Francis, He hath willed that the Stigmata of His passion, the which He had imprinted upon his body in his life, should now be seen and touched by many in his death. In like manner, the Mother of Christ promised to renew her virginal purity and her humility in a woman, to wit in St. Clare, on such wise that, by her example, she should deliver many thousands of women out of our hands. And thus, God the Father, being appeased by these promises, delayed His final sentence". Then Messer Landolfo, desiring to know certainly whether the devil, who is the storehouse and father of lies, spake the truth in these things, and especially touching the death of St. Francis, sent one of his faithful squires to Assisi, to Santa Maria degli A ngeli, to know whether St. Francis were dead or alive; the which squire, on his arrival there, found that St. Francis had actually

M departed from this life on the very day and hour which the devil had said; and so returning he reported it unto his lord.

HOW POPE GREGORY IX., WHO DOUBTED TOUCHING THE STIGMATA OF ST. FRANCIS, WAS CONVINCED THEREOF

LEAVING all the miracles of the most holy Stigmata of St. Francis, the which may be read in his Legend, for conclusion of this fifth consideration, it is to be known that to Pope Gregory IX. (doubting somewhat of the wound in the side of St. Francis, even as he afterward related) St. Francis appeared one night and, lifting up his right arm a little, uncovered the wound in his side, and asked of him a phial; and he caused it to be brought; and St. Francis caused it to be set under the wound in his side; and it seemed to the Pope that, of a verity, it was filled even unto the brim with blood mixed with water, which came forth from the said wound; and from thenceforth every doubt departed from him.

And thereafter, with the counsel of all the cardinals, he approved the most holy Stigmata of St. Francis, and therefore he gave to the friars a special privilege with the hanging seal; and this he did at Viterbo in the eleventh year of his pontificate; and afterward, in the twelfth year, he gave another more ample. Again, Pope Nicolas III. and Pope Alexander gave ample privileges whereby whosoever should deny the most holy Stigmata of St. Francis, against him might proceedings be taken even as against a heretic. And this sufficeth as touching the fifth consideration of the glorious and most holy Stigmata of our father St. Francis; whose life may God give us grace so to follow in this world that, by virtue of his glorious stigmata, we may merit to be saved with him in paradise. To the praise of Jesus Christ and of the mendicant St. Francis. Amen.

THE LIFE OF FRIAR JUNIPER

1

How Friar Juniper cut off the foot of a pig, only to give it to a sick man

ONE of the most elect disciples and first companions of St. Francis was Friar Juniper, a man of profound humility, of great fervour and charity; of whom St. Francis speaking on a time with those holy companions of his, said: "He would be a good minor friar who had conquered himself and the world as Friar Juniper hath done". Once at Santa Maria degli Angeli, being as it were on fire with the charity of God, he was visiting a sick friar, and asked him with great compassion: "Can I do thee any service?" The sick man made answer: "Great comfort would it give me if thou couldst obtain for me a pig's trotter". Friar Juniper forthwith said: "Leave that to me and I will get it for you immediately". And he went and took a knife, I believe from the kitchen, and, in fervour of spirit, went through the wood, where certain swine were feeding, and he flung himself upon one of them and cut off its foot and fled away, leaving the pig with its foot thus maimed; and returning, he washed and dressed and cooked this foot; and with great diligence, having prepared it well, he carried the said foot to the sick man with much charity; and the sick man ate it very greedily, to the great consolation and joy of Friar Juniper; who, for the diversion of the sick man, narrated with much delight the assaults which he had made upon the pig. Meanwhile, the swineherd, who had seen this friar cut off the foot of the pig, told all the story to his master in order, with great grief. And he, when he had heard thereof, came to the Place of the friars, and, calling them hypocrites, and petty thieves, and forgers, and highwaymen and evil folk, demanded: "Why have ye cut off the foot of my pig?" At the great noise which he made St. Francis and all the friars came out; and with much humility St. Francis sought to excuse his friars, and, as one ignorant of the deed, he promised, to appease him, that he would make good every damage. But for all this he was in nowise appeased, but, with great wrath, abuse and threats, departed from the friars in anger; and, repeating again and again that they had cut off the foot of his pig of malice prepense, he refused to accept any recompense or any promise, and went away full of indignation. And St. Francis full of prudence, while all the other friars were amazed, considered and said within his heart: "Can Friar Juniper have done this thing of indiscreet zeal?" And he caused Friar Juniper to be called unto him secretly and asked him saying: "Didst thou cut off the foot of a pig in the wood?" Whereto Friar Juniper, not as one who had committed a fault, but as one who seemed to himself to have done a great charity, made answer very joyfully, and spake thus: "My sweet father, true it is that I cut off the foot of the said pig; and the reason, my father, do thou hear, if thou wilt, indulgently. I went for charity to visit such and such a sick friar;" and therewith he recounted unto him all the matter in order, and then added: "I tell thee that considering the consolation that this our friar had and the comfort he took from the said foot, I verily believe that, if I had cut off the feet of a hundred pigs instead of one, God would have been well pleased thereat". Whereto St. Francis with righteous zeal and with great displeasure, said: "O Friar Juniper, why hast thou given such great scandal? Not without reason doth that man lament and is so wrath with us; and peradventure he is even now speaking ill of us throughout the city by reason of this evil deed; and verily he hath good cause so to do. Wherefore I command thee, by holy obedience, that thou run after him until thou come up with him, and cast thyself on the ground before him and tell him thy fault, promising him to make satisfaction on such wise that he may have no ground of complaint against us; for of a surety this hath been a very grievous offence." Friar Juniper was very much surprised at the aforesaid words, and the other friars were amazed, marvelling that any one should be angered at all at so charitable an act; for to him it seemed that these temporal things were naught save only in so far as they were charitably shared with one's neighbour. And Friar Juniper made answer: "Doubt not, my father, that I will pay him at once and content him. "And wherefore should he be so disquieted, seeing that this pig whose foot I have cut off was rather God's than his, and that such great charity hath been done therewith?" And so he set off at a run and came up with this man, who was beyond measure enraged, so that there remained in him no patience at all; and he told him how and for what reason he had cut off the foot of the said pig; and this with as much fervour and delight and joy as if he were one who had done him a great service, for the which he ought to be well rewarded. But he, full of wrath, and beside himself with fury, bitterly reviled Friar Juniper, calling him madman and fool, petty thief and basest highwayman. And for those abusive words Friar Juniper cared nothing, but wondered within himself; for, albeit he rejoiced in the insults, he believed that the man had not understood him aright, since it seemed to him a matter for gladness and not for wrath; wherefore he told his story over again, and threw himself upon his neck and embraced him and kissed him, telling him how this thing was done only for charity, and inviting and beseeching him to give the rest of the pig for the same purpose, with so much simplicity and charity and humility that this man, having come to himself, cast himself upon the ground not without many tears; and confessing the wrong he had done and said to the friars, he went and took this pig and killed it, and, having cooked it, carried it with much devotion and with great weeping to Santa Maria degli Angeli, and gave it to those holy friars to eat, for pity of the wrong he had done them. St. Francis, considering the simplicity and patience under adversity of the said holy Friar Juniper, said to his companions and to the others who were standing round: "Would to God, my brethren. that I had a great forest of such Junipers!"

2

Ensample of the great power of Friar Juniper against the devil

THAT the demons were not able to endure the purity of innocence and the profound humility of Friar Juniper appeareth in this ensample following, to wit that once a demoniac, contrary to every wont of his, and with passing strange violence, suddenly leaped out of the road, and, running very swiftly, fled for seven miles through divers by-paths; and, being asked by his kinsfolk, which with great grief followed after him, wherefore he had so strangely fled away, he made answer: "The reason is this; because that madman Juniper was passing along that road; and not being able to endure his presence or to wait, I fled into these woods". And certifying themselves of this truth, they found that Friar Juniper had passed at that hour, even as the demon had said. Wherefore St. Francis, when demoniacs were brought unto him that he might heal them, if the devils departed not immediately at his command, was wont to say: "If thou dost not forthwith depart from this creature, I will cause Friar Juniper to come against thee"; and then the devil, fearing the presence of Friar Juniper, and unable to endure the virtue and humility of St. Francis, departed immediately.

3
_____

How, through procurement of the devil, Friar Juniper was condemned to the gallows

ON a time the devil wishing to frighten Friar Juniper, and to put him to shame and affliction, went unto a very cruel despot, by name Nicolas, who was then at war with the city of Viterbo, and said: "Sir, look well to this your town, for presently a great traitor cometh hither, sent by the men of Viterbo to the end that he may slay you and set fire to this town. And that this is true I give you these tokens: He goeth in guise of a mendicant, with garments all tattered and patched and with a torn cowl hanging on his shoulders; he carrieth with him an awl wherewith to slay you, and hath besides a flint and steel wherewith to set fire to this town; and if you find not this to be true, punish me as you will." At these words Nicolas was all amazed and feared much, because he who spake these words unto him appeared a worthy person. And he commanded that watch should be diligently kept, and that if this man, with the aforesaid tokens, came, he should forthwith be brought before him. In the meanwhile Friar Juniper came alone; for by reason of his perfection he had licence to go and to stay alone even as he pleased. And, as he came, he met certain dissolute youths who derided him and began to make great mock of him, but for all this he disquieted not himself, but rather led them on to make greater sport of him. And coming to the gate of the town, when the guards saw him so ill-seeming, with but little clothing and that all torn (for, on his way, he had given part of his habit to the poor for the love of God, and looked nothing like a minor friar); because the tokens which had been given unto them manifestly appeared in him, he was violently dragged before this despot Nicolas; and being searched by the attendants to see if he had weapons of offence, they found in his sleeve an awl wherewith he was wont to mend his sandals; also they found a flint which he carried to light a fire, because the weather was fine, and he ofttimes dwelt in woods and waste places.

Now when Nicolas saw these tokens in him according to the information given by the devil who had accused him, he ordered that a cord should be twisted round his head; and so was it done, and with such cruelty that the whole of the cord entered into his flesh. And afterward he put him to the strappado, and caused his arms to be pulled and wrenched and all his body to be tortured, without any mercy. And when he was asked who he was, he replied: "I am a very great sinner"; and when he was asked whether he wished to betray the town and to give it to the people of Viterbo, he replied: "I am a very great traitor, and undeserving of any good". And when he was asked if he wished to kill Nicolas, the despot, with that awl and to burn the town, he replied: "Very much greater things and worse should I do, if God permitted it". Then Nicolas, overcome with anger, would not examine him further; but full of fury incontinently condemned Friar Juniper, as a traitor and a murderer, to be tied to the tail of a horse and dragged through the town to the gallows, there to be forthwith hanged by the neck. And Friar Juniper made no defence; but, as one who for love of God rejoiced in tribulations, was all joyful and glad. And when the command of the despot was put into execution, and Friar Juniper was dragged through the town, tied by his feet to the tail of a horse, he complained not neither lamented, but like a gentle lamb which is led to the slaughter, went with all humility. To this spectacle and sudden justice ran all the people to see him executed with speed and severity; and no man recognised him. Nevertheless, as God willed it, a good man, who had seen Friar Juniper taken, and who now saw him forthwith dragged away to execution, ran to the place of the minor friars and said: "For God's sake, I beseech you, come quickly; for a poor beggar hath been taken, and straightway sentence hath been passed upon him, and he is being led away to his death. At least come, that he may be able to commit his soul into your hands; for to me he seemeth a good man, and he hath had no time to confess himself, and he hath been dragged to the gallows, and he seemeth neither to care for death nor for the salvation of his soul. Oh! come quickly, I entreat you."

The guardian, who was a compassionate man, went at once to seek to save his soul; but, when he arrived, the folk which were come thither to see the execution were already so numerous that he could not make his way through them; wherefore he stood and watched his opportunity; and, as he thus watched, he heard a voice from among the folk, which said: "Don't, don't, you little rascals, you hurt my legs". At the sound of this voice the guardian began to suspect that it was Friar Juniper, and with fervour of spirit he threw himself among them, and tore the bandage from the man's face, and then he knew of a truth that it was Friar Juniper. Therefore the guardian, for pity's sake, would have taken off his own habit to cover Friar Juniper therewith, but he with merry countenance, as if joking, said: "O guardian, thou art a fat man, and it would be most unseemly to see thee naked. I will not have it." Then the guardian, with great weeping, besought those executioners and all the people that for pity's sake they would wait a little, while he went to intercede with the despot for Friar Juniper, if peradventure he might grant him grace concerning him. The executioners and certain bystanders agreed thereto, believing of a truth that he was his kinsman; and the devout and compassionate guardian went to Nicolas, the despot, with bitter weeping and said: "Sir, I am in such wonder and grief as my tongue could never tell, because meseemeth that in this town hath to-day been committed a greater sin and a greater wrong than was ever done in the days of our forefathers; and I believe that it hath been done through ignorance". Nicolas heard the guardian with patience, and asked him: "What is the great crime and wrong which hath been committed to-day in this town?" The guardian made answer: "My lord, that one of the holiest friars at this time in the Order of St. Francis (whereunto you bear a singular devotion) hath by you been condemned to such a cruel death, and certainly, I believe, without cause". Said Nicolas: "Now tell me, guardian, who is this? Peradventure, not recognising him, I have done a great wrong." Said the guardian: "He whom you have condemned to death is Friar Juniper, the companion of St. Francis". Nicolas, the despot, was astounded, for he had heard of the fame and holy life of Friar Juniper; and, all pale, as one overcome with horror, he ran with the guardian and came to Friar Juniper and loosed him from the tail of the horse and set him free, and, in the presence of all the people, he cast himself down upon the ground before him, and, with very great weeping, confessed his fault touching the injury and insult which he had caused to be done unto this holy friar, and added: "I believe, in truth, that the days of my evil life are drawing to an end, because I have thus tortured this holy man without any cause. For my evil life, God will permit that I shall soon die an ill death, albeit I have done it ignorantly." Friar Juniper freely pardoned Nicolas, the despot; but God permitted it that, a few days thereafter, this Nicolas, the despot, finished his life with a very cruel death; and Friar Juniper departed, leaving all the people edified.

4
———

How Friar Juniper gave whatever he could to the poor, for the love of God

SUCH pity and compassion had Friar Juniper for the poor, that, whenever he saw any one who was ill-clad or naked, he was wont to forthwith take off his tunic or the cowl of his habit and give it to such poor man; wherefore the guardian commanded him by virtue of obedience that he should neither give all his tunic nor part of his habit to any poor man. Now it came to pass that, a few days later, he met a poor man, who was well-nigh naked and begged alms of Friar Juniper for the love of God; to whom, with great compassion, he said: "I have nothing which I can give thee save my tunic; and my superior hath ordered me in virtue of obedience neither to give it nor part of my habit to any one; but if thou shouldst take it off my back I would not say thee nay". He spake not to deaf ears; for the poor man forthwith pulled his tunic over his head and made off with it, leaving Friar Juniper naked. And, when he returned to the Place and was asked where his tunic was, he answered: "A good man pulled it off my back and went away with it". And the virtue of compassion increased so much in him that at the last he was not content with giving away his tunic, but gave books and vestments and mantles; and whatever he could lay his hands on he gave to the poor. And for this reason the friars left nothing exposed to the public, because Friar Juniper gave away everything for the love of God and for His glory.

5

How Friar Juniper plucked off certain bells from the altar, and gave them away for the love of God

ONCE Friar Juniper was at Assisi for the Nativity of Christ, in deep meditation before the altar of the Convent, the which altar was passing well draped and adorned; at the prayer of the sacristan, Friar Juniper remained to guard the said altar, while the sacristan went to eat. And, while he was in devout meditation, a beggar woman asked alms of him for the love of God. To whom Friar Juniper made answer after this wise: "Wait a little, and I will see whether I cannot give thee something from this altar which is so richly decked". There was upon the altar a border of gold, very beautiful and lordly, with little silver bells of great price. Said Friar Juniper: "These bells are a superfluity"; and he took a knife and cut them all off from the border; and for compassion's sake he gave them to the beggar woman. The sacristan, when he had eaten three or four mouthfuls, recalled to mind the ways of Friar Juniper, and began to fear greatly lest Friar Juniper, for zeal of charity, should do him some injury in regard to that altar, so richly adorned, which he had left in his charge. And anon, being full of suspicion, he rose up from table and gat him to the church and looked to see if any of the ornaments of the altar had been removed or taken away; and he saw that the bells had been cut and plucked off the border; whereat he was beyond measure disquieted and scandalised.

Friar Juniper, seeing him thus perturbed, said: "Do not disquiet thyself touching those bells, for I have given them to a poor woman who had very great need thereof, and here they were no use at all save for vain and worldly pomp". When the sacristan heard this he was sore grieved, and forthwith ran through the church and through all the city, if perchance he might find her; but not only could he not find her, but he found no one who had seen her. He returned to the Place, and, in great anger, took the border and carried it to the General, who was then in Assisi, and said: "Father General, I ask of you justice against Friar Juniper who hath destroyed this border for me, the which was the most honourable that was in the sacristy. See now how he hath spoiled it, and hath plucked off from it all the silver bells; and he saith that he hath given them to a poor woman." The General made answer: "Friar Juniper hath not done this, but rather thy folly; for by this time thou shouldst know his ways; and I tell thee that I marvel that he did not give away all the rest; nevertheless I will correct him well for this fault". And, all the friars having been assembled in Chapter, he caused Friar Juniper to be summoned, and, in the presence of all the convent, rated him soundly touching the aforesaid bells, and so much did his wrath increase that he shouted himself well-nigh hoarse. Friar Juniper cared little or nothing for those words, because he delighted in insults and in being put to shame; but, when he considered the inflammation of the General, he began to think of a remedy. Wherefore, as soon as he had received the rebuke of the General, Friar Juniper went into the city and ordered and caused to be made a good porringer of gruel with butter; and, when a good part. of the night was over, he went for it and returned, and, having lighted a candle, gat him to the cell of the General with this porringer of gruel, and knocked upon the door.

The General opened it and saw him standing there with the lighted candle and the porringer in his hand, and demanded in a low voice: "What is this?" Friar Juniper replied: "My father, to-day when you rebuked me for my faults, I perceived that your voice became hoarse, as I believe, from over-exertion, and therefore I thought of a remedy and caused this gruel to be made for thee. Eat it, I pray thee, for I assure thee it will relieve thy throat and chest." Said the General: "What hour is this to come disturbing others?" Friar Juniper made answer: "See it hath been made for thee; eat it, I pray thee, without more ado, for it will do thee much good". The General, angered at the lateness of the hour and at his importunity, bade him depart, because at such an hour he did not wish to eat, calling him by name, a very low fellow and a scoundrel. Friar Juniper, perceiving that neither entreaties nor soft words prevailed, spake thus: "My father, since thou wilt not eat this gruel which was made for thee, at least do this for me; hold the candle for me and I will eat it myself". Then the General as a compassionate and devout person, considering the piety and simplicity of Friar Juniper, and that all this was done by him of devotion, replied: "Behold now since thou wilt have it so, let us eat it, thou and I, together"; and so they two ate this porringer of gruel by reason of his importunate charity. And far more were they comforted by devotion than by the food.

6

How Friar Juniper kept silence for six months

FRIAR JUNIPER once resolved to keep silence for six months after this manner. The first day for love of the Heavenly Father. The second day for love of Jesus Christ His Son. The third for love of the Holy Ghost. The fourth day for reverence of the most holy Virgin Mary; and so each day, in succession, for love of some saint, he observed the six months without speaking.

7

Ensample against the temptations of the flesh

ONCE, when Friar Giles and Friar Simon of Assisi and Friar Ruffino and Friar Juniper were met together to talk of God and of the soul, Friar Giles said to the other friars: "How do ye deal with temptations to carnal sin?" Said Friar Simon: "I consider the baseness and infamy of carnal sin, and therefrom follows a great abhorrence, and so I escape". Said Friar Ruffino: "I fling myself flat upon the ground and continue in prayer, beseeching the mercy of God and of the Mother of Jesus Christ until I feel myself wholly freed therefrom". Made answer Friar Juniper: "When I feel the turmoil of the diabolical carnal suggestion, I forthwith run and shut fast the door of my heart; and, for the safety of the fortress of my heart, I occupy myself in holy meditations and holy desires, so that, when the carnal suggestion cometh or knocketh at the door of my heart, I answer it, as if from within: 'Begone; for this lodging is already taken, and here no more folk may enter'; and on this wise never do I allow the carnal thought to enter into my heart;

whereupon, seeing itself conquered, it departeth from me as one discomfited, and not from me alone but from all the neighbourhood". Friar Giles made answer: "Friar Juniper, I hold with thee, because no man may contend better with the fleshly enemy than by flight; for within the traitor carnal desire and without the senses of the body make themselves felt as enemies so great and so strong, that, if we flee not, we cannot conquer them. Therefore, he who would fight in any other way, for the toil of battle rarely has the victory. Flee vice then, and thou wilt be victorious."

8

How Friar Juniper abased himself for the glory of God

ONCE Friar Juniper, desiring to utterly abase himself, stripped himself stark naked save for his breeches, and, having made as it were a bundle of his habit, put his clothes upon his head, and thus naked entered Viterbo, and gat him to the public piazza to be jeered at. As he stood there naked, the children and youths, deeming him out of his senses, treated him with great despite, casting much mud upon him, and pelting him with stones, and pushing him about, now this way and now that, with words of great derision; and thus tormented and derided he stayed there the greater part of the day, and afterward, all naked as he was, he betook himself to the convent. And seeing him in such case the friars were very wrath with him. And especially because he had come thus naked through all the city with his bundle on his head, they rebuked him very harshly, and threatened him with grievous penalties. And one said: "Let us put him in prison"; and another said: "Let us hang him; no punishment could be too great for such an ill example as he hath set this day, both touching himself and all the Order". And Friar Juniper replied joyfully and with all humility: "Ye speak well and truly, for I am worthy of all these punishments and of many more".

9

How Friar Juniper, to abase himself, played at see-saw

ONCE when Friar Juniper was going to Rome, where the fame of his sanctity was already noised abroad, many Romans, for their great devotion, went forth to meet him? and, seeing so many folk coming, Friar Juniper bethought him to turn their devotion to scorn and derision. There were there two little boys who were playing at see-saw, that is to say they had laid one log across another log, and each of them sat at his end, and thus they went up and down. Friar Juniper went and lifted one of those boys off the log and got up there himself, and began to see-saw. Meanwhile the people came up and marvelled to see Friar Juniper playing at see-saw; nevertheless, they saluted him with great devotion and waited until he should have finished his game of see-saw, to the end that they might thereafter attend him honourably to the convent. And Friar Juniper cared but little either for their salutation and reverence or for their waiting, but took great pains with his see-sawing. And, after they had thus waited a long time, some of them began to grow weary and to say: "What fool is this?" Some, knowing the ways of the man, increased in devotion toward him; nevertheless, in the end, they all went away and left Friar Juniper on the see-saw, and, when they were all gone, Friar Juniper remained full of consolation because he had seen some who made a mock of him. So he gat him up and entered Rome with all meekness and humility, and came to the convent of the minor friars.

10

How Friar Juniper once cooked for the friars food enough for fifteen days

ONCE when Friar Juniper was in a very little Place of friars, for a certain good reason all the friars had to go forth, and only Friar Juniper remained in the house. The Guardian said: "Friar Juniper, we are all going out, and therefore look thou to it that when we return thou hast cooked a little food for the refreshment of the friars". Friar Juniper made answer: "Very gladly will I do so; leave it to me". And, when all the friars were gone forth, as hath been told, Friar Juniper said: "What unnecessary labour is this that a friar should be lost in the kitchen and kept away from all prayer? In sooth, now that I am left behind to cook, I will prepare so much that all the friars, even if there were more of them than there are, shall have enough for fifteen days." So he went to the town in haste and begged divers great cooking-pots and got fresh meat and salt, and fowls, and eggs, and herbs; and he begged firewood enough, and put everything on the fire, to wit the fowls with their feathers on, the eggs in their shells, and all the other things in like fashion. When the friars returned to the Place, one who well knew the simplicity of Friar Juniper went into the kitchen and saw all those great pots standing on a roaring fire; and he sat him down and looked on with amazement and said nothing, watching with what diligence Friar Juniper did this cooking. Because the fire was exceeding great, and he could not very easily approach his pots to skim them, he took a plank and tied it tightly to his body with his cord, and thereafter kept jumping from one pot to another, so that it was a joy to see him. And, when he had observed all this, to his very great amusement, that friar went out of the kitchen and, having found the other friars, said: "I can tell you that Friar Juniper is preparing a wedding feast". The friars took that saying as a jest. Then Friar Juniper lifted those pots from off the fire, and caused the bell to be rung for dinner, and the friars came to the table; and he gat him to the refectory with the food which he had cooked, all ruddy with his exertions and with the heat of the fire, and said to the friars: "Eat well; and afterward let us all go to prayer. And let no one think any more of cooking for a while, for I have made so great a banquet to-day that I shall have enough for much more than two weeks"; and he sec this poultice of his upon the table before the friars; and there is no pig in all the city of Rome so famished that he would have eaten it. Friar Juniper belauded the viands he had cooked like a shopman puffing his wares, for he saw already that the other friars were not eating, and he said: "Now these fowls are excellent to invigorate the brain; and this broth will keep you the body moist, so good is it". And while the friars were yet marvelling at the devotion and simplicity of Friar Juniper; the Guardian, full of wrath at such folly and at the loss of so much good food, rebuked Friar Juniper with great severity. Thereupon Friar Juniper forthwith flung himself upon the ground and kneeled before the Guardian and humbly confessed his fault to him and all the friars saying: "I am the worst of men; such an one committed such a sin, for the which his eyes were torn out, but I was much more guilty than he; such an one was hanged for his crimes, but much more do I deserve it for my wicked deeds; and now I have wasted the good things of God and of the Order"; and thus bitterly lamenting he went forth, and all that day never showed himself where any friar was. And then the Guardian said: "Most dear friars of mine, I would that every day, even as now, this friar wasted an equal quantity of good things, if we had them, if only he might be edified thereby; for out of great simplicity and charity hath he done this".

11

How Friar Juniper once went to Assisi for his confusion

ONCE, while Friar Juniper was sojourning in the Val di Spoleto, he heard that there was a great festival at Assisi, and that many folk were going thither with great devotion; and there came to him a desire to go to this festival; and hearken how he did it. Friar Juniper stripped himself all naked save only for his breeches, and so set out, passing through Spoleto through the midst of the city; and thus naked he came to the convent. The friars were much disquieted and scandalised and rebuked him very harshly, calling him madman and fool and troubler of the Order of St. Francis, and saying that he should be chained up, as a madman. And the General, who was then in the Place, caused all the friars to be called and Friar Juniper with them; and, in the presence of all the convent, he gave him a severe and stern reproof. And, after many words, speaking as one with authority to punish, he said to Friar Juniper: "Thy fault is such and so great that I know not what fitting penance to give thee". Whereupon Friar Juniper, even as one who delighteth in his own confusion, made answer: "Father, I will tell thee: as I have come hither naked, so for penance let me return again, in the same guise, to the place wherefrom I set out to come to this festival".

12

How Friar Juniper was rapt in ecstasy during the celebration of the Mass

ONCE while Friar Juniper was hearing Mass with great devotion, he was rapt in ecstasy through elevation of mind and for a long time; and having been left in a cell far away from the other friars, when he returned to himself he began, with great fervour, to say: "O friars mine, who is there in this life so noble that he would not gladly carry a basket of dung through all the town, if he were given a house full of gold?" And he said: "Alack! wherefore are we unwilling to suffer a little shame, if so be we may gain the blessed life?"

13

Of the grief which Friar Juniper had for the death of his companion, Friar Amazialbene

FRIAR JUNIPER had as his companion a friar whom he dearly loved, and his name was Amazialbene. Abundantly was this man dowered with the virtue of highest patience and obedience; for, if he were beaten all day long, never did he murmur or utter one single word of complaint. He was ofttimes sent to Places where the friars were surly and hard to please, and from whom he suffered many persecutions; the which he bore most patiently without any murmuring. At the bidding of Friar Juniper he would weep and laugh. Now, as God willed it, this Friar Amazialbene died in exceeding good report; and when Friar Juniper heard of his death he took greater grief therefrom than ever he had had in all his life before for any carnal thing; and so by his outward bearing he manifested the great bitterness which was within, and said: "Woe is me! miserable wretch that I am, for now no good thing remaineth unto me, and all the world is undone in the death of my sweet and well-beloved Friar Amazialbene!" And he said: "Were it not that I should have no peace with the friars, I would go to his grave and take therefrom his head, and of his skull would I make two porringers; from the one, in memory of him and for my love's sake, I would always eat, and from the other I would drink whenever I was thirsty or desired to drink".

14

Of the hand which Friar Juniper saw in the air

ONCE, when Friar Juniper was praying, and peradventure thinking too highly of himself, it seemed to him that he saw a hand in the air, and heard a voice with his bodily ears, which spake unto him after this manner: "O Friar Juniper, with this hand thou canst do nothing". Whereat he forthwith rose up, and, having lifted up and turned his eyes toward heaven, he cried in a loud voice, as he ran through the convent: "Indeed it is true, indeed it is true". And this he kept on repeating for a long time.

THE LIFE OF FRIAR GILES, THE COMPANION OF ST. FRANCIS

1

How Friar Giles and three companions were received into the Order of the Minors

FORASMUCH as the ensamples of holy men fill the hearts of devout hearers with contempt for transitory delights, and are effectual to awake desire of eternal salvation; to the honour of God and of His most venerable Mother, Our Lady, St. Mary, and for the profit of all hearers, I will speak certain words touching the work which the Holy Ghost hath wrought in our saintly Friar Giles; who, while yet he wore the garb of a layman, was touched by the Holy Ghost and began to ponder within himself how in all his works he might please God alone. At this time, St. Francis, as a new herald prepared of God as an ensample of life, of humility and of holy penance, two years after his conversion, drew and induced to evangelical observance and poverty a man adorned with wonderful prudence and very rich in temporal goods, to wit Messer Bernard, and also Peter Cattani; so that by the counsel of St. Francis they distributed unto the poor, for love of God, all their temporal treasures, and took unto themselves the glory of patience and evangelic perfection and the habit of the Minor Friars; and with very great fervour have they promised to observe the Religion all the days of their lives; and even so did they with all perfectness. Eight days after the aforesaid conversion and distribution of goods to the poor, Friar Giles, who was then a layman, beholding the contempt in which such noble knights of Assisi held the good things of this world, so that all the city marvelled thereat, was all enkindled with Divine love, and, on the following day, which was the Feast of St. George, in the year of our Lord M.CC.IX., (1209) very early in the morning, and as one in earnest about his salvation, went to the Church of San Gregorio, where was the Convent of St. Clare; and, when he had prayed, having a great desire to see St. Francis, he went toward the hospital of the lepers where he dwelt apart with Friar Bernard and Friar Peter Canard in a very lowly hut. And being come to a crossing of ways, and knowing not whither to go, Friar Giles offered up a prayer to Christ, the precious Guide, who led him to the said hut by a straight way. And while he pondered on that for which he .was come, St. Francis chanced to meet him, as he was coming from the wood whither he had gone to pray; whereupon he forthwith cast himself upon the ground and kneeled before St. Francis, and humbly asked him to receive him to his company, for the love of God. St. Francis, beholding the devout bearing of Friar Giles, made answer and said: "Dearest brother, God hath done thee singular grace. If the Emperor should come to Assisi, and should desire to make a certain citizen his knight or his lord of the bedchamber, should not such an one rejoice exceedingly? How much more then oughtest thou to be glad that God hath chosen thee for His knight and well-beloved servitor, to observe the perfection of the Holy Gospel. And therefore be thou firm and constant in the vocation whereunto

God hath called thee." And he took him by the hand and lifted him up and brought him into the little house aforesaid; and he called Friar Bernard and said: "Messer the Lord God hath sent us a good friar, wherefore rejoice we all in the Lord; let us eat in charity". And, when they had eaten, St. Francis and this Giles went to Assisi to beg cloth wherewith to make a habit for Friar Giles. They found by the way a beggar woman who asked alms of them, for the love of God; and not knowing wherewithal to succour the poor woman, St. Francis turned him to Friar Giles, with a face like that of an angel, and said: For the love of God, dearest brother, let us give this mantle to the poor woman"; and Friar Giles [who was hoping that St. Francis would bid him do so] obeyed the holy father with so ready a heart that it seemed to him that he saw that alms fly straightway up to heaven, and Friar Giles flew with it into heaven by the nearest way; whereby he felt within himself unspeakable joy, with new stirrings of spirit. And St. Francis, when the cloth had been procured and the habit made, received Friar Giles into the Order; the which was one of the most glorious Religious that the world at that time had in the contemplative life. After the reception of Friar Giles, St. Francis forthwith went with him into the March of Ancona, singing with him and magnificently praising the Lord of heaven and earth; and he said to Friar Giles: "Son, our Religion will be like unto the fisher which setteth his nets in the water and taketh a multitude of fishes, and the large ones he keepeth and the little ones he leaveth in the water". Friar Giles marvelled at this prophecy because as yet there were in the Order only three friars and St. Francis; and albeit, as yet, St. Francis preached not publicly to the people, he admonished and corrected men and women, as he went by the way, saying simply and lovingly: "Love and fear God and do fitting penance for your sins". And Friar Giles used to say: "Do that which my spiritual father here tells you, for he says exceeding well".

2

How Friar Giles went to St. James the Greater

ONCE, in process of time, by leave of St. Francis, Friar Giles went to St. James the Greater in Galicia, and in all that journey, once only did he fully satisfy his hunger by reason of the great want which there was in all that region. For going to beg alms and finding none who would do him any charity, he came by chance in the evening to a threshing-floor where a few beans had been left, the which he gathered up, and on them he supped; and there he slept the night; for he willingly dwelt in solitary places and remote from men to the end that he might the better devote himself to prayers and vigils. And by this meal he was so much comforted of God that he deemed that, had he eaten of divers dishes, he had not had so great refreshment. As he went on his journey, he met a mendicant who begged alms of him in God's name. And Friar Giles, full of charity, and having nothing wherewith to cover his nakedness save only his habit, cut the cowl from that old threadbare habit, and gave it to the poor man, for the love of God; and so, for twenty days in succession, he journeyed without his cowl. And, when he was returning through Lombardy, he was called by a man, to whom he went willingly, thinking to receive from him an alms; and, when he held out his hand, the man put therein a pair of dice, inviting him to play. Friar Giles made answer very humbly: "God pardon thee, my son". And so as he went through the world, he was much derided and ever he bore it with all tranquillity.

3
___

Of the manner of life which Friar Giles led when he went to the Holy Sepulchre

BY leave of St. Francis, Friar Giles went to visit the Holy Sepulchre of Christ, and came to the port of Brindisi, and there he abode many days, because no ship was ready. And Friar Giles, wishing to live by the labour of his hands, begged a water-pot and filled it with water, and went crying through the city: "Who wants water?" And by his labour he gat him bread and the things necessary for the bodily life, both for himself and for his companion; and thereafter, he crossed the sea and visited the Holy Sepulchre of Christ and the other holy places with great devotion. And, as he returned, he abode in the city of Ancona for many days, and, because he was wont to live by the labour of his hands, he made baskets of rushes and sold them, not for money but for bread for himself and his companion, and he carried the dead to their burying for the same wage. And, when this failed him, he returned to the table of Jesus Christ, asking alms from door to door. And on this wise, with much labour and poverty he returned to Santa Maria degli Angeli.

4
―――――

How Friar Giles praised obedience more than prayer

ONCE a friar was in his cell at prayer, and his Guardian sent unto him bidding him by virtue of obedience to go and beg for alms. Wherefore he straightway went to Friar Giles and said: "My father, I was at prayer, and the Guardian hath commanded me to go for bread; and to me it seemeth that it were better to continue in prayer". Friar Giles made answer: "My son, hast thou as yet neither learned nor understood what manner of thing is prayer True prayer is that a man should do the will of his Superior; and it is a sign of great pride in him who hath put his neck beneath the yoke of holy obedience, when, for any cause, he shunneth it, to do his own will, albeit to him it seemeth that thereby he doth a more perfect work. The perfectly obedient Religious is like unto the knight who is mounted upon a goodly horse, by the excellence whereof he goeth without fear along the midst of the road; and, on the contrary, the disobedient Religious, grumbling and unwilling, is like unto one who is mounted upon a thin, weak and vicious horse, because, when he hath endured but a little fatigue, he either falleth down dead or is taken by the enemy. I tell thee that if a man were so devout and of such elevation of mind that he spake with Angels, and, while he thus spake, were called by his Superior, he ought forthwith to leave the converse of the Angels and to obey him who is set over him."

5
―――

How Friar Giles lived by the labour of his hands

FRIAR GILES being once at a convent in Rome, wished to live by bodily labour, even as it had been his wont to do from the time he entered the Order; and he did after this manner. In the morning betimes he heard Mass with great devotion; then he gat himself to the wood, which was eight miles distant from Rome, and brought back a bundle of wood on his shoulders, and sold it for bread and other things to eat. One time among others, as he was returning with a load of wood, a woman wished to buy it of him; and, when the bargain for the price had been made, he carried it to her house. Notwithstanding the bargain which had been made, the woman, because she saw that he was a Religious, gave him far more than she had promised him. Said Friar Giles: "Good woman, I would not that the vice of avarice should overcome nee; wherefore I desire not a higher price than that which I bargained for with thee"; so that not only did he not take more, but only took half the price which had been agreed upon, and so departed;

whereat that woman conceived toward him a great devotion. In all the work which he did for hire Friar Giles was ever mindful of holy honesty; he helped the husbandmen to pick the olives and to tread out the wine. One day, when he was in the piazza, a certain man wanted to have his walnut trees beaten, and asked another to beat them at a price; he excused himself because it was a very long way off and the climbing was very difficult.

Said Friar Giles: "My friend, if thou art willing to give me part of the walnuts, I will go with thee and beat thy trees"; and, when he had covenanted with him, he went; and, having first made the sign of the most holy Cross, he climbed up, with great fear, into a high tree to beat it; and, when he had beaten it, so many nuts fell to his share that he could not carry them in his lap; so he took off his habit, and, having tied the sleeves and the cowl, made a sack of his habit, remaining naked save only for his breeches; and so he put this habit full of walnuts upon his back, and carried them to Rome, and, with great joy, gave them all to the poor for the love of God. When the wheat was reaped, Friar Giles went with other poor folk to glean the ears, and if any one offered him a handful of grain, he made answer: "My brother, I have no granary wherein to store it"; and those ears he generally gave away for the love of God. Rarely did Friar Giles help another all the day; for he was wont to bargain for sufficient time in which to say the canonical hours, and not to miss his private prayers. Once Friar Giles went to the Fountain of St. Sixtus to draw water for those monks, and a man asked drink of him. Friar Giles replied: "And how can I carry the vessel half empty to the monks?" The man, being angered, spake many abusive words and insults to Friar Giles; wherefore Friar Giles returned to the monks very sorrowful. He borrowed a large vessel and forthwith returned to the said fountain for water, and found that man again and said: "My friend, take and drink as much as thy heart desireth and be not wrath; for to me it seemed a discourtesy to carry to those holy monks water wherefrom another had drunk". The man, moved to contrition and constrained by the charity and humility of Friar Giles, confessed his fault, and from that day forward held him in great devotion.

6
---

*How Friar Giles was miraculously provided for in his great need,
when by reason of the snow he could not go to beg alms*

FRIAR GILES being at Rome and sojourning in the house of a Cardinal, when the greater Lent drew nigh, found not that quiet of mind which he desired, and said unto the Cardinal: "My father, by your leave I desire for my peace to go with my companion to keep this Lent in some solitary place". Messer the Cardinal made answer: "Alas! my dearest friar, whither wouldst thou go? The famine is sore in the land, and as yet ye are strangers here, be ye content, I pray you, to abide in my court, for it will be for me a singular privilege to cause to be given unto you, for the love of God, that whereof ye have need." But Friar Giles was determined to go; and he departed from Rome, and went into a high mountain where of old time there had been a town, and he found there a deserted Church, which was called after St. Lawrence; and he and his companion entered therein, and continued in prayer and in much meditation; and, since they were not known, they received but little reverence and devotion; wherefore they suffered great want; and in addition thereto there came a great snowstorm which lasted many days. They were not able to leave the Church and nothing was sent them to eat, and they themselves had nothing; and they remained so shut up for three whole days and nights. Friar Giles, perceiving that he could not live by the labour of his hands and that he could not go out to beg alms, said to his companion: "Dearest brother mine, let us call upon our Lord with a loud voice, that of His compassion He may provide for us in our great extremity and need; for once certain monks being in great need called upon God and the Divine Providence supplied all their wants". Wherefore, after the ensample of those monks, they betook themselves to prayer, beseeching God with all their hearts that He would help them in their so great need. God, who is highest pity, regarded their faith and simplicity and fervour on this wise. A certain man, as he looked toward the Church where were Friar Giles and his companion, being inspired of God, said within himself: "Peradventure there are in that church some good persons who are doing penance, and who, by reason of this exceeding great snow, lack the necessities of life, and are therefore like to die of hunger"; and, being moved thereto by the Holy Ghost, he said: "Of a surety I will go thither to learn whether my imagination be true or no"; and he took slime loaves and a vessel of wine and set out on his way; and with exceeding great difficulty he came unto the Church aforesaid, where he found Friar Giles and his companion praying most devoutly; and they were so much worn with hunger that their appearance was rather that of dead men than of living. He had great compassion on them, and, when they were refreshed and comforted, he returned and told unto his neighbours the extremity and great need of these friars and urged and besought them for God's sake to provide for them:

wherefore many, after his ensample, brought them bread and wine and other things necessary for their sustenance, for the love of God; and through all that Lent they took such order among them that they were provided for in their necessities. And Friar Giles, considering the great mercy of God and the charity of those folk, said unto his companion: "My dearest brother, even until now have we prayed God that He would provide for us in our need, and we have been heard; therefore is it meet that we give Him thanks and glory, and pray for those who have fed us with their alms and for all Christian people". And for his great fervour and devotion, God granted so much grace to Friar Giles that many, after his ensample, left this blind world, and many others which were not minded to be religious did very great penance in their own homes.

7

Of the day of the death of the holy Friar Giles

ON the vigil of St. George at the hour of matins, when two and fifty years had gone by (for on the first day of the month he had received the habit of St. Francis), the soul of Friar Giles was received by God into the glory of Paradise, to wit upon the Feast of St. George.

8

How a holy man, being in prayer, beheld the soul of Friar Giles go to the life eternal

A GOOD man, being in prayer, when Friar Giles passed from this life, saw his soul go up to heaven, together with a multitude of other souls which at that hour came forth from Purgatory; and he saw Jesus Christ come to meet the soul of Friar Giles, and, with a multitude of Angels and all those souls, ascend into the glory of Paradise, to a great sound of sweet music.

9

How through the merits of Friar Giles, the soul of a friend of a certain Preaching Friar was delivered from the pains of Purgatory

WHEN Friar Giles lay sick of that sickness whereof a few days after he died, a friar of St. Dominic fell sick even unto death. Now this man had a friend who was a friar; and the said friend, seeing him draw nigh unto death, said unto the sick friar: "My brother, I desire that, if God permit, thou return to me after thy death and tell me how thou farest". The sick man promised to return if it should be possible. Friar Giles died the same day, and, after his death, [the said Preaching Friar] appeared unto the living Preaching Friar, and said: "It was the will of God that I should keep my promise to thee". Said the living to the dead: "How is it with thee?" The dead made answer: "It is well, because I died on the same day whereon a holy Minor Friar, by name Friar Giles, departed from this life, unto whom, by reason of his great sanctity, Jesus Christ granted that he should lead to Paradise all the souls which were in Purgatory, among whom was I, in great torment; and by the merits of Friar

Giles I am delivered therefrom". And when he had said this he suddenly vanished away; and that friar revealed not the vision to any man. The said friar fell sick, and anon suspecting that God had smitten him because he had not revealed the virtue and. the glory of Friar Giles, he sent for the Minor Friars and there came unto him five couples; and, when they were assembled, together with the Preaching Friars, he revealed unto them the aforesaid vision with great devotion; and after that they had inquired diligently, they found clearly that they two had departed this life on the self-same day.

10

How God had given graces unto Friar Giles, and of the year of his death

FRIAR BUONAVENTURA of Bagnoreggio was wont to say of Friar Giles that God had given and granted unto him special grace for all those who commended themselves unto him with devout intention as touching those things which appertain unto the soul. He wrought many miracles in his life, and after his death, as appeareth from his Legend; and he passed from this life to the glory supernal in the year of Our Lord M.C-C.LII., (1252) on the day of the Feast of St. George, and was buried at Perugia in the convent of the Minor Friars.

TEACHINGS AND SAYINGS OF FRIAR GILES

A CHAPTER OF VICES AND OF VIRTUES

THE grace of God and the virtues are a road and a ladder to ascend to heaven; but vices and sins are a road and a ladder to descend to the depths of hell. Vices and sins are a deadly potion and a mortal poison but virtues and good works are a healing theriac. One grace accompanies and brings after it another; one vice brings after it another. Grace desireth not to be praised; and vice cannot endure to be despised. In humility the mind rests and reposes; patience is her daughter. And holy purity of heart sees God; but true devotion tastes Him. If thou lovest, thou wilt he loved. If thou servest, thou wilt be served. If thou fearest, thou wilt be feared. If thou shalt do good unto others, it is fitting that others do good to thee. But blessed is he who truly loves and desires not to be loved. Blessed is he who serves and desires not to be served. Blessed is he who fears and desires not to be feared. Blessed is he who does good to others and desires not that others do good to him. But inasmuch as these things are very high and of great perfection, therefore the foolish can neither know nor attain unto them. Three things are exceeding high and very profitable, and they who have acquired the same shall never be able to fall. The first is if thou bear willingly and with joy every tribulation which befalleth thee for the love of Jesus Christ. The second is if thou humble thyself every day in everything that thou dost and in everything that thou seest. The third is that thou faithfully love that Highest Good, celestial, invisible, with all thy heart; the which no man is able to behold with the eyes of the body. Those things which are most despised and reviled by worldly men are of a truth most acceptable and most welcome to God and to His Saints; and those things which are most loved and most honoured and most pleasing to worldly men, are those which are most despised and reviled and hated by God and by his Saints. This foul contradiction proceeded) from human ignorance and wickedness; for wretched man loveth rather those which he ought to hate, and hateth those things hick he ought to love. Once Friar Giles asked another friar, saying: "Tell me, most dear brother, hast thou a good soul?" The friar made answer: "This I do not know". Then Friar Giles said: "My brother, I would have thee know, that holy penitence, and holy humility, and holy charity, and holy devotion, and holy joy make the soul good and blessed".

CHAPTER OF FAITH

ALL those things which may be thought with the heart, or spoken with the tongue, or seen with the eyes or handled with the hands, are well-nigh nothing with regard and in comparison to those things which cannot be thought, or seen or touched. All the saints and all the wise men who have passed away, and all those who are in the present life, and all those who shall come after us, who have spoken or written or who shall speak or write concerning God, have never said nor shall ever be able to say so much concerning God as would be a grain of millet with regard and in comparison to the heaven and the earth, yea even a thousand thousand times less. For all the Scriptures which spake of God, speak of Him as it were babblingly, even as doth a mother who babbles with her infant, that would not understand her words if she spoke in any other way. Once Friar Giles said to a doctor of law, a layman: "Believest thou that the gifts of God are great?" The lawyer made answer: "I believe". Whereto Friar Giles said: "I will show thee that thou dost not believe faithfully"; and thereafter he said unto him: "What is the worth of that which thou possessest in this world?" The lawyer replied: "It is worth perhaps a thousand lire". Then Friar Giles said: "Wouldst thou give these possessions of thine for ten thousand lire?" The lawyer replied without hesitation, saying: "Certainly I would give them willingly"; and Friar Giles said: "It is a thing indisputable that all the possessions of this world are as nothing in comparison with celestial things: wherefore then dost thou not give these possessions of thine to Christ that thou mayest therewith buy those which are celestial and eternal?" Then the lawyer, wise in the foolish science of the world, answered pure and simple Friar Giles: "God hath filled thee full of the foolishness of Divine wisdom," saying: "Dost thou believe, Friar Giles, that there is any man whose visible and external works are proportionate to his inward belief?" Friar Giles made answer: "Behold, my dearest brother, it is certain that all the saints have striven to fulfil in their actions all that which they understood to be the will of God, to the utmost of their power; and all those things which they were not able to fulfil in their actions, they fulfilled with the holy desires of their wills; on such wise that with the desire of the soul they supplied that which was lacking in their actions, and so fulfilled the will of God". Then said Friar Giles: "If any man had perfect faith, in a little while he would attain to a state of perfection, whereby he would be given full assurance of salvation. The man that with firm faith awaits that eternal and supreme and highest Good, what harm or what ill could any temporal adversity in this present life do him? And the wretched man who awaits the eternal evil, what shall any prosperity or temporal good in this world profit him? Nevertheless, albeit a man is a sinner, he ought not therefore to despair, as long as he lives, of the infinite mercy of God; for where is no tree in all the world so thorny and gnarled and knotty that men cannot smooth it and polish it and beautify it and make it fair: and even so there is no man so evil, nor any sinner in this world so great that God cannot convert him and adorn him with singular graces and with the gift of many virtues."

CHAPTER OF HOLY HUMILITY

NO man may come unto any knowledge and understanding of God save through the virtue of holy humility; for the same straight way which goeth upwards is also that which goeth downwards. All the dangers and the great falls, which have happened in this world, have come from no other cause than the uplifting of the head, to wit of the mind, in pride; and this is proved by the fall of the devil who was cast out of Heaven, and by the fall of our first parent, to wit Adam, who was cast out of Paradise for the uplifting of his head, to wit for disobedience; and also by the Pharisee, of whom Christ speaks in the Gospel, and by many other ensamples: and so likewise, on the contrary, all the great benefits, which ever befel in this world, proceeded from the lowering of the head, to wit from the humbling of the mind; as is proved by the blessed most humble Virgin Mary, and by the Publican, and by the holy Thief upon the Cross, and by many other ensamples in the Scriptures. And therefore would it be well if we could find some great and heavy weight which we might keep continually tied to the neck, so that it might alway drag us down, to wit that it might ever make us humble. A friar asked of Friar Giles: "Tell me, father, in what manner may we flee from this pride?" Whereto Friar Giles replied: "My brother, be thou sure of this, to wit, that never wilt thou learn how to flee from pride until thou first put thy mouth where now thou hast thy feet; but if thou considerest well the benefits of God, then thou wilt know well that for duty's sake thou art bound to bow thy head. And again, if thou wilt give good thought to thy shortcomings and to the many offences which thou hast committed against God, thou wilt have great cause to humble thyself. But woe unto those which desire to be honoured for their wickedness! One degree of humility is in that man who knoweth himself to be the adversary of his own good. One degree of humility is to render unto another the things that are his and not to appropriate them to oneself; that is to say that every good thing and every virtue which a man findeth in himself he ought not to attribute unto himself, but to God alone, from whom cometh every grace and every virtue and every good thing; but every sin and every desire of the soul or whatsoever vice a man findeth in himself, he ought to attribute to himself, considering that it cometh from himself and of his own wickedness and not from others. Blessed is the man who knoweth himself and accounteth himself vile in the sight of God, and so also before men! Blessed is he who alway judgeth himself and condemneth himself, and not another; for he shall not be judged by that terrible and last eternal judgment. Blessed is he who shalt go diligently under the yoke of obedience and under the governance of others, even as did the Apostles both before and after they received the Holy Ghost!" Also Friar Giles said: "It behoves him who would gain and possess perfect peace and rest to account every man his superior, and it behoves him always to acknowledge himself subject and inferior to all. Blessed is that man who desireth neither to be seen nor known in his words or ways, save only in that simple form and in that artless adornment wherewith God adorned and formed him! Blessed is that man who knoweth how to keep and to hide the Divine revelations and consolations! for there is no thing so secret that God reveals it not when it seemeth good unto Him. If a man were the most perfect and the most holy man in the world,- and accounted himself and believed himself the most miserable sinner and the vilest man in the world, in this man would be true humility. Holy humility knoweth not how to talk, and the blessed fear of God knoweth not how to speak". Said Friar Giles: "Unto me it seemeth that humility is like unto a thunderbolt; for even as the thunder-bolt striketh a terrible blow, breaking, splintering and burning that which it encounters, and afterward naught can be found of that thunder-bolt; even so humility in like manner strikes and scatters and burns and consumes every wickedness and every vice and every sin; and afterward it is found to be nothing in itself. That man who possesseth humility, through humility findeth grace with God, and perfect peace with his neighbour".

CHAPTER OF THE HOLY FEAR OF GOD

HE who feareth not, showeth that he hath not aught to lose. The holy fear of God orders, rules and directs the soul, and maketh it to come into grace. If any man possesseth any grace or Divine virtue, holy fear is that which preserves it. And whosoever hath not yet obtained virtue or grace, holy fear maketh him obtain it. The holy fear of God is a guide which guideth us to the Divine graces, in that it maketh the soul wherein it dwells to speedily attain to holy virtue and to the Divine graces. All creatures which ever fell into sin, would never have fallen if they had possessed the holy fear of God. But this holy gift of fear is not given save only to the perfect, because as a man is more perfect so is he more fearful and humble. Blessed is that man who knoweth himself to be in a prison in this world, and who alway remembereth how grievously he hath offended his Lord! Much ought man to fear pride, lest it give him a push and cause him to fall from the state of grace in which he is, for a man may never be safe when he is among our enemies; and our enemies are the allurements of this miserable world, and our own flesh, the which, together with the fiends, is ever an enemy of the soul. Greater fear doth it behove a man to have lest his own wickedness should conquer and deceive him, than of any other enemy of his. A thing impossible is it that man can mount up and ascend to any grace or Divine virtue, or persevere therein, without holy fear. He who hath not the fear of God goeth in peril of death and much more of being utterly lost. The fear of God maketh a man to obey with humility, and causeth him to bow his head beneath the yoke of obedience; and the greater fear a man hath the more fervently doth he pray; no little gift is that of prayer to him unto whom it is given. The virtuous actions of men, however great they seem to me, are not accounted or rewarded according to our judgment, but according to the judgment and good pleasure of God; for God regards not the quantity of the work done, but the greatness of the love and humility of the doer: and therefore the safest part for us is always to love and fear with humbleness, and never to trust in ourselves for any good, ever suspecting those thoughts which are born in the mind under the appearance of good.

CHAPTER OF HOLY PATIENCE

HE who with steadfast humility and patience suffereth and beareth tribulations for fervent love of God, will soon come to great graces and virtues, and will be lord of this world and will have an earnest of the other glorious world. Everything which a man doth, whether good or ill, unto himself he doth it; and therefore be thou not offended with him who doth thee wrong; rather shouldst thou have humble patience, and for his sin alone shouldst thou grieve, having pity upon him and praying God effectually for him. In proportion as a man is strong to bear and to endure injury and tribulation patiently for love of God, even so is he great in the sight of God, and not more; and the weaker a man is to bear sorrow and adversity for the love of God, the less is he in the sight of God. If any man praise thee speaking well of thee, give that praise to God only; and if any man speak evil of thee or revile thee, do thou aid him, speaking the same evil of thyself and worse. If thou desire to make good thy cause, ever strive to make it bad; and make good that of thy companion, always accusing thyself, and always praising or excusing thy neighbour.

When any man would contend or go to law with thee, if thou desire to win, lose, and thou wilt win; for if thou shouldst desire to go to law to win, when thou didst believe that thou hadst won, then wouldst thou find that thou hadst greatly lost. And therefore, my brother, believe me that of a surety the straight way of salvation is the way of perdition. But when we bear not tribulation well, then we cannot be followers of the eternal consolations.

A far greater consolation is it. and a more meritorious thing, to bear injuries and reproaches patiently and without murmuring, for the love of God, than to feed, a hundred poor and to fast continually every day. But what shall it profit a man, or what shall it avail him to despise himself, and to grievously vex his body with great fasts and watchings and scourgings, if he cannot bear a little wrong at the hands of his neighbour? For the which thing a man shall receive a far greater reward and greater merit than for all the afflictions wherewith he may afflict himself of his own will; for to bear the upbraidings and abuse of his neighbour with humble patience and without murmuring much more quickly cleanseth from sin than doth the fountain of many tears. Blessed is that man who always keeps before the eyes of his mind the memory of his sins and the benefits of God! for he will bear with patience every tribulation and adversity; from which things he looks for great consolations. The man who is truly humble looks not for any merit or reward from God, but only strives continually how he may please Him in everything, knowing himself to be His debtor; and every good thing which he hath he knows that he hath only through the goodness of God, and not through any merit of his own; and every adversity which befalleth him he knows to have befallen him through his sins. A friar asked Friar Giles saying: "Father, if great adversities and tribulations shall come in our times, what ought we to do?" To whom Friar Giles made answer, saying: "My brother, I would have thee know that, if the Lord should cause stones and thunderbolts to rain down from heaven, they could not hurt us nor do us any harm, if we were such men as we ought to be; because were a man in truth that which he ought to be, every evil and every tribulation would be turned to good; for we know that the Apostle said that *all things work together for good to them that love God;* and so likewise for the man whose desire is evil, all good things are turned to evil and to judgment. If thou wouldst save thyself and go to the celestial glory, it behoveth thee never to desire any vengeance or retribution upon any creature; for the inheritance of the saints is always to do good and always to receive evil. If in very truth thou knewest in what manner and how grievously thou hast offended thy Creator, thou wouldst know that it is a right and just thing that all creatures should persecute thee and work thee pain and tribulation; inasmuch as such creatures would be taking vengeance for the offences which thou hast committed against their Creator. Very great virtue is it for a man to conquer himself; for he who conquereth himself shall conquer all his enemies and attain unto all good. Yet much greater virtue would it be if a man should permit himself to be conquered by all men; because then he would be lord of all his enemies, to wit of vices, of demons, of the world and of his own flesh. If thou wouldst save thyself, renounce and despise every consolation which all worldly things and all mortal creatures can give thee; for greater and more frequent are the falls which come from prosperity and from consolations, than those which come through adversities and tribulations." Once a Religious murmured against his Superior in the presence of Friar Giles by reason of a harsh obedience which he had commanded him; unto whom Friar Giles said: "Dearly beloved, the more thou shalt murmur, the more thy burden increaseth and the heavier will it be for thee to bear; and the more humbly and devoutly thou shalt put thy head beneath the yoke of holy obedience, the lighter will this obedience be and the sweeter for thee to bear. But to me it seemeth that thou art not willing to be reviled in this world for love of Christ, and yet desirest to be honoured by Christ in the world to come; thou art not willing to be persecuted and cursed in this world for Christ's sake, and yet in the other world thou desirest to be blessed and received by Christ; in this world thou wouldst not labour, and in the other world thou wouldst rest and take thine ease. I tell thee, friar, that thou art badly deceived; for by the path of misery and shames and revilings man cometh to the true heavenly honour, and by patiently bearing derision and curses for love of Christ, man cometh to the glory of Christ; therefore well saith the worldly proverb: *He who gives away nothing which he feels the loss of, receives nothing which he wants.* Excellent is the nature of the horse, because how fast soever he may run he allows himself to be ruled, guided and turned up and down, forward and backward, according to the will of his rider; and so likewise ought the servant of God to do, to wit he ought to allow himself to be ruled, guided, twisted and bent, according to the will of his superior, and also by every one else, for the love of Christ. If thou wouldst be perfect strive earnestly to be gracious and virtuous, and fight valiantly against vice, bearing patiently every adversity for love of thy Lord, who was tormented, afflicted, reviled, beaten, crucified and slain for love of thee, and not for His fault, or for His glory, or for His profit, but only for thy salvation; and to do this which I have told thee, above all it is needful that thou conquer thyself; because it profiteth a man little to lead and draw souls to God if he doth not first conquer and lead and draw himself."

CHAPTER OF SLOTH

THE man who is slothful loseth this world and the next; for he bringeth not forth any fruit himself, and he is of no profit to his neighbour. It is impossible for man to attain unto virtue without diligence and without great labour. When thou art able to abide in a safe place, abide not in a place which is doubtful; he abideth in a safe place who is diligent and afflicts himself and works and strives according to the will of God and for God, and neither for fear of punishment nor for reward, but for God. The man who refuseth to afflict Himself and to spend himself for Christ verily refuseth the glory of Christ; and even as diligence is profitable and helpful to us, so carelessness is always contrary to us. Thus, even as sloth is the way which leadeth unto hell, so is holy diligence the road to heaven. Very diligent ought man to be to obtain and keep the virtues and the grace of God, ever using that grace and virtue faithfully; because oftentimes it befalleth to that man who laboureth not faithfully that he loseth the fruit for the leaves, or the wheat for the straw. To one God, of His grace, granteth good fruit with few leaves, and to another He gives fruit and leaves together; and others there be which have neither fruit nor leaves. Meseemeth a greater thing to know well how to guard and keep secret the good gifts and graces of the Lord, than to know how to obtain them; for, albeit a man knoweth well how to earn, if he knoweth not well how to store up and keep, he will never be rich; but some there be who earn little by little and become rich, because they keep safe their earnings and their treasure. O what great quantity of water would the Tiber have collected, if it ran not away in any part! Man asketh of God an infinite gift, without measure and without end; and he desired) not to love God save with measure and with end. Whosoever would be loved of God, and would receive from Him merit boundless and measureless, must love God without measure and without limit, and must always render Him infinite service.

Blessed is he who loveth God with all his heart and with all his mind, and always afflicted) his body and his mind for love of God, seeking therefor no recompense under heaven, save only that he may know himself His debtor. If a man were exceeding poor and needy, and another man should say unto him: "I am willing to lend thee a very precious thing for the space of three days; and know that if, during this period of three days, thou shalt make good use of this thing, thou wilt gain an infinite treasure which will make thee rich for evermore"; it is certain that that poor man would be very anxious to use that precious thing well and diligently, and much would he study to profit thereby. So, in like manner, I say that the thing lent us by the hand of the Lord is this body of ours, the which the good God hath lent us for three days; for all our times and years are in comparison but as three days. If then thou wouldst be rich and enjoy eternally the Divine sweetness, study to use well this body of thine lent by the hand of God and to make it bring forth fruit, in this space of three days, to wit in the brief period of thy life; for if thou art not diligent to lay up treasure in this present life, while yet thou hast time, thou wilt not be able to enjoy those eternal riches, nor to rest for evermore in that holy celestial peace. But if all the estates in the world belonged to one person and he cultivated them not neither caused them to be cultivated by others, what fruit or what profit would he have from these things? Certain it is that he would have no profit therefrom, nor any fruit. But well might it be that a man should have but few fields and, cultivating them well, should have much profit for himself, and for others ample fruit and abundant. A worldly proverb saith: *Set not an empty pot on the fire to boil in the hope that thy neighbour will fill it;* and so, in like manner, God willeth not that any grace shall remain empty; for the good God never giveth grace to a man that he may keep it empty; rather doth He give it to the end that he may fill it with fruit of good works; for goodwill sufficeth not, unless a man seek to follow it out and to fill it with the fruit of holy works. Once a wanderer said to Friar Giles;" Father, I beseech thee give me some consolation"; to whom Friar Giles made answer: "My brother, seek to stand well with God, and forthwith thou wilt have the consolation whereof thou hast need; for if a man prepare not a spotless dwelling-place within his soul for God to live and rest therein, he will never find shelter, nor rest, nor true consolation in created things". When a man is minded to do ill, never doth he ask much advice before doing it; but for doing well many take counsel and make long delay. Once Friar Giles said to his companions; "My brethren, meseemeth that in our day none is found who is willing to do those things which he seeth to be more profitable, not only for the soul but also for the body. Believe me, my brethren, that I could swear in very truth that the more a man flees from and shuns the burden and the yoke of Christ, the more grievous doth he make it for himself, and the more weighty and heavy doth he feel it; and the more zealously a man taketh it, ever increasing the weight thereof of his own free-will, the lighter he feels it and the greater sweetness he hath in being able to bear it. Now would to God that man might obtain and have the good things of the body in this world, because he would also gain those of the soul; inasmuch as the body and the soul, without any doubt, must be joined together to suffer always or to rejoice always; to wit to suffer in hell for all eternity punishments and torments inestimable, or to enjoy for ever with Saints and. Angels in Paradise, delights and consolations unspeakable, through the merits of good works. Nevertheless if a man did well or forgave his enemies without humility, these things would turn to evil; for there have been many who have done many deeds which seemed good and praiseworthy, but, because they had not humility, it was made manifest and known that they were done through pride, and the works themselves have shown it, for things which are done with humility never become corrupt." A friar said to Friar Giles: "Father, meseemeth that as yet we know not how to recognise what is good for us". Whereto Friar Giles replied: "My brother, certain it is that each man practiseth the craft which he hath learned, for no man can do good work unless he first learn; wherefore, my brother, I would that thou shouldst know that the noblest craft which there is in the world is to do good work: and who can know it, if he have not first learned it? Blessed is that man whom no created thing can teach to do wrong! but more blessed is he who in everything which he sees and hears receiveth edification for himself."

CHAPTER OF THE IRKSOMENESS OF TEMPORAL THINGS

MANY griefs and many sorrows will that wretched man have who setteth his desire and his heart and his hope on earthly things, for the which he abandoneth and loseth heavenly things; and finally he will also lose these earthly things. The eagle flieth very high; but, if she had some weight tied to her wings she could not fly very high: and thus man by reason of the weight of earthly things cannot fly high, to wit cannot attain unto perfection; but the wise man, who tieth the weight of remembrance of death and of judgment to the wings of his heart, could not, by reason of great fear, go astray or fly among the vanities and riches of this world, which are the cause of damnation. Every day we see the men of the world labour and strive much, and risk great bodily perils to gain these transitory riches; and after they shall have laboured and gained much, in a moment they will die and will leave that which they shall have gained during their life: and therefore this deceitful world is not to be trusted, for it defraudeth every man which believeth it, since it is false. But whoso desireth and is minded to be great and abundantly rich, let him seek and love the riches and the possessions of eternity, which always satisfy and never cause satiety and never become less. If we would not err, let us take ensample from the beasts and birds, which, when they have fed are content, and seek nothing save their sustenance front one hour to another, when they have need thereof; and even so should man be content with the necessities of life temperately and without superfluity. Friar Giles said that the ants pleased not St. Francis as did the other animals, by reason of the great care which they had to gather together and to lay by great store of grain in the summer time for the winter: but he used to say that the birds pleased him much more, because they gathered together nothing on one day for another. But the ant setteth us this ensample that we ought not to stand idle in the summer-time of this present life, to the end that we may not find ourselves empty and without fruit in the winter of the last and final judgment.

CHAPTER OF HOLY CHASTITY

OUR miserable and weak human flesh is like unto the hog which ever delighteth to lie down in the mud and to befoul itself therewith, deeming the mud its great delight. Our flesh is the devil's knight; because it wars against and resists all those things which are according to the will of God and for our salvation. A friar inquired of Friar Giles and said unto him: "Father, teach me in what manner we may keep ourselves from carnal sin". Whereto Friar Giles made answer: "My brother, he who would stir any great weight or any great rock and move it into another place should study to move it more by skill than by strength. And so we, in like manner, if we would conquer carnal sins and obtain the virtues of chastity, may better obtain them by humility and by good and wise spiritual regimen than by our presumptuous austerity and violence of penance. Every sin troubles and obscures holy and resplendent chastity; for chastity is like unto a bright mirror which is obscured and bedimmed, not only by the touch of filthy things, but even by the breath of man. It is impossible for man to attain unto any spiritual grace as long as he continues to be disposed to carnal concupiscence, and therefore, turn and turn thyself again as thou wilt, never shalt thou find any other means whereby to attain to spiritual grace save only by subduing every carnal sin. Therefore fight valiantly against thy weak and sensual flesh, thy proper enemy, which would ever thwart thee by day and by night. He who shall conquer our mortal enemy, the flesh, may be certain that he hath conquered and discomfited all his enemies, and that he will soon attain to spiritual grace, and to every good state of virtue and of perfection." Friar Giles was wont to say: "Among all the other virtues I would give the first place to the virtue of chastity, for most sweet chastity path in itself alone some perfection; whereas there is not any other virtue which can be perfect without chastity". A friar asked Friar Giles, saying: "Father, is not the virtue of charity greater and more excellent than that of chastity?" And Friar Giles said: "Tell me, brother, what thing in this world is there to be found more chaste than holy charity?" Oftentimes Friar Giles sang this song, to wit: *O holy chastity, lo! how great is thy goodness! Verily thou art precious, and such and so sweet is thy fragrance, that he who savoureth thee not, knoweth not how rare it is. Therefore the foolish know not thy worth.* A friar asked Friar Giles, saying: "Father, thou that so greatly commendest the virtue of chastity, I beseech thee declare unto me what is chastity"; whereto Friar Giles replied: "My brother, I tell thee that that which is correctly called chastity is diligent care and continual watching of the bodily and spiritual senses to preserve them pure and immaculate for God alone".

CHAPTER OF TEMPTATIONS

THE great graces which man receives from God, man cannot possess in tranquillity and peace, because many contrary things arise and many troubles and adversities hostile to these graces; for the more pleasing a man is to God, the more grievously is he assailed and attacked by the fiends. Therefore man ought never to cease from fighting, that he may be able to keep the grace which he hath received from God: for the harder the battle, the more precious will be the crown, if he conquer in the fight. But we have not many battles, nor many hindrances, nor many temptations, because we are not such as we should be in the spiritual life. But very true it is that if man walked well and wisely along the way of God, he would have neither weariness nor toil in his journey; but the man who walketh in the way of the world, will never be able to avoid many toils, wearinesses, anxieties, tribulations and sorrows, even to the day of his death. Said a friar to Friar Giles: "My father, to me it seemeth that these two sayings of thine are contrary to one another, for first thou didst say that the more virtuous and the more pleasing to God a man is, the greater the obstructions and the battles which he will have in the spiritual life; and thereafter thou saidst the opposite, to wit that the man who walked well and wisely along the way of God would not feel either toil or weariness in his journey". To whom Friar Giles, explaining the contrariety of these two sayings, made answer thus: "My brother, certain is it that the demons make greater battle with strong temptations against those who have the will to do right than they do against others who have not good will, to wit after the mind of God. But to the man who goeth wisely and fervently along the way of God, what toil and what weariness and what harm can the demons and all the adversities of the world cause? since he knoweth and seeth that he is selling his merchandise at a price a thousand times greater than it is worth.

Moreover I tell thee certainly that he who hath been enkindled with the fire of Divine love, the more he is assailed by sins the more he bolded) them in hatred and abhorrence. It is the custom of the worst demons to run and tempt man when he is in some sickness and in some bodily weakness, or when he is in some trouble, or very cold or sorrowful, or when he is an hungered or athirst, or when he hath received some shame or wrong, or temporal or spiritual injury; for these wicked ones know that in such hours and moments as these, man is more prone to yield to temptation; but I tell thee that for every temptation and for every sin that thou shalt conquer thou shalt obtain a virtue; and if thou conquerest that sin which assaileth thee, thou shalt receive therefor so much the greater grace and fairer crown." A friar asked counsel of Friar Giles, saying: "Father, often I am tempted by a very evil temptation, and many times have I prayed God to deliver me from it; yet the Lord taketh it not from me; counsel me, father, what I ought to do". To whom Friar Giles made answer: "My brother, the more nobly a king doth furnish his knights with excellent and strong armour, the more manfully would he have them fight against his enemies for his love". A friar asked Friar Giles, saying: "What remedy shall I use, that I may be able to go to prayer more willingly, and with more desire and with more fervour? For when I go to pray I am hard, slothful, dry and lacking in devotion." To whom Friar Giles made answer, saying: "A king hath two servants; and the one hath arms wherewith to fight, and the other hath not arms wherewith to fight, and both of them wish to enter into the battle and to fight against the enemies of the king. He that is armed enters into the battle and fights valiantly; but the other who is unarmed, speaks on this wise to his lord: 'My lord, thou seest that I am naked without arms; but for love of thee, gladly would I enter into the battle and fight all unarmed as I am'. And then the good king, beholding the love of his faithful servant, saith to his attendants: 'Go with this my servant and clothe him with all those arms which are necessary for him to be able to fight, so that he may enter into the battle with safety; and sign all his arms with my royal sign so that he may be known as my faithful knight'. And so oftentimes it befalleth a man when he goeth to pray, that he findeth himself naked, undevout, slothful and hard of heart, but nevertheless he compelleth himself for love of His Lord to enter into the battle of prayer; and then our gracious King and Lord, seeing the endeavour of His knight, giveth him by the hands of His attendants, the Angels, fervour of devotion and good-will. Sometimes it happens that a man will begin some great and toilsome labour, such as clearing and cultivating the earth or a vineyard, to gather therefrom fruit in due season. And many by reason of the great toil and the many anxieties weary thereof and almost repent of having begun that labour; but if they persevere until harvest, they forget thereafter it weariness and are comforted and glad beholding the fruit which they can enjoy; and even so the man who is strong in the day of temptations will attain unto many consolations; for after tribulations, says St. Paul, are given consolations and crowns of life eternal: and not only will the reward be given in heaven to those who resist temptations, but also in this life, as saith the Psalmist: Lord, according to the multitude of my temptations and sorrows Thy consolations shall make glad my soul; so that the greater the temptation and the fight the more glorious will be the crown."

A friar asked counsel of Friar Giles concerning a certain temptation of his, saying: "O father, I am tempted by two exceedingly grievous temptations. One is that, when I do any good thing, I am forthwith tempted to vainglory; the other is that when I do any evil I fall into such great sadness and listlessness, that I am well-nigh driven to despair." To whom Friar Giles made answer: "My brother, well doest thou and wisely to lament thy sin; but I counsel thee to grieve prudently and in moderation, and always shouldst thou remember that the mercy of God is greater than thy sin. But if the infinite mercy of God receiveth to repentance the man who is a great sinner and who sinneth of his own free will, when he repenteth; believest thou that that good God abandons the good man who sinneth against his will, and is already contrite and repentant? Further, I counsel thee that thou cease not ever to do well, for fear of vainglory; for if a man desiring to sow grain, should say: 'I will not sow because if I should sow, peradventure the birds will devour it '; and if, thus saying, he should not sow his seed, certain is it that he would gather no harvest that year. But if he soweth his seed, albeit the birds eat of that seed, nevertheless the husbandman harvesteth the greater part thereof; and in like manner when a man is assailed by vainglory, if he doth not well for vainglory's sake, but always fighteth against it, I say that he loseth not the merit of the good which he doth, because he is tempted." A friar said to Friar Giles: "Father, I find that St. Bernard once said the seven penitential psalms with so great tranquillity of mind and with such devotion, that he thought not nor mused on any other thing save only the proper meaning of the aforesaid psalms". Unto whom Friar Giles made answer thus: "My brother, I deem that that lord showeth much greater prowess who holdeth a walled place, and being besieged and attacked by his enemies, defendeth himself so valorously that he alloweth no enemy of his to enter therein, than doth that man who liveth in peace with none to hinder him".

CHAPTER OF HOLY PENANCE

MUCH ought a man always to afflict and mortify his body, and willingly to suffer every wrong, tribulation and anguish, grief, shame, contempt, insult, adversity and persecution, for love of our good Master and Lord Messer Jesus Christ, who set us the ensample in His own self; for from the first day of His glorious nativity, even unto His most holy passion, He always suffered anguish, tribulation, sorrow, despite, trouble and persecution, only for our salvation. And therefore, if we would come to a state of grace, it behoves us to walk, as far as in us lies, in the same path and in the footsteps of our good Master, Jesus Christ. A layman asked Friar Giles, saying: "Father, in what manner may we laymen come into a state of grace?" To whom Friar Giles made answer: "My brother, man ought first to bewail his sins with great contrition of heart, and thereafter he must confess them to he priest with bitterness and sorrow of heart, accusing himself only, without concealment and without excuse; and he must perfectly fulfil the penance which is given him and laid upon him by his confessor; also he must keep himself from every vice and from every sin, and from every occasion of sin; and likewise he must exercise himself in good and virtuous works toward God and toward his neighbour; and by so doing that man will attain unto a state of grace and of virtue. Blessed is that man who shall sorrow continually for his sins, ever bewailing them day and night, with bitterness of heart, solely for the offence that he hath committed against God! Blessed is that man who shall have alway before the eyes of his mind the afflictions, the pains and sorrows of Jesus Christ, and whŏ, for love of Him, shall neither desire nor receive any temporal consolation in this bitter and tempestuous world, until he shall come to the celestial consolation of eternal life, where all his desires shall be fulfilled with perfect joy!"

CHAPTER OF HOLY PRAYER

PRAYER is the beginning, the middle and the end of every good; prayer illuminateth the soul, and through it the soul distinguisheth good from evil. Every sinful man should make this prayer continually every day with fervour of heart; to wit, should pray God humbly to give him perfect knowledge of his own misery and sins, and of the blessings which he hath received and is receiving from the good God. But the man who knows not how to pray, how shall he be able to know God? And all those who would save themselves, if they are persons of true understanding, must, in the end, be converted to holy prayer. Said Friar Giles: "If there were a man who had a son, who had committed so great a crime that he was condemned to death or was banished from the city; certain is it that that man would be very anxious to do his utmost, both by day and by night and every hour, to obtain the grace of his son's life or to bring him back from banishment; making very great prayers and supplications, and giving gifts or indemnities to the extent of his ability, both he and his friends and kinsmen. If, then, a man doth this for his son, who is mortal, how careful should he be not only to pray to God Himself for his own soul, which is immortal and which hath been banished from the celestial city and condemned to eternal death for his many sins, but also to prevail upon good men in this world, and upon the saints in the other world, to pray for it also."

A friar said to Friar Giles: "Father, meseemeth that a man ought to grieve much and to be exceeding sorrowful when he may not have the grace of devotion in his prayers". To whom Friar Giles made answer: "My brother, I counsel thee that thou do thy business gently; for if thou hadst a little good wine in a barrel, and in this barrel there were also lees under the good wine, it is certain that thou wouldst not shake or move that barrel, for fear of mixing the good wine with the lees; and so, I say, until thy prayer shall be separated from every sinful and carnal concupiscence, it will not receive Divine consolation; for that prayer is not clear in the sight of God, which is mingled with the lees of sensuality. And therefore man should strive with all his might to separate himself from all the lees of sinful concupiscence; to the end that his prayer may be clean in the sight of God, and that he may receive therefrom Divine devotion and consolation." A friar asked Friar Giles, saying: "Father, wherefore doth it come to pass that, when a man worshippeth God, he is more tempted, assailed and tormented than at any other time?" To whom Friar Giles made answer thus: "When any man hath to plead his cause before a judge, and beginneth to state his case to the judge, as it were asking of him advice and help; as soon as his adversary heareth this, he presently appeareth to gainsay and to oppose that which that man demandeth, and he letteth him sore, as it were confuting everything that he saith; and so likewise it befalleth when a man goeth to pray; for he asketh help of God in his need; and therefore his adversary the devil straightway appeareth with his temptations, to offer great opposition and to gainsay him, to use every effort, device and argument that he can to hinder his prayer, to the end that that prayer may not be acceptable in the sight of God, and that the man may not gain therefrom any merit or any consolation.

And this may we see well and clearly; for when we are speaking of worldly things we endure no temptation nor any distraction of mind; but, if we go to pray, to delight and console the soul with God, presently we shall feel the mind stricken by divers arrows, to wit by divers temptations; wherewith the devils pierce us to cause our minds to wander, so that the soul may have neither joy nor consolation from that which the said soul speaketh with God." Friar Giles said that the man who prayeth should do as the good knight doth in battle; who, albeit he be pierced or smitten by his enemy, doth not therefore straightway depart out of the battle, but resisteth manfully that he may gain the victory over his enemy, and, having gained it, may rejoice and console himself with the glory he hath won; but, if he departed out of the battle as soon as he was smitten and wounded, certain it is that he would be put to confusion and shamed and reviled. And so likewise ought we to do; to wit not to leave off praying for every temptation, but we ought to resist courageously, because, as saith the Apostle: *Blessed is the man that endured, temptation; for when he is tried he shall receive the crown of life;* but if a man, by reason of temptations, ceaseth to pray, it is certain that he will be confounded, conquered and discomfited by his enemy the devil. A friar said to Friar Giles: "Father, I have seen certain men who have received of God the Grace of devotion in their prayers even unto the shedding of tears; and I cannot feel any of these graces when I worship God". To whom Friar Giles made answer: "My brother, I counsel thee that thou labour humbly and faithfully in thy prayers; for, without toil and without labour first spent thereon, the earth yieldeth not her fruit; and even after the work hath been done, the wished-for fruit cometh not immediately, but delayeth until the proper season hath arrived; and so God giveth not at once these graces to man when he prayeth but withholdeth them until; the fitting time hath come, and until his mind is purged of every carnal affection and sin. Therefore, my brother, labour humbly in prayer; for God, who is all good and gracious, knoweth and discerneth all things best, and when the time and the season shall be come, He, of I His loving kindness, will give thee much fruit of consolation." Another friar said to Friar Giles: "What doest thou, Friar Giles? What doest thou, Friar Giles?" And he replied: "I do ill". And that friar said: "What evil dost thou do?" And then Friar Giles turned him to another friar and said unto him: "Tell me, my brother, who dost thou believe is the more ready, our Lord God to grant us His grace, or we to receive it?" And then friar made answer: "Certain it is that God is more ready .to give us His grace than we are to receive it". And then Friar Giles said: "do we then well?"

And that friar said: "Nay, we do ill". Then Friar Giles turned him again to the first friar and said: "Behold, friar, it is clearly shown that we do ill; and that which I answered thee just now is true, to wit that I did ill". Said Friar Giles: "Many works are praised and commended in the Holy Scriptures, which are works of mercy and other holy works; but when He spake of prayer the Lord said: The heavenly Father seeketh men that will worship Him on earth in spirit and in truth." Also Friar Giles said that the true Religious are like unto wolves; for rarely do they go abroad among men, unless it be for some great necessity; and then they forthwith seek to return again to their secret place without delaying much or holding familiar intercourse with men. Good works adorn the soul; but, above all the rest, prayer adorneth and illuminateth the soul. A friar, who was an intimate companion of Friar Giles, said: "Father, wherefore dost thou not sometimes go to speak of the things of God, and to teach and labour for the salvation of the souls of Christians?" Unto whom Friar Giles made answer: "My brother, I desire to do my duty to my neighbour with humility, and without damage to my own soul, to wit by prayer". And that friar said: "At least thou shouldst sometimes go to visit thy kinsfolk". And Friar Giles replied: "Knowest thou not that. the Lord saith in the Gospel: Whosoever shall leave father and mother, brethren, sisters and possessions for My name's sake shall receive an hundredfold?" And again he said: "A gentleman entered the Order of the friars, whose riches were worth peradventure 60,000 lire; great gifts then await those who for God's sake leave great things, for God giveth them an hundredfold more. But we who arc blind, when we see any man virtuous and full of grace in the sight of God, cannot understand his perfection. by reason of our imperfection and blindness. But if any man were truly spiritual, scarcely would he ever wish to see or hear any one, save only in great need; for the truly spiritual man always desires to be separated from men and united to God through contemplation." Then Friar Giles said to a friar: "Father, gladly would I know what contemplation is"; and that friar made answer: "Father, I do not yet know". Then Friar Giles said: "Meseemeth that the dignity of contemplation is a Divine fire, and a sweet devotion of the Holy Ghost, and an ecstasy and abstraction of the mind, intoxicated by the contemplation of that ineffable savour of the Divine sweetness; and a soft and still and sweet delight of soul, which is uplifted and rapt in great admiration of glorious, supernal, celestial things; and a burning inward sense of that heavenly and unspeakable glory."

CHAPTER OF HOLY SPIRITUAL PRUDENCE

O THOU servant of the heavenly King, that wouldst learn the mysteries and the profitable and virtuous prudence of the holy spiritual doctrine, open well the ears of the intellect of thy soul, and receive with desire of heart; and keep carefully in the house of thy memory the precious treasure of these precepts and teachings and spiritual warnings, the which I speak unto thee, whereby thou shalt be illuminated and directed on thy journey, to wit of the spiritual life, and shalt be armed against the evil and subtle assaults of thy corporeal and incorporeal enemies, and shalt go with humble boldness, safely voyaging over the tempestuous sea of this present life, until thou shalt reach the longed-for harbour of salvation. Then, my son, attend well and mark that which I say unto thee: If thou wouldst see well, put out thine eyes and be blind; if thou wouldst hear well, become deaf; if thou wouldst speak well, become dumb; if thou wouldst walk well, stand still and walk with thy mind; if thou wouldst work well, cut off thy hands, and work with thy heart; if thou wouldst love well, hate thyself; if thou wouldst live well, mortify thyself; if thou wouldst gain much and be rich, lose and be poor; if thou wouldst enjoy thyself and take thine ease, afflict thyself and be always sorrowful; if thou wouldst be safe, be ever fearful and suspect thyself; if thou wouldst be exalted and have great honour, humiliate and revile thyself; if thou wouldst be held in great reverence, despise thyself and do reverence to them that do thee despite and dishonour; if thou wouldst have good always, endure evil always; if thou wouldst be blessed, desire that all folk curse thee; and if thou wouldst have true rest and eternal, labour and afflict thyself, and desire every temporal calamity. O how great wisdom is it to know how to do and to perform these things! but because these things are great and very high therefore are they granted by God to but few persons. But verily he who shall study well all the aforesaid things and shall do them, of him I say that he needeth not to go to Bologna or to Paris to learn other theology; for if a man should live 1,000 years, and should do no outward bodily action and should speak no word with his tongue, nevertheless I say that he would have enough to do, disciplining himself inwardly in his heart, labouring within himself in the purifying and directing and justifying of his mind and of his soul. A man ought not to wish either to see, or to hear, or to speak of anything save only what is profitable for his soul. The man who knoweth not himself is not known. And therefore woe unto us, when we receive the gifts and graces of the Lord and know not enough to recognise them: but greater woe to those who neither receive them nor recognise them, nor even care to obtain and to possess them. Man is made in the image of God, and as he willeth so he changeth; but the good God changeth never.

CHAPTER OF PROFITABLE AND UNPROFITABLE KNOWLEDGE

THE man who would know much, must labour much and humble himself much, abasing himself and bowing down his head until he goeth with his belly upon the ground; and then the Lord will give him much knowledge and wisdom. The highest wisdom is to do good alway, labouring virtuously and keeping oneself carefully from every sin and from every occasion of sin, and to ever think upon the judgments of God. Once Friar Giles said to one who wished to go to school to get knowledge: "My brother, wherefore wouldst thou go to school? for I do thee to wit that the sum of all knowledge is to fear and to love, and these two things suffice thee; for so much wisdom as he can make use of sufficeth a man, and more he needeth not. Be not thou over careful to study much for the benefit of others, but alway study and be diligent to labour at those things which are useful unto thyself; for ofttimes this befalleth, that we would get much knowledge to help others, and little to help ourselves; and I say unto thee that the word of God is not for him that speaketh nor yet for him that heareth, but is for him that truly doeth it.

Certain men which knew not how to swim went into the water to aid those who were drowning; and it came to pass that they all drowned together. If thou dost not take good thought for the salvation of thine own soul, how shalt thou take thought for that of thy neighbours? And if thou dost not thy own business well, how shalt thou do well that of others? For it is not believable that thou lovest the soul of another more than thine own. The preachers of the word of God ought to be the banner, the candle and the mirror of the people.

Blessed is that man who so leadeth others along the way of salvation that he himself doth not cease to walk in that way of salvation! Blessed is that man who on such wise urgeth others to run that he doth not cease to run himself! More blessed is he who on such wise helpeth others to earn and to be rich and ceaseth not to enrich himself. I believe that the good preacher admonisheth and preacheth to himself more than he doth to others. Meseemeth that the man who would convert and bring the souls of sinners into the way of God, ought alway to fear lest he be grievously perverted by them, and brought into the way of sin and of the devil and of hell."

CHAPTER OF GOOD AND EVIL SPEAKING

THE man who speaketh good words and profitable to souls is in truth as it were the mouthpiece of the Holy Ghost, and so likewise the man who speaketh evil and unprofitable words is certainly the mouthpiece of the devil. When, at any time, good and spiritually minded men be met to hold converse together, they ought always to speak of the beauty of virtues, so that virtues may please them more and they may take more delight therein; for by delighting themselves and taking pleasure in the said virtues they will discipline themselves the more therein; and by disciplining themselves in them they will attain unto greater love thereof; and through this love, and through continual discipline and pleasure in virtues, ever will they advance to more fervent love of God and into a higher state of soul; for the which cause more gifts and more Divine graces would be granted unto them by the Lord. The more a man is tempted the more need he hath to speak of holy virtues; for even as through evil talk of sins a man ofttimes falleth lightly into sinful deeds, so ofttimes through speaking of virtues a man is lightly brought and disposed to the holy deeds of virtue. But what shall we say of the good which proceedeth from virtues? for it is so passing great that we cannot speak worthily of its great excellence, marvellous and infinite. And likewise what shall we say of the evil and of the eternal punishment which proceeds from sin? for it is so great an evil and so bottomless an abyss that it is for us incomprehensible and beyond either thought or speech. I deem it no less a virtue to know well how to keep silence than to know well how to speak; and therefore meseemeth that a man hath need of a long neck like the crane, to the end that when he would speak his words might pass through many joints before they reached his mouth; that is to say that, when a man wished to speak, it might be necessary for him to think and think again, and to examine and consider very carefully, the how, and the why, and the when, and the manner, and the condition of his hearers, and the effect upon himself, and the motive wherefor he spake.

CHAPTER OF GOOD PERSEVERANCE

WHAT doth it profit a man to fast much and to pray and to give alms, and to afflict himself, with his mind ever fixed upon things celestial, if he cometh not to the blessed haven of salvation which he longeth for, to wit the haven of good and steadfast perseverance? Sometimes it befalleth that some great ship appeareth upon the sea, passing fair and great and strong and new, and laden with much riches; and it cometh to pass that by reason of a storm or through some fault of the helmsman, that ship doth perish and sink and foundereth miserably and cometh not to the haven where she would be; what then do all her beauty and excellence and riches profit her, after she hath thus miserably perished in the depths of the sea?

Also sometimes there appeareth upon the sea a small ship and old, and with but little cargo, and she, having a good and prudent helmsman, overcometh Fortune, and escapeth from the profound abyss of the sea, and cometh to the desired haven; and so doth it befal to men in the tempestuous ocean of this world. And therefore Friar Giles was wont to say: "Man ought alway to fear, and albeit he is in great prosperity, or in high estate, or in great dignity, or in great perfection of condition, if he hath not a good helmsman, to wit prudent self-government, he may perish miserably in the deep sea of sin; and therefore for well-doing there is great need of perseverance, as saith the Apostle: Not he who beginneth, but he who endureth unto the end, shall have the crown. When a tree springeth up, it becometh not great at once; and after that it be grown it doth not therefore yield fruit at once; and when it yieldeth fruit, all that fruit cometh not to the mouth of the owner of that tree; for much of the fruit falleth to the ground, and becometh rotten and is wasted, and such the beasts of the field do eat; but if it continueth to grow unto the proper season, the greater part of its fruit will be gathered by the owner of that tree."

Likewise Friar Giles said: "What would it profit me if I should taste the kingdom of Heaven for full a hundred years, and persevered not therein, so that thereafter I came not to a good end?" And also he said: "I deem that these are two exceeding great graces and gifts of God unto him who can obtain them in this life, to wit to persevere with love in the service of God, and alway to keep oneself from falling into sin."

CHAPTER OF THE TRUE RELIGION

FRIAR GILES used to say, speaking of himself: "I would rather have a little of the grace of God, being a Religious in the Religion, than I would have many graces of God being a layman and living in "the world; for in the world there are many more hindrances and perils, and much less remedy and help than there is in the Religion." Also Friar Giles said: "Meseemeth that sinful man feareth more his own good than he doth his loss and hurt; for he feareth to enter into the Religion and to do penance; but he feareth not to offend God and his soul, by remaining in the hard and obstinate world, and in the loathesome mire of his sins, awaiting his last eternal damnation". A layman asked Friar Giles, saying: "Father, what dost thou counsel me to do? to enter the Religion or to remain in the world doing good works?" To whom Friar Giles made answer: "My brother, certain is it that if any needy man knew that a great treasure was hidden in the public land, he would not ask counsel of any person to assure himself whether it would be well to dig it up and hide it in his house; how much more should a man endeavour and hasten with all zeal and diligence to possess himself of that celestial treasure which is to be found in the holy Religious and spiritual congregations, without asking so much advice!" And that layman, hearing this answer, forthwith distributed that which he possessed among the poor, and thus despoiled of everything, forthwith entered the Religion. Friar Giles was wont to say: "Many men enter the Religion, and yet do not put into effect and operation those things which belong to the perfect state of the holy Religion; but these men are like unto that ploughman who clad himself in the armour of Orlando, and knew not how to fight or joust therewith. Every man knoweth not how to ride a restive and vicious horse; and, even if he rideth him, perchance he would not know how to keep himself from falling, when the horse ran or grew restive." Also Friar Giles said: "I hold it not a great thing that a man gaineth entrance to the court of the king; nor do I hold it a great matter that he should know how to obtain some graces or benefits from the king; but the great matter is that he should know well how to remain and dwell and bear himself aright in the court of the king, continuing to act prudently according to that which is meet. The court of the great Celestial King is the holy Religion, wherein it is not difficult to enter and to receive some gifts and graces from God; but the great matter is that a man know well how to live and bear himself and persevere therein with prudence even unto his death." Likewise Friar Giles said: "Rather would I be a layman and continually hope and desire with devotion to enter the Religion, than I would be clad with the habit in the holy Religion, without the practice of virtuous works, continuing in sloth and in negligence. And therefore the Religious man should always strive to live well and virtuously, knowing that he cannot live in any other state save only in his Order." Once Friar Giles said: "Meseemeth that the Religion of the Minor Friars was verily sent by God for the profit and great edification of the people; but woe unto us friars, if we shall not be such men as we ought to be! Certain it is that in this life men more blessed than we could not be found; because holy is he who followeth him who is holy, and he is truly good who walketh in the path of the good; and rich is he who goeth in the footsteps of the rich; and the Religion of the Minor Friars, more than any other Religion, followeth the footsteps and the way of the most good, of the most rich and of the most holy that ever was or ever shall be, to wit of our Lord Jesus Christ."

CHAPTER OF HOLY OBEDIENCE

THE more the Religious abideth beneath the yoke of holy obedience, for the love of God, the greater fruit will he give of himself to God; the more he shall be subject to his Superior for the honour of God, the more free will he be and clean from sin. The true obedient Religious is like unto a knight well armed and mounted the which overcometh and breaketh the ranks of his enemies, safely and without fear, because none of them can hurt him. But he who obeyeth with murmuring and on compulsion, is like unto an unarmed knight and ill-mounted, the which, when he entereth into the battle, will be cast to earth by his enemies, and wounded by them and taken, and sometimes imprisoned and slain. That Religious who desireth to live according to his own will and pleasure, showeth that he would build himself an everlasting habitation in the abyss of hell. When the ox putteth his neck beneath the yoke, then is the ground well ploughed and yieldeth good fruit in its season, but when the ox wandereth where it will, the earth remaineth untilled and wild, and yieldeth not its fruit in due season. And even so, the Religious who submitted his neck to the yoke of obedience, bringeth forth much fruit to the Lord God in due season; but he who obeyeth not his Superior with a good heart, remaineth sterile and wild and without fruit of his profession. Wise men and magnanimous submit their necks readily, without fear and without doubting, to the yoke of holy obedience; but foolish and fearful men seek to draw their necks from under the yoke of holy obedience, and thereafter are not willing to obey any creature. I hold it greater perfection, in the servant of God, to simply obey his superior, for reverence and love of God, than to obey God Himself, if God should lay his commands upon him; for he who is obedient to a vicar of the Lord, would, of a surety, be more obedient to the Lord himself if He should command him. Also meseemeth that, if any man had promised obedience to another, and had grace to speak with angels; and if it befel that, while he was speaking with those angels, he to whom he had promised obedience called him; I say that he ought forthwith to stop speaking with the Angels, and ought to hasten to do obedience for the honour of God. He who hath set his neck beneath the yoke of holy obedience, and thereafter would withdraw his neck from under that obedience, through desire of following a life of greater perfection; I say that, if he be not first altogether perfect in the state of obedience, it is a sign of the great pride which secretly lieth hid in his soul. Obedience is the path which leadeth to every virtue; and disobedience is the path of every evil and of every sin.

CHAPTER OF THE REMEMBRANCE OF DEATH

IF man had alway before the eyes of his mind the remembrance of his death, and of the last eternal judgment, and of the pains and torments of damned souls, it is certain that never would the wish to sin or to offend God come upon him. But if it were possible that some man had lived from the beginning of the world even until now, and, during all that time, had suffered every adversity, tribulation, pain, affliction and sorrow, and, if he should die, and his soul should go to receive the eternal happiness of Heaven, what harm would all that evil do him which he had borne in the time that was past? And so, likewise, if a man had had, through all the aforesaid time, every good thing and every delight and pleasure and consolation of the world, and thereafter he should die and his soul should receive those eternal pains of Hell, what would all the good things, which he had enjoyed, in the time that was past, profit him? A man who was a wanderer said to Friar Giles: "I tell thee that willingly would I live long in this world and have great riches and abundance of everything; and I would desire to be much honoured". Unto whom Friar Giles said:

"My Brother, if thou wast lord of all the world, and couldst live in it for a thousand years, in all the delight of temporal joys, pleasures and consolations, lo! tell me, what reward or what merit wouldst thou expect to have in this thy miserable flesh, the which thou wouldst serve and please? But I tell thee that the man who liveth well in the sight of God, and guardeth himself against offending God, will surely receive from God the highest good and infinite eternal reward, and great riches and great honour and life everlasting, in that never-ending celestial glory, whereto may the good God, our Lord and King Jesus Christ, bring us, to the praise of the same Jesus Christ and of his mendicant Francis."

HERE ENDETH THE TEACHINGS AND NOTABLE SAYINGS OF FRIAR GILES

ADDENDA TAKEN FROM THE MANUSCRIPTS

Chapter 1. An Ensample Of Friar Leo, How St. Francis Bade Him Wash The Stone

IN the mountain of Alvernia, as St. Francis was speaking with Friar Leo, St. Francis said: "Friar little sheep, wash this stone with water". Friar Leo hastened to obey and washed the stone with water. Said St. Francis, with great joy and gladness: "Wash it with wine"; and so was it done. " Wash it," said St. Francis, "with oil;" and so was it done. Said St. Francis: "Friar little sheep, wash that stone with balm". Friar Leo replied: "O sweet father, how can I get balm in so wild a place as this is?" St. Francis made answer: "Know, friar little sheep of Christ, that this is the stone where Christ sat when He appeared to me on a time in this very place; and therefore have I said unto thee four times: 'Wash it and hold thy peace '; for Jesus Christ hath promised me four singular graces for my Order. The first is that all those who shall love my Order from their hearts, and the friars who shall persevere, shall by the Divine grace make a good end. The second is that the persecutors of this holy Religion shall be notably punished. The third is that no evil man shall be able to remain long in this Order, continuing in his frowardness. The fourth is that this Religion shall last even unto the last judgment."

Chapter 2. How St. Francis Appeared To Friar Leo

ON a time, after St. Francis had departed this life, there came upon Friar Leo a desire to see that sweet father, whom, when alive, he had so dearly loved; and, by reason of this desire, he began, beyond his wont, to afflict his body with prayers and fastings; beseeching God with great fervour that He would fulfil his desire. And so, while he was all enkindled in that prayer, St. Francis appeared unto him all glorious with wings, and he had talons upon his hands and upon his feet, like unto those of an eagle, but gilded. And Friar Leo, being all gladdened and consoled by this so marvellous apparition, said with wonder: "Wherefore, my most venerable father, hast thou appeared unto me in so strange a shape?" St. Francis made answer: "Among the other graces, which have been given and granted unto me by the Divine compassion, are these wings; to the end that, being invoked, I may straightway succour the lovers of this holy Religion in their tribulations and necessities; and may carry their souls and those of my friars, as it were flying, to the supernal glory. These talons so great and strong and golden are given me against the devil, against the persecutors of my Religion and against the reprobate friars of this holy Order, that I may chastise them with hard and grievous clawings and cruel punishments." To the praise of Christ. Amen.

Chapter 3. How Friar Leo Saw A Terrible Vision In A Dream

ONCE, in a dream, Friar Leo beheld a vision of the making ready of the Divine judgment. He beheld the Angels making music with trumpets and divers instruments, and calling together a marvellous great crowd in a meadow. And on one side of the meadow was set a ladder all rosy red, which reached from earth even unto heaven, and on the other side of the meadow was set another ladder all white, which descended from heaven to earth. On the top of the red ladder, Christ appeared a Lord offended and exceeding wrath. And St. Francis was nigh unto Christ but a few steps lower down; and he came farther down the ladder, and with a loud voice and great fervour called and said: "Come ye, my friars, come confidently, fear not, come, draw nigh unto the Lord, for He calleth you". At the voice of St. Francis and at his bidding, the friars went and climbed up the red ladder with great confidence. And, when they were all thereon, some fell off the third step, and some off the fourth step, others off the fifth and the sixth; and at the last all fell, so that there remained not one upon the ladder. And so great ruin of his friars, St. Francis, as a pitiful father, was moved to compassion, and besought the Judge for his sons, that He would receive them to His mercy. And Christ showed His wounds all bloody, and said unto St. Francis: "This have thy friars done unto Me". And St. Francis delayed not, but, even as he interceded, came down certain steps, and cried unto the friars that were fallen from the red ladder and said: "Come ye, rise up, my sons and friars, be of good courage and despair not, but run to the white ladder and climb up it, for by it ye shall be received into the Kingdom of Heaven; run, friars, through paternal admonishment, to the white ladder". And on the top of the ladder appeared the glorious Virgin Mary, the Mother of Jesus Christ, all pitiful and kind, and welcomed those friars; and without any difficulty they entered into the eternal kingdom. To the praise of Christ. Amen.

Copyright © 2021 by FV Éditions
Cover Design : Canva.com, FVE
Ebook ISBN : 979-10-299-1205-4
Paperback ISBN : 979-10-299-1206-1
Hardcover ISBN : 979-10-299-1207-8
All rights reserved.

Also Available

www.ingramcontent.com/pod-product-compliance
Lightning Source LLC
LaVergne TN
LVHW041655060526
838201LV00043B/440